CANDLE IN THE WIND

EUGENE B. SHIRLEY, JR., is an independent television and film producer living in Los Angeles. He produced *Candle in the Wind,* an award-winning PBS prime-time special on religion in the USSR.

MICHAEL ROWE is the senior researcher on the Soviet Union at Keston College. Since 1979 he has edited Keston's series *Religious Prisoners in the USSR.*

RICHARD SCHIFTER is U.S. assistant secretary of state for human rights and humanitarian affairs.

CANDLE IN THE WIND

Religion in the Soviet Union

Edited by

EUGENE B. SHIRLEY, JR.
and
MICHAEL ROWE

Foreword by Richard Schifter

ETHICS AND PUBLIC POLICY CENTER

THE **ETHICS AND PUBLIC POLICY CENTER,** established in 1976, conducts a program of research, writing, publications, and conferences to encourage debate on domestic and foreign policy issues among religious, educational, academic, business, political, and other leaders. A nonpartisan effort, the Center is supported by contributions (which are tax deductible) from foundations, corporations, and individuals. The authors alone are responsible for the views expressed in Center publications. The founding president of the Center is **Ernest W. Lefever.**

Library of Congress Cataloging-in-Publication Data

Candle in the wind : religion in the Soviet Union / edited by
Eugene B. Shirley, Jr. and Michael Rowe.
p. cm.
Bibliography: p.
Includes index.
1. Soviet Union—Religion. 2. Religion and state—Soviet Union.
3. Persecution—Soviet Union. I. Shirley, Eugene B. II. Rowe, Michael.
III. Ethics and Public Policy Center (Washington, D.C.)
BL940.S65C36 1989
291'.0947—dc19 89–1277
ISBN 0–89633–135–0 (alk. paper)
ISBN 0–89633–136–9 (pbk.: alk. paper)

Distributed by arrangement with:

University Press of America, Inc.
4720 Boston Way
Lanham, MD 20706

3 Henrietta Street
London WC2E 8LU England

All Ethics and Public Policy Center books are produced on acid-free paper. The paper used in this publication meets the minimum requirements of American National Standard for Information Sciences—Permanence of Paper for Printed Library Materials, ANSI Z39.48–1984. ♾

Ethics and Public Policy Center
1030 Fifteenth Street N.W.
Washington, D.C. 20005
(202) 682–1200

Contents

Chronology

863	Cyril and Methodius sent as missionaries by Constantinople patriarchate to Slavic tribes in Moravia
955	Princess Olga baptized on visit to Constantinople
988	Christianity begins in Russia with baptism of Olga's grandson Prince Vladimir I
1017	Church of St. Sophia begun in Kiev
1037	Kiev becomes a metropolitanate under patriarchate of Constantinople
1054	Great Schism: Church divides into Western (Catholic) and Eastern (Orthodox)
1240	Kiev devastated by Mongols
1308–26	Moscow becomes center of religious life under Metropolitan Peter
1380	Prince Dimitri Donskoi defeats Mongols at Battle of Kulikovo
1408	Mongols reassert rule over Russia
1438–45	Council of Ferrara-Florence attempts to unify Catholics and Orthodox
1453	Fall of Constantinople to Turks
1480	Mongol rule ends

1517	Protestant Reformation begins in Germany
1533–84	Reign of Ivan IV (the Terrible)
1589	Moscow becomes a patriarchate
1595	Uniate church established in Ukraine
1603	Romanov family elected to throne
1652	Nikon becomes Patriarch of Moscow
1654–56	Church council in Moscow revises liturgical books, leading to Old Believers schism
1682–1725	Reign of Peter I (the Great)
1700	Tsar Peter refuses to allow new patriarch after death of Adrian
1703–1917	St. Petersburg (Leningrad) capital of Russia
1721	Patriarchate abolished; replaced by Holy Synod, under Tsar Peter's close supervision
1762–96	Reign of Catherine II (the Great)
1791	Catherine creates Pale of Settlement to contain Jews
1812	Napoleon invades Russia
1815	Congress of Vienna readjusts boundaries and restores monarchies after exile of Napoleon
1848	Marx and Engels, *Communist Manifesto*
1854–56	Crimean War
1861	Alexander II liberates serfs
1880	Dostoevsky publishes *The Brothers Karamozov*
1891–1903	Trans-Siberian railroad constructed

1894–1917	Reign of Nicholas II
1903	*Protocols of the Elders of Zion* published
1904–5	Russo-Japanese War
1905	Revolution against Tsar Nicholas II
1906	First *duma* (elected assembly)
1914–18	World War I
1917	February revolution / Nicholas II abdicates / provisional government / patriarchate restored / Bolshevik October Revolution (Lenin, Trotsky, Stalin) / Bolshevik government begins to repress Russian Orthodox Church
1918	Decree on the Separation of Church From State and School From Church / Tsar Nicholas and his family executed
1918–20	Civil War
1922	Arrest of Patriarch Tikhon and dissolution of Holy Synod / Union of Soviet Socialist Republics created / Stalin becomes secretary of Communist Party
1924	Lenin dies
1925	Patriarch Tikhon dies; state refuses to permit election of new patriarch
1927	Metropolitan Sergei of Moscow (acting in lieu of patriarch) proclaims loyalty to Soviet state
1928–32	First Five-Year Plan
1929	Trotsky expelled from USSR / Law on Religious Associations
1930	Kulaks liquidated
1934	USSR joins League of Nations / Biro-Bidzhan proclaimed a Jewish autonomous region

1934–38	Communist Party purges
1939	Nazi-Soviet Non-Aggression Pact / Nazis and Soviets invade Poland / World War II begins / Soviets invade Finland; League of Nations expels USSR in response
1940	USSR annexes Estonia, Latvia, Lithuania
1941	Stalin becomes premier / Nazis invade USSR
1943	Patriarchate reestablished
1944	All-Union Council of Evangelical Christians–Baptists (AUCECB) formed
1945	World War II ends
1946	Ukrainian Greek Catholic (Uniate) Church liquidated
1949	Pope Pius XII excommunicates Communists
1953	"Doctors' Plot" charged / Stalin dies; replaced by group in which Khrushchev becomes dominant
1956	USSR invades Hungary / Khrushchev denounces Stalin at party congress
1958	Khrushchev becomes premier
1959–64	Renewed persecution of religion
1964	Khrushchev ousted; Brezhnev succeeds him
1968	USSR invades Czechoslovakia
1972	First Strategic Arms Limitation Treaty (SALT I)
1974	Solzhenitsyn's *Gulag Archipelago* published / Solzhenitsyn forced to leave USSR
1975	USSR and other nations sign Helsinki Accords

1979	USSR invades Afghanistan / SALT II signed, never ratified by U.S. Senate
1981	Under Soviet pressure, Poland declares martial law and outlaws Solidarity
1982	Brezhnev dies; Andropov succeeds him
1983	USSR shoots down Korean commercial airliner
1984	Andropov dies; Chernenko succeeds him
1985	Chernenko dies; Gorbachev succeeds him
1986	Chernobyl nuclear power plant accident
1987	Gorbachev initiates political and economic reforms called *glasnost* and *perestroika*
1988	Millennium of Christianity in Russia celebrated / Proposed reform of 1929 Law on Religious Associations / Earthquake in Armenia kills at least 55,000 / Pope's Christmas Mass from Vatican broadcast in USSR for first time
1989	USSR completes troop withdrawal from Afghanistan

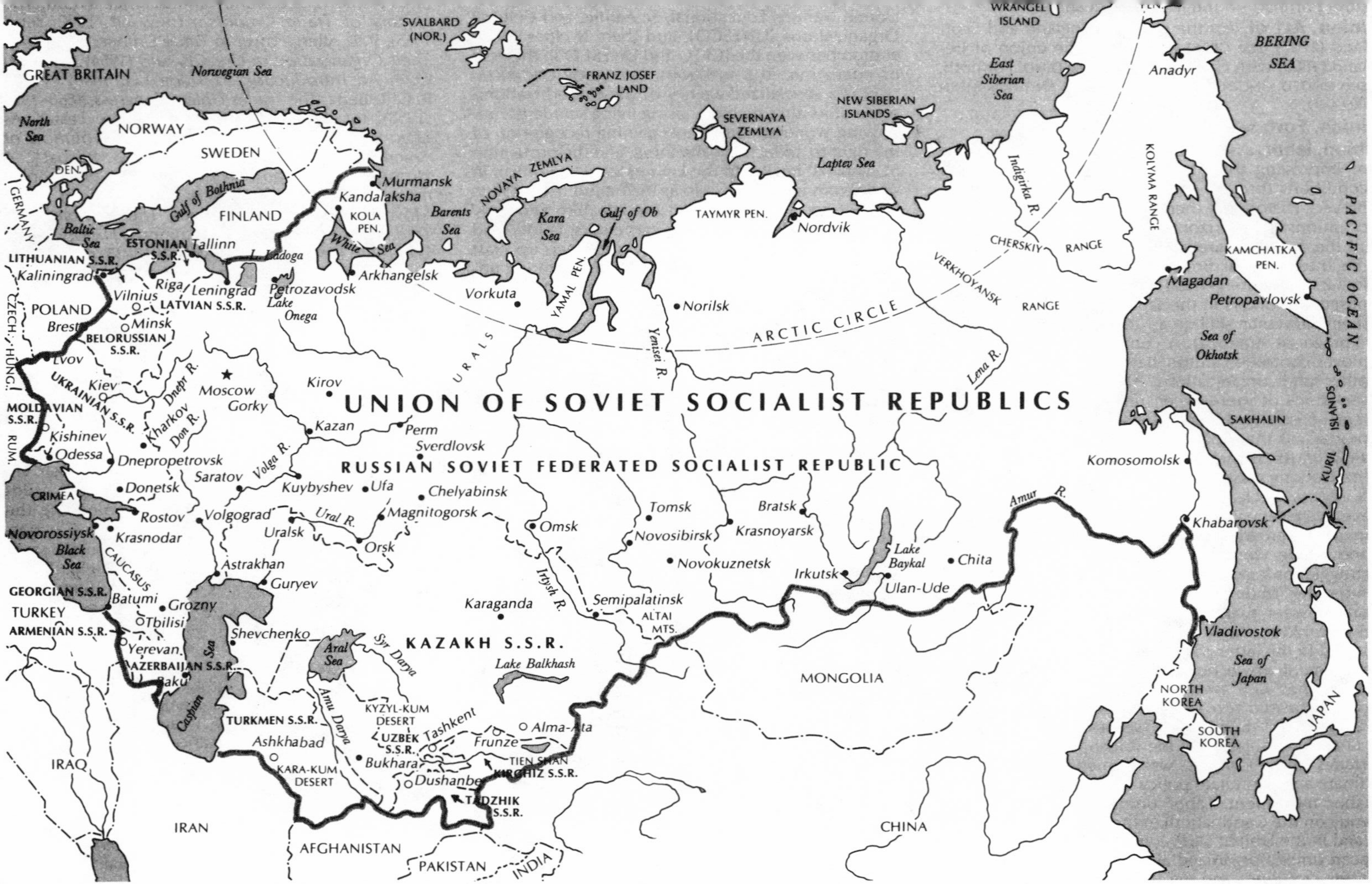
UNION OF SOVIET SOCIALIST REPUBLICS
RUSSIAN SOVIET FEDERATED SOCIALIST REPUBLIC
GREAT BRITAIN
Norwegian Sea
SVALBARD (NOR.)
FRANZ JOSEF LAND
WRANGEL ISLAND
BERING SEA
East Siberian Sea
Anadyr
NEW SIBERIAN ISLANDS
SEVERNAYA ZEMLYA
Laptev Sea
KOLYMA RANGE
PACIFIC OCEAN
North Sea
NORWAY
SWEDEN
NOVAYA ZEMLYA
Indigirka R.
DEN.
GERMANY
Murmansk
Kandalaksha
Gulf of Bothnia
FINLAND
KOLA PEN.
Barents Sea
Kara Sea
Gulf of Ob
TAYMYR PEN.
Nordvik
Baltic Sea
White Sea
ESTONIAN S.S.R.
Tallinn
L. Ladoga
Arkhangelsk
CHERSKIY RANGE
KAMCHATKA PEN.
LITHUANIAN S.S.R.
Kaliningrad
Riga
Leningrad
Petrozavodsk
Vorkuta
YAMAL PEN.
Norilsk
VERKHOYANSK RANGE
Magadan
Petropavlovsk
Vilnius
LATVIAN S.S.R.
Lake Onega
POLAND
Minsk
Brest
BELORUSSIAN S.S.R.
ARCTIC CIRCLE
Sea of Okhotsk
CZECH.
HUNG.
Lvov
URALS
Yenisei R.
Lena R.
UKRAINIAN S.S.R.
Kiev
Dnepr R.
Moscow
Gorky
Kirov
MOLDAVIAN S.S.R.
Kharkov
Don R.
SAKHALIN
KURIL ISLANDS
RUM.
Kishinev
Kazan
Perm
Odessa
Dnepropetrovsk
Sverdlovsk
Komosomolsk
Saratov
Volga R.
Donetsk
Kuybyshev
Ufa
Chelyabinsk
CRIMEA
Amur R.
Tomsk
Bratsk
Rostov
Volgograd
Ural R.
Magnitogorsk
Khabarovsk
Novorossiysk
Omsk
Krasnodar
Uralsk
Novosibirsk
Krasnoyarsk
Black Sea
Orsk
CAUCASUS
Lake Baykal
Chita
Astrakhan
Novokuznetsk
Irkutsk
GEORGIAN S.S.R.
Guryev
Ulan-Ude
Batumi
Irtysh R.
Semipalatinsk
TURKEY
Grozny
Karaganda
Tbilisi
ALTAI MTS.
ARMENIAN S.S.R.
Shevchenko
Vladivostok
Yerevan
Aral Sea
Syr Darya
KAZAKH S.S.R.
AZERBAIJAN S.S.R.
Caspian Sea
Lake Balkhash
Baku
MONGOLIA
Sea of Japan
NORTH KOREA
KYZYL-KUM DESERT
Amu Darya
TURKMEN S.S.R.
Tashkent
Alma-Ata
Ashkhabad
UZBEK S.S.R.
Frunze
SOUTH KOREA
JAPAN
IRAQ
KARA-KUM DESERT
Bukhara
TIEN SHAN
KIRGHIZ S.S.R.
Dushanbe
TADZHIK S.S.R.
IRAN
CHINA
AFGHANISTAN
PAKISTAN
INDIA

Foreword

Richard Schifter

Perestroika and *glasnost* have made all predictions about the future of the Soviet Union precarious. Even three or four years ago, the sweeping changes Soviet leaders have made in confronting past and present failures, in allowing open discussion of issues, and in releasing prisoners would have been unthinkable. If President Gorbachev's initiatives succeed, we have reason to hope they may lead to a Soviet Union far different from the one we have known.

A changed attitude toward religion is one aspect of the Soviet Union's efforts at reform. Konstantin Kharchev, who as chairman of the Council of Ministers' Council on Religious Affairs is the top administrator of Soviet religious policies, admitted in late 1988 that existing laws on freedom of conscience "have no real backup." His suggestion to allow religious bodies the status of "a legal entity" is therefore important. Kharchev also indicated the possible return of religious buildings to their proper denominations: "Religious structures must not be used for other purposes if there are objections from believers." Churches and synagogues, he said, must also be permitted to run their own schools.

Sharp disagreements in the Soviet establishment are now clearly in evidence. While there are many who want to preserve the old ways, others are committed to carrying out "restructuring."

To be sure, Lenin continues to be revered. Soviet officials still sprinkle their speeches with quotations from him, and they justify the changes now under way by citing one or another of his precepts. But the approach to the relation between government and the governed seems no longer to reflect the core of Leninist teachings. What Lenin would have derided as bourgeois liberalism is beginning to find concrete expression in Soviet society.

Will it last? None of us can predict. We can observe what has changed, however, and what has not. The KGB appears to be under instructions to behave differently than it did heretofore. But that organization has not been dismantled. It still wields a great deal of power, and it continues to intimidate a great many people, particularly in regions distant from Moscow. I have frequently heard of warnings issued by KGB personnel to those who act or speak more freely than the KGB deems appropriate, warnings that the country's leadership will change again and that the KGB will then pursue those who made use of the freedoms now allowed. There is no doubt that if the Soviet leadership truly wants to turn the corner, wants to reassure the people that the present course will continue, it must begin to dismantle the apparatus of internal repression, the secret police.

The KGB is needed in the war against corruption. To allow it to function in a manner that advances the goal of clean government and yet have it respect civil liberties is a major challenge to the Soviet Union's reformers.

Given the relatively recent move toward greater openness, the limited successes thus far, and the powerful anti-*glasnost* forces at work, we cannot say that the Soviet reform movement is about to succeed. But those of us who believe that "governments are instituted among men, deriving their just powers from the consent of the governed" in keeping with what Thomas Jefferson called the "laws of nature and of nature's God," should view the trends now in evidence in the Soviet Union as natural, understandable, in the interest of the Soviet people, and, in fact, in the interest of people throughout the world. It is now imperative that we try to follow developments in the Soviet Union, that we recognize the forward movement that is taking place while at the same time being aware of its limits.

We also need to ask ourselves how we can be of help. In 1987 we saw for the first time in years that Soviet dissidents were no longer prevented from functioning, at least on the fringes of Soviet society—harassed, but not prevented from functioning. We applauded them. We gave them moral encouragement. Now we see reformers operating within the Soviet system, persons in positions of authority sticking their necks out to enlarge civil liberties, to respect religious belief, to institute the rule of law. We need to extend a helping hand to these reformers. Our approach must combine firmness and delicacy. Some progress can be made by public pressure. Other kinds of progress may require subtle influences on the current system. As one Soviet official described the latter process: "We are prepared to learn, as long as we are not being taught."

Wherever we can stimulate change within the Soviet Union we should surely do so. Just how we can effectively provide encouragement for democratic change in Soviet society is the question we need to keep constantly in mind in the period ahead. Religious bodies both in the Soviet Union and in the Free World will play a role in that change. Those bodies and all of us should master the kind of material contained in this book if we wish to discharge our responsibilities with clearsightedness and intelligence.

Ambassador Schifter has been assistant secretary of state for human rights and humanitarian affairs since October 1985.

Introduction

Eugene B. Shirley, Jr.

> I would like to make one preliminary remark concerning the character of our country. I think it will be a mistake to say . . . that our state—where believers and non-believers live—is "atheistic." This country has a cultural/historical tradition which includes many centuries of the existence of the Orthodox Church. There are tens of millions of believers, as well as atheists. And besides, this is a state that in its legislation acknowledges the existence of religion. Therefore it is not right to call our state "atheistic." It is better to say that this is a state where believers and non-believers live. —ARCHBISHOP KIRILL, rector, Leningrad Theological Academy.

OF THE 280 million people in the USSR, some 18 million are members of the Communist Party, while perhaps as many as 100 million or even more are adherents of Christian, Muslim, Jewish, Buddhist, and other religious traditions. Size does not correspond to power, of course; the Party holds the reins of absolute control, while religious believers live on the fringe of society, only minimally influential. Although the new initiatives of *glasnost* may alter that status somewhat, and current discussions about reducing discrimination against believers are promising, the extent to which discrimination will end remains an open question. Still, it is one of the great ironies of Soviet culture: an enduring and at times vibrant religious faith within an officially atheistic state.

I began researching this situation in the fall of 1980 with the aim of producing a television documentary. My interest grew out of a certain world view, a vision of the universe as an organism, profoundly interconnected, with every part affected by and affecting the others, every member having intrinsic value. No individual, religious group, or nation stands alone. When Buddhists or Muslims or Jews or Christians are denied a basic freedom in the Soviet Union, the freedom of us all is constricted.

In 1981, two prominent religious figures, Metropolitan Filaret of Kiev and Lubamir Mirajowsky, head of the Prague-based Christian Peace Conference, promised me assistance with my filming. Probably neither anticipated that the completed film would be as open about church-state relations and as critical of religious repression as it is. Largely through their efforts and, especially, those of Bruce Rigdon of the (U.S.) National Council of Churches of Christ (NCC), in May 1982 we were able to film in five Soviet cities, the first independent U.S. production company to film officially in the USSR.

Over the next 2½ years, the documentary *Candle in the Wind* took shape, under the skillful writing and directing of Arthur Barron, as a collection of "official" footage, underground film, rare archival material, and interviews with experts on Soviet affairs. Consultants to the project included scholar-specialists affiliated with Keston College—an eminent research center outside London for the study of religion in Communist countries—and the (U.S.) National Conference on Soviet Jewry, and numerous other academic experts. Michael Rowe, head of Soviet research at Keston College and the co-editor of this volume, was also centrally important to the development of *Candle in the Wind*.

This book draws heavily upon the resources and research that went into the making of the film but moves beyond it with more detailed and recent information. The title, of course, is rich with symbolism, the *candle* being religious faith, *wind* having the paradoxical connotation of both quickening and snuffing out.

The Place of Religion

Since the Bolshevik Revolution in 1917, laws and articles within successive constitutions have guaranteed Soviet believers "freedom to perform religious rites." In our interviews, Soviet government and religious leaders often referred to this constitutional right, enshrined in Article 52. "The church doesn't interfere in the affairs of the state, and the state, in its turn, doesn't mix with the affairs of religion. This is our constitutional principle,'' said Pyotr Makartsev, vice chairman of the government's Council for Religious Affairs. Archbishop Pitirim of Volokolamsk stated, ''Religion in our country is very free and separated from the state.''

Such responses, sincere or not, point to the unique place that religion holds in Soviet society: it is the only tolerated form of organized divergent ideology. Both Communist Party theory and Soviet institutional practice are fundamentally opposed to religion. Religious understandings are considered not only *wrong* but also socially *harmful*. Religion is to be kept at the extreme outer limits of social influence. Still, incense is burned, prayers are offered, and sermons are preached each day for the coming of a kingdom that will depose all existing powers and establish a different world order. Religion is at once ''a form of spiritual oppression,'' a ''kind of spiritual vodka in which the slaves of capitalism drown their human shape and their claims to any decent life whatsoever'' (Lenin), and the only voice of organized ideological dissent that has not been totally silenced by force. Hence it is not surprising that the relation between religion and the Soviet state has been ambiguous and dynamic, not static.

Russian Orthodoxy, with 50 million or more adherents, remains the dominant form in the Soviet Christian tradition, which also includes substantial groups of Roman Catholics, Protestant evangelicals, and others. Because of its long history of identification as the state church, revolutionary leaders sought to overthrow the Russian Orthodox Church along with the tsar. It survived largely because of the indomitable religious spirit of the Russian people. At first, the post-revolution church resisted state control and interference. But resistance proved futile as bishops and priests were executed, thousands of churches were closed, church property was nationalized, and charitable activities were prohibited. The only options open to the church were accommodation or martyrdom.

Not many years later, in the 1930s, the Russian church again was nearly destroyed, this time by Stalin. Only the tragedy of the ''Great Patriotic War'' (World War II) revived the major religious institutions. Then once again, in the 1960s, Khrushchev attempted the systematic destruction of religion. The last two decades can be classified as relatively better, with prospects for positive change increasing under Gorbachev. (It should be noted that religious intolerance and persecution in Russia and Russian-dominated areas has a centuries-long history. Under various tsars, Jews were forcibly baptized—the alternative was drowning—and proselytism by religious faiths other than Russian Orthodoxy was illegal. Tsarist governments routinely used religion for political purposes.)

The accommodating or "officially sanctioned" religious leader has two candles, one for God and one for the government. "The patriotic activity of religion and religious organizations is highly valued by our government," said Pyotr Makartsev of the Council for Religious Affairs. Just as *mullahs* of the Islamic faith serve as ambassadors in the Middle East, Russian Orthodox bishops frequently travel to the West. Where they can, some probably use their influence as loyal functionaries of the state to try to win minor concessions from the government on behalf of their religious communities. Their failure to protest the anti-religious policies of the Soviet system has been seen as proof of their loyalty to the state.

But in spite of the church's precarious existence, Western travelers are frequently struck by an obvious fervor in Russian Christianity, unmatched in any Western European country. Worshipers stand shoulder to shoulder for hours at a time, not only for Sunday services but for other church events as well.

The Religious Profile

Predictably, Soviet sociological data on religious believers are difficult to acquire and even more difficult to interpret. Most of what is officially available has been collected by the Institute of Scientific Atheism, which raises serious questions about its accuracy. There are vested interests in describing religion both as having little effect, for propaganda purposes, and as continuing with a certain strength, to justify the costly anti-religious bureaucracy. Still, a number of conclusions are generally accepted by specialists in this field. (I am indebted to William C.

Fletcher's *Soviet Believers* [Regents Press, 1981] for much of the following sociological information.)

Among Western countries, only the United States rivals the Soviet Union in the number and variety of religious communities. The large number of religious traditions in the USSR is due in part to the diversity of cultures and nationalities in this vast country—one-seventh of the earth's land mass. How many religious believers there are remains unknown; experts give vastly differing high and low estimates, especially of the Christian community. What is clear is that religious activity is most prevalent among people over age fifty, and that women outnumber men in the churches by perhaps as many as three or four to one. At the same time one often sees people of all ages at worship services, and there is evidence of a sustained and perhaps growing interest in a religious world view among young people, intellectuals, and others. *Glasnost* appears to have increased public manifestations of belief by these groups.

The median educational level of religious people appears to be somewhat lower than that of the rest of the population. This may be due in part to pervasive discrimination against believers in the educational system, and in part to the fact that older persons are generally less educated than younger ones. However, among some believers there is an aversion to secular education; certain minorities wish to minimize contact with unbelievers and the "world." By and large, Russian believers have remained isolated from modern theological understandings, as only very limited ecumenical and Western contact has been allowed. The religious communities tend to adopt rigid and authoritarian patterns of interaction and to reject a pluralistic philosophical perspective.

Statistics also show that from 30 to 40 per cent of religious people are not members of the labor force; those who are employed are likely to be in unskilled or semi-skilled work. These statistics undoubtedly reflect discrimination in employment. Those with satisfactory employment, however, are probably very hesitant to reveal their religious orientation for an official poll.

A greater proportion of rural than urban people are religious.

But most rural churches are closed, and the few that remain open usually have services infrequently. Therefore, observes William Fletcher, urban believers are generally characterized by a "stronger and more active faith. There seems to be less vacillation in their world view, and religion plays a more vigorous role in their lives than is the case with the average rural believer" (*Soviet Believers*, p. 203). The city also affords greater anonymity than the rural setting, not an insignificant factor in Soviet religious practice.

Most religious people trace their beliefs to early childhood. In large part this reflects the influence of grandparents, under whose care a high proportion of children are raised. Grandmothers sometimes secretly bring children to be baptized and in other ways attempt to pass on a religious heritage—a heritage that often also includes folk belief and superstition, especially in areas where there is no functioning religious community.

Not surprisingly, marriage is the least practiced of the sacraments. People generally marry at a time of life when secular attitudes are more prevalent and when, in the Soviet Union, they are most vulnerable to discrimination in education and employment. Baptism is widely practiced, but the religious funeral is the most common rite. The sacramental life of the church, however, has been bought at the price of an uneasy alliance with an atheistic regime—frequently at the expense of "unregistered" or underground believers.

The Two Tiers of Religion

Religious dissenters think the established churches have compromised with the state too much, and they view themselves as working to maintain a true witness to "pure biblical teaching" without state interference. They engage in activity on behalf of believers' rights, publish *samizdat* (clandestine, privately reproduced and circulated materials), and organize unofficial churches with charitable and evangelistic activities. A telling question for differentiating between the official and underground Christian bodies is, "Can a Christian fully obey Soviet laws?" The dissenter answers, "No."

It is not the position of either the film or this book that only those living in sustained conflict with the Soviet government can be "true believers," that one is either on the side of "godless Communism" or counted among the faithful. Both "official" and "unofficial" leaders and laity work to keep symbols of the religious world alive within their communities. Both are torn by the effects of the state's inherent antagonism toward religion.

Of all the officially registered religious communities in the Soviet Union, Jews are the most deprived. There are only six or seven rabbis for some 1.8 million Soviet Jews. In Odessa, a city with 100,000 to 200,000 Jews, there is only one synagogue—and it is in a non-Jewish part of the city.

The chairman of the Odessa Jewish community told us during an interview: "Jewish congregations don't need anything; they have everything." We later learned he is a lieutenant in the KGB, the Soviet secret police.

For Soviet Jews, the two-tiered structure, with both official and underground movements, is not nearly so pervasive as it is among Christians and Muslims. There are underground services, *bar mitzvahs*, and religious classes. But most Soviet Jews either assimilate into Russian culture or, at the cost of usually severe harassment, seek to emigrate to Israel or the West. A very few are reconciled to remaining in the USSR and attempting to affirm their tradition there.

The Soviet Union's some 47 million Muslims are the fifth-largest Muslim population in the world. At current growth rates—one out of two Soviet-born children is Muslim—they may one day challenge Russians as the leading ethnic community in the USSR.

In general, Muslims do not feel their culture and religious tradition threatened. Communism was forced on them by the Soviets but did not destroy the *umma*, the community of believers. Communist ideology is understood by Muslims not as a political doctrine but as a technique of power for preserving an ethnic Russian regime—considered to be directly descended from the imperial tsarist court. Mixed marriages between Muslims and Russians are extremely rare, and there is little cultural and linguistic assimilation.

Like the Christians, the Muslim community exists on both

official and underground levels. Official Muslim leaders are often used to promote Soviet foreign policy in Arab countries. Unofficial leaders, however, are committedly anti-Soviet and in some areas command significant local followings. Underground and sometimes violent Muslim organizations known as Sufi brotherhoods pose serious internal threats to Soviet policy.

Further east and north, in Siberia, are some 500,000 Buddhists. At first the Bolsheviks sensed a certain kinship with Buddhism, primarily because of the atheism of Zen. For the Buddhist, however, the world is ultimately an illusion; for the Marxist this world is all there is. Thus even Buddhism has not managed to escape the Soviet Union's anti-religious drive.

Can a contemporary state survive without a pantheon of gods? While Communist Party ideology claims that it can, and can thrive in doing so, the Soviet Union remains a country whose people are more steeped in religious tradition than those of most Western nations. Even among atheists, the cult of Lenin, expressed in statues to the "saint" in most parks, portraits of him in every schoolroom and office, and long lines waiting to venerate his remains, seems to suggest some deep human need for a deity, what Paul Tillich would call an object of ultimate concern.

About This Book

The pervasiveness and dynamism of religious traditions within this Marxist-Leninist setting produces a field of topics ripe for discussion. But I wish to make three cautionary remarks about what will follow in this book.

First, there is no hidden agenda, political or religious. The people involved with the project represent a diversity of political and religious views. It would be unfair to draw conclusions about issues of religious belief, domestic policy, or foreign affairs that are not immediately available from the facts conveyed here.

Second, the issue in this study is not socialism versus capitalism. We who enjoy the fruits of capitalism and the democratic process tend to attribute to Soviet believers, especially religious dissidents, a throughgoing anti-Sovietism. This does them and their cause great disservice, and gives substance to their government's claim that Western concern is not really about religious freedom but rather about an economic system.

Perhaps one reason for the confusion of the issues is that to be religiously observant in the Soviet Union is to place oneself unquestionably in opposition to the ultimate ideological aims of the state. In addition, there is the difficult question of what is meant by "socialism." Soviet-style socialism is different from a variety of other economic situations that may also be called socialist. Both of these points are expressed in the proceedings of the trial of the prominent dissident Vladimir Poresh:

> *Katukova* [prosecutor]: Do you believe that your activity could be consistent with a socialist society?
>
> *Poresh*: It is written in the Constitution of the USSR that the final aim of socialist society is Communism, which means the creation of a godless state, so in this sense I am subversive. The Kingdom of God will replace Communism.

To appreciate Poresh's statement fully, however, we should juxtapose it with that of another well-known dissident, Anatole Levitin. Levitin stated during an interview that while he rejected "categorically the brutality of the Soviet regime," he is "a supporter of socialism; I am a Christian socialist." As one priest put it, "In our country . . . an Orthodox Christian is taking part in the work of building a new socialist society."

The issue is not one of socialism versus capitalism but of Soviet practice and ideological aims versus the rule of national and international law. Some economic and political systems are more conducive to freedom of religious belief than others. But the important fact in this study remains that Christians and other religious believers can and do survive under varying forms of governments, accommodating to different politico-economic systems as their consciences and situations allow.

Third, while I would never suggest that there is an ethical equivalency between the internal policies of the Soviet Union and those of the United States, both the film project and the book were approached with a keen sense of the moral compromise inherent in all state powers. All nations bow the knee to parochial and economic interests, to "tribal gods." We are concerned about all people who suffer from state tyranny. Our primary concern, however, has been with a system where repression has taken an obvious and demanding institutional form.

A case could be made for the futility of focusing upon the abuses of an "enemy." The sins of one's own state are difficult enough to remedy—why investigate those of a historical antagonist?

I hope that what the reader gains from the following study is simply a more complete and realistic comprehension not only of religious life among the Soviet people but also of the Soviet system itself. The reader will then have a better understanding of why Gorbachev's *perestroika* and *glasnost* initiatives are necessary, and will have a yardstick against which to measure changes in the religious sphere as they occur.

Until laws are actually altered and the way new laws are to be enforced is demonstrated, the scope of Gorbachev's reforms cannot be predicted. Several writers in this book do point to areas where improvement in the lot of believers either has begun or is anticipated. But the main focus of the eleven authors here is the more than six decades of Soviet religious policy before Gorbachev, an era whose legacy continues to dominate Soviet religious life.

A study of religion in the Soviet Union suggests a new set of questions to be asked. As the failures of a compartmentalized approach to academic study become increasingly evident, so it becomes obvious that an examination of Soviet economics or political structures or foreign-policy objectives is incomplete without an interrelated understanding of the people's many and varied "ultimate concerns." Spanning vast historic periods as well as geographic, national, and cultural boundaries, religious traditions offer their own peculiar and rarely insignificant perspectives on the world.

Religion in the Union of Soviet Socialist Republics has not been "destroyed from the thoughts of mankind." It has neither withered away in the face of advancing socialism, as Marx predicted, nor been extinguished under the anti-religious pressures of Communism, first set in motion by Lenin. While it has been forced to the periphery of social influence, the past seventy years have demonstrated the power of the religious spirit to survive great calamity and to continue to offer living symbols of worth and purpose in an all too Orwellian world.

Religion itself is the story of beginning again, a story in which the cycles of rebirth save the world from irreversible movement toward a determined end. Death means resurrection. Earth blossoms anew. "You can be born again" is a motif consistent with universal religious thought. The degree of success in seizing this vision within a "totalitarian" structure depends in part upon the flexibilities of that structure. Perhaps more important, however, is the creative ability of religious believers to rise above external coercion through the persuasive power that religion has always had for the human spirit.

1

Religion in Russia: To 1917

Karl-Heinz Schroeder

All too often accounts of the history of civilization pay relatively little attention to the Russian people, presenting their story in relation to that of presumably more important Western peoples. A typical introductory history course omits the Russian past before the seventeenth century and Peter the Great. Students of the history of Christianity are likely to be even less aware of the Russian people's religious history. This ethnocentric approach has deprived Western students of the insights they need to understand the Russian and Slavic political, cultural, and religious traditions.

One of the most important influences upon the Russian character from the Middle Ages to the present has been the Russian Orthodox Church. For centuries the church was the people's unifying force, providing a focus of identity and stimulating art, music, and literature. In times of decline and foreign oppression, the church fostered the strength to persevere against hardship and gave meaning to seemingly inexplicable difficulties. In times of imperial expansion and national glory, the church was the incarnate symbol of God's blessing. Even today, comments

---

Karl-Heinz Schroeder teaches modern Europe, the history of Christianity, and other subjects at Union College in Lincoln, Nebraska. He was born in Weinheim, Germany, and did graduate and postgraduate work at the University of California at Santa Barbara.

Hedrick Smith, "the Party has acknowledged Orthodoxy as an essential ingredient in the particular mixture of loyalties that holds the Soviet state together, a vital element of its Russianness" (*The Russians*, 1976, p. 583).

The Arrival of Cyril and Methodius, 863

The brothers Constantine (who later took the name Cyril) and Methodius and their disciples, who worked among the Moravians and Bulgarians in the ninth century, are generally credited with laying the foundation for Slavic Christianity. According to tenth- and eleventh-century legend, however, Christianity had penetrated into Russia as early as the age of the apostles; the *Primary Chronicle*, a medieval Russian history, cites the missionary journey of Saint Andrew the Apostle to the Crimea and other areas. Undoubtedly this story was useful to establish for the church a direct apostolic foundation. Still it is a known fact that the early church did indeed penetrate into the Black Sea region, establishing Christian communities in the Greek cities along its coast. Through trade and other contacts, the Christian faith undoubtedly became known to the Slavic peoples inhabiting that region and beyond.

The Slavs at that time occupied vast territories to the north of the Byzantine Empire, which at its height in the sixth century nearly encircled the Mediterranean Sea. The Slavs were in the process of forming a state and were becoming a serious challenge to Byzantium. The Byzantine church—that is, the part of the church whose primary bishop was the patriarch of Constantinople (Byzantium)—made its first major missionary thrust into Slavic territory in 863. At the request of Prince Rastislav of Moravia (now part of Czechoslovakia), it sent as missionaries two experienced brothers from the Greek city of Thessalonica: Constantine, a teacher and philologist, and Methodius, a monk. The brothers were fluent not only in Greek but also in Slavonic, the language of the Slavs to whom they were sent. Also, they had already done some important work for the Byzantine Empire and church among the Khazars north of the Caucasus Mountains. Perhaps even more important than their diplomatic experience was their scholarly training. Constantine had become an outstanding scholar, teaching philosophy at the patriarchal school in Constantinople. As the father of the Cyrillic alphabet, he was to make a great contribution to Slavic culture: the alphabet made possible the development of a Slavic literature.

Since the Slavic lands were far removed from Constantinople, it was almost inevitable that the influence of the Franks (a Germanic people with a sizable empire in Western Europe) and other Western Europeans would be working against the Byzantine missionaries. Jealousy on the part of Frankish Latin clergy and of the Greek brothers' use of Slavonic as a language of the church brought about determined opposition, even though the pope of Rome had given his approval to the brothers' missionary activities.

Constantine died in Rome in February 869, only a few weeks after he had become a monk and taken the name Cyril. Methodius continued his work among the Slavs, and Pope Hadrian II strengthened his hand by making him archbishop of Pannonia, with jurisdiction over Pannonia, Moravia, and Slovakia. Then in 870 new political realities dramatically altered the religious situation: Rastislav, the prince of Moravia, was overthrown by his nephew Sviatopluk, who acknowledged the Frankish king Louis the German as overlord. Seizing this opportunity, the Frankish clergy brought about the persecution and imprisonment of the newly consecrated archbishop. Not until three years later was a new pope, John VIII, able to gain his release. The Frankish clergy remained adamant in their refusal to accept a Slavonic liturgy, and the support of the papacy for the work of Methodius weakened.

Central to these developments was a doctrinal split between the Eastern and Western churches: the Frankish church and Rome adhered to the doctrine of *filioque* ("and from the son"), which holds that the Holy Spirit proceeds from the Father *and* the Son, while the Byzantine church, committed to the original formulation of the Nicene Creed, rejected this interpolation as heresy. The dispute culminated in 1054 in the Great Schism.

Isolated and far from home, Methodius found himself in a precarious situation. In 881 he journeyed to Constantinople, possibly to discuss the missionary work among the Slavs. Upon his return he devoted his remaining years to translating religious and juridical works from Greek into Slavonic. Methodius died in 885, having seen his ecclesiastical organization fall into the hands of his enemies. Still, the literary, juridical, and religious work that he and his brother had accomplished were foundational to the culture of the Slavic peoples.

While the Moravian work of Saint Cyril and Saint Methodius would disappear, in the 890s their disciples carried their literary and religious legacy to the Bulgarians. The Bulgarians formed the first "national" church of the Slavs to be recognized as autocephalous (self-governing) by the patriarchate of Constantinople (927). The significance of the creation of a national Slavic church with a Slavonic liturgy and literature cannot be overemphasized. The Latin-Germanic world of western and central Europe did not see a comparable development until the Protestant Reformation in the sixteenth century.

Baptism of Princess Olga, 955

While the foundation for Slavic Christianity was to a large extent laid by Cyril and Methodius and their disciples among the Moravians and Bulgarians in the ninth century, the future of this new form of Christianity lay with the people of Kievan Rus'. This earliest Russian state, centered in Kiev, flourished from the tenth to the thirteenth century.

The first convert who was significant in the historical development of Christianity in the area was Princess Olga, a local princess who served as regent for her son from 945 to 962. Princess Olga was a far-sighted regional ruler, the first to recognize that the Christianization of her lands would help to bring her people into contact with the great powers to the south and west. Conversion would mean new markets, and trade, and entrance into the civilized world of Europe.

Princess Olga herself was baptized by the Byzantine patriarch when she visited Constantinople in 955. But later, after her request was turned down by Constantinople, she asked the German emperor Otto I to send a bishop and missionary priests to work among her people. Her reasons for turning from the Byzantine church to the Roman church—other than Constantinople's negative response to her request for missionaries—are not clear. Perhaps she wanted the church in her kingdom to be rather independent, and the empire of the West was much farther away than the empire of Byzantium. Whatever her reasons, the Latin church was willing to oblige. At this time the church of Rome was also expanding into Scandinavia and was active in the conversion of the Poles and other Baltic Slavs.

By the time the Latin priests arrived, however, Olga had stepped down, and her son, Sviatoslav, had taken power. He was not well disposed toward the new religion. The Western priests returned home, and Olga's plans had to be postponed.

Baptism of Prince Vladimir, 988

It was Olga's grandson, Vladimir, who realized her dream of a Christian Kievan Rus'. His conversion in 988 is considered the beginning of Christianity in Russia. Although that conversion is shrouded in mystery, the *Primary Chronicle* records an interesting, if apocryphal, story. The prince, in looking for a new religion for his people, considered Islam, Judaism, Western Christianity, and Byzantine, or Greek, Christianity. He sent a team of ten wise men to visit the centers of these religious traditions. When they returned, their unanimous opinion was in favor of Byzantium. Their description of what they saw and experienced is worth quoting:

> Then we went on to Greece, and the Greeks led us to the edifices where they worship their God, and we know not whether we were in heaven or earth. For on earth there is no such splendor or beauty, and we are at a loss to describe it. We know only that God dwells there among men, and their service is fairer than the ceremonies of other nations. For we cannot forget that beauty. Every man, after tasting something sweet, is afterward unwilling to accept that which is bitter, and therefore we can dwell no longer here [Serge Zenkovsky, *Medieval Russia's Epics, Chronicles, and Tales* (Dutton, 1975), pp. 67–68].

Vladimir appears to have been an astute politician who understood clearly the political potential of Christianity, both for legitimizing and consolidating power at home and for gaining access to the family of civilized powers. His conversion meant the forced conversion of the entire population under his control. Mass baptisms were ordered at the Dneiper River; those who refused were drowned. To ensure that the people's allegiance to the new faith would not waiver, Vladimir ordered the conversion of pagan shrines into Christian places of worship, with resident priests. It is recorded that "unbelievers" wept as their idols were destroyed and they were forced to succumb to a new and foreign but politically expedient way of reverencing the Absolute. Children from the upper classes were educated in the new faith, probably in monastery schools. The immediate impact upon the masses was superficial, and pagan practices survived among the people even into the modern period.

Importance of the Monasteries

The influence of Christianity was more immediately felt in the urban areas, where government control was much stronger. Here churches were built and monasteries established. From these urban centers, the message of Orthodox Christianity slowly penetrated into the countryside.

The monasteries played a key role in the gradual conversion of the people who would later be called "Russians" and "Ukrainians." As in the Roman Catholic West during the Middle Ages, the monasteries were not only the transmitters of religious education but also the promoters of "civilization." One important difference, however, between Eastern and Western monasteries in the practice of this civilizing role was the use, in the East, of the language of the people. In the West, the church and education used the Latin language and were therefore accessible only to an elite. In the East, the liturgy and religious literature were available to the people in their own language. The Russian monasteries produced Slavonic translations from Greek or Bulgarian and copies of manuscripts already in Slavonic.

According to Professor George P. Fedotov (*The Russian Religious Mind,* 1960, p. 37ff.), this vernacular emphasis in the young Russian Orthodox Church had serious negative implications for the intellectual development of Russia. Fedotov argues that the more rapid cultural development of Western Europe was largely the result of the use of Latin as the language of religion and education throughout the Middle Ages. Western European clergy and scholars through their use of Latin gained access to the classical secular learning of antiquity—history, philosophy, geography, science—which greatly stimulated the development of scholarly and scientific thinking.

Fedotov states that Russia, on the other hand, "did not receive Greek classical culture with its acceptance of Greek Christianity" (p. 39); rather, it received Slavonic translations of the Scriptures or spiritual writings that had already been made in Moravia and Bulgaria, to which the Russians added their own translations of Greek religious writings. But no Greek secular writings were among these translations. As a result, the Russian mind was not challenged by a more secular world view, as seen in Greek classical civilization. It may not be surprising, then, that Russia did not produce any "scientific" works and that its "medieval" period lasted so much longer than that of Western Europe.

While secular works of the Greeks were ignored, the catalogue of Greek religious texts translated into Slavonic is enormous, consisting of canonical and apocryphal Scriptures, sermons, moral treatises and admonitions, and sayings of religious thinkers. Most numerous are lives of saints. Indeed, the unifying characteristic of the Slavonic literary corpus in medieval Russia is its practical and didactic nature. Works recounting the lives of saints—of men and women who escaped the snares of the devil and gained eternal life—were important for teaching Christian heroism and the rewards of Christian virtue, while the Old Testament, particularly the Psalter, was important for liturgical worship.

But the use of the vernacular in lieu of Latin or Greek as the language of worship and education also had an important advantage for Russia: religious services were conducted in a language understood by the people and certainly helped in the early development of a national culture and consciousness.

Two Forms of Monasticism

The growing division between the Eastern and Western parts of the church was formalized in the Great Schism of 1054, when the church divided into Orthodox and Catholic entities. The Orthodox Church in Kievan Rus' was organized on the Byzantine model. The titular leader was the metropolitan of Kiev, and below him were the bishops of other major urban communities. The metropolitan of Kiev was, until the thirteenth century, almost always a Greek, appointed by and subject to the patriarchate of Constantinople. This direct control of the Russian church by the Greek patriarch lasted until the fifteenth century.

Below the metropolitan and other bishops were the monasteries. Like its Byzantine model, the Russian monastic movement was not grouped onto various "orders" with distinct disciplines, as in the Latin West. Instead, each monastery was formed around its own spiritual founder but subject to the authority of the local bishop. One of the most important was the Monastery of the Caves in Kiev, established early in the eleventh century. Here Saint Theodosius created the Eremetic Cave form of monasticism—one of two major Russian monastic traditions. So pervasive was the influence of Theodosius that it is said that "all Russian monks are his children" (Fedotov, p. 111). Emphasizing poverty, humility, and especially social service, he used the example of Jesus to instill in his disciples the Christian vocation of service, love, humility, and suffering.

Besides the Theodosian monastic form there arose, also in the eleventh century, the Founder's Monastery form—institutions founded by princes and subject to them, particularly in the areas of administering property and appointing abbots (heads of monasteries). Ernst Benz maintains that the Founder's Monastery, coupled with the ecclesiastical hierarchy, "formed the backbone of the evolving state church" centered in Kiev (*The Eastern Orthodox Church*, 1963, p. 94). Siding with and legitimizing the authority of the established powers, the Founder's Monastery frequently found itself in opposition to the Eremetic Cave movement, whose support was among the poor and oppressed. The monasteries provided the ecclesiastical leadership, since only monks were eligible to serve in higher church offices. The religious needs of the local parishes were attended to by married priests. Parish priests could not become bishops unless they took monastic vows.

By the middle of the eleventh century, Kievan Rus' had begun to decline. Among the major factors historians cite to explain this were civil wars among the princes of the ruling dynasty, numerous attacks by a nomadic Turkic people from Asia called Cumans or Polovtsy, and a serious decline in Kiev's economic welfare as a result of a shift in East-West trade to the Mediterranean, where Italian merchants had become active (Nicholas V. Riasanovsky, *A History of Russia*, 1963, pp. 42–46). These events led to a population shift from the south to the north that was given further impetus by Mongol raids and conquest in the thirteenth century. Kiev was devastated by the Mongols in 1240. The northern city of Novgorod emerged as the new Russian center, and Christianity spread from Kiev to the north and northeast. With the northward move, society changed from a more urban to a more rural one, and Moscow developed into a political center.

Two Centuries of Mongol Rule

While the Russians were being subdued by the Mongols, they also had to face the combined attack of the Christian Swedes and the Teutonic and Livonian Knights (German military-religious orders) in the northwest. Prince Alexander rallied the Russian forces and defeated the invaders in 1240 and 1242. (He earned the surname Nevsky—"of the Neva"—by defeating the Swedes on the Neva River.) Mongol domination, on the other hand, lasted about 200 years and was in some ways quite severe. Forced conscription of Russian men into the Mongol armies and punitive expeditions to suppress the slightest attempts at independence were a feature of Mongol rule, which stretched from the Pacific Ocean to the Balkans. As part of the Mongol Empire, however, Russian craftsmen and merchants were provided with new markets and important opportunities for trade, and the Mongol overlords were tolerant of the religious beliefs of their subjects. Still, the experience of foreign invasion and occupation left an indelible mark on the Russian soul.

Russia was permanently changed by Mongol rule in several ways. The economy took a definite turn toward the agrarian, as cities were devastated or destroyed. Many crafts and trades declined or disappeared. A significant political change was the dissolution of the old Russian city assemblies, once an important check on princely powers. The destruction of many cities, coupled with the dislike of the assemblies by Mongol rulers and Russian princes alike, doomed the "democratic" element in the political system at the end of the fifteenth century. Once the Mongols were expelled, the princes emerged with no remaining political challenge to their power.

The church was not dramatically affected during the two centuries of Mongol rule. In fact, its power and influence actually increased, as it was seen to provide necessary spiritual support in a period of instability. With the increasing importance of the peasants in the more agrarian economy, the Christianization of Russia was completed by the inclusion of the rural population in the church.

The monasteries played a significant role in the rural development of the church. Young men who were deeply dissatisfied with life under the Mongols dedicated themselves to religious life in the "wilderness." Often beginning as hermits, some would in time attract followers, and in this way many monastic communities developed. Inevitably, villages would grow up around these religious institutions, and again individual monks, dissatisfied with their rapidly changing environment, would leave and go further into the wilderness. There the process might start all over again. In this way, religious centers were established throughout the country, extending all the way to the Arctic Circle.

Ascendancy of Moscow

Kiev never fully recovered from its Mongol sacking, and during the fourteenth century Moscow assumed prominence. When Metropolitan Peter (1308–26) made Moscow his place of residence, the city became the center of Russia's religious life. Saint Sergius of Rodonezh, the saint of the wilderness, also contributed to the rising importance of Moscow in the fourteenth century, giving Grand Duke Dmitri Donskoi of Moscow his blessing before the battle of Kulikovo (September 1380), where the prince's army defeated the Mongols. While this battle proved the vulnerability of the Mongols and confirmed the importance of Moscow, not for another century would Russia be free of the Mongol yoke.

Through the fourteenth century, the Russian church remained subject to the patriarch of Constantinople, and the metropolitans continued to be, for the most part, Greek. But by the middle of the fifteenth century, as a result of major shifts in the international political arena, the Russian church had been freed from the domination of Constantinople.

The beginning of the fifteenth century witnessed the Byzantine Empire fighting for survival against the Ottoman Turks, who by 1400 had conquered large areas of the Balkans (the Balkan peninsula today comprises Greece, Yugoslavia, Romania, Bulgaria, Albania, and part of Turkey). The only possible assistance for the Byzantine Empire was the Roman Catholic West. But Western assistance would have its price: Greek Orthodox recognition of papal authority, of the use of unleavened bread in the Eucharist, of the doctrine of purgatory, and of the *filioque* clause in the creed—the four points that four centuries earlier had caused the division of the church.

The Florentine Union

The majority of an Orthodox episcopal delegation signed a treaty of union with the Western church in 1439, during the Council of Florence (1438–45), but the agreement was almost universally rejected by the masses of believers back home. Metropolitan Isidore of Kiev, the Russian delegate to the council, was arrested upon his return to Moscow and later exiled. When Grand Duke Basil II called a council of the Russian bishops in 1448 to elect a new and "orthodox" metropolitan, independent of Constantinople, Bishop Jonas became the first autonomously elected metropolitan of Russia.

When the hoped-for military assistance from the West never arrived, Constantinople fell to the Turks in May 1453. The sacred church of Hagia Sophia ("Holy Wisdom") was converted into a mosque. To the Orthodox believer, the fall of Constantinople to the Turks and the end of the Byzantine Empire was a sign that God was displeased with the 1439 union. In Russia, it was believed that the torch of the true faith had been passed on to the Russian Orthodox Church. Even after the Greek Orthodox patriarch of Constantinople officially repudiated the Florentine Union in 1453, the Russian church continued to pursue its independent course of electing its own leader.

Indeed, with the rest of the Orthodox world under the domination of the Turks, Moscow began to emerge as the political center of Orthodoxy; the idea developed that Moscow had become the "Third Rome" (after Constantinople, or "New Rome"). To many Russians it must have been quite significant that in 1472 Sophia, the niece of the last ruling Byzantine emperor, married Ivan III and thus established a direct link between the imperial house and the Grand Duke of Moscow. The double-headed eagle of Byzantium became the emblem of Moscow.

Possessors and Non-Possessors

For Russia, emerging triumphantly from two centuries of Mongol domination, the fifteenth and sixteenth centuries were a dynamic period. The church had become autonomous and the most powerful in the Orthodox world. But there were voices of discontent, and by the beginning of the sixteenth century two philosophies within the church had begun to clash. On the one hand were the Non-Possessors, led by Saint Nil Sorsky, who stood in a prophetic, mystical, and idealist tradition. In opposition to them were the Possessors, emphasizing practicality and realism, led by Saint Joseph, abbot of Volokalamsk. The issue at stake was the monastic ownership of land, at a time when monasteries possessed one-third of Russian territory.

For the Non-Possessors, monastic wealth was a corruption of the original intent of the monastic movement. The monk's duty was to exemplify the Christian ideal of separation from the concerns of the world and complete surrender to God and his care. As the acquisition of property and wealth inevitably leads back into the world and involvement with "corruptions," such as political concerns, it was not appropriate for those devoted to the spiritual quest to acquire possessions. The Possessors argued from a more pragmatic position: the church had a religious and social obligation to care for the less fortunate, which it could not do effectively without wealth and government assistance. At the church council of 1503, these two factions split, and for two decades the issue remained unresolved.

The differing ideals of the two movements are seen in their attitudes toward the government and toward heretical movements. The establishment-oriented Possessors argued for close cooperation between church and state, even to the point of the state's enforcing religious conformity. The Non-Possessors, however, rejected government involvement with church affairs. This issue came to a head with concern over the "Judaizers," a heretical Christian movement that had adopted some Jewish concepts and had made numerous converts. The Non-Possessors argued for persuasion as the only means of dealing with heresy; the Possessors argued that the full weight of the state ought to prevail on the side of Truth. The church council of 1504 came down in favor of the Possessors, which meant the eventual elimination of the Judaizer sect.

But the differences between the Possessors and the Non-Possessors ran deeper still. Nil Sorsky and the Non-Possessors emphasized a more personal, pietistic, and mystical form of worship, with puritanical tendencies. They played down the importance of beauty in the liturgical services, including the decoration of churches and the painting of icons. Nothing, they held, should distract the believer from his contemplation of God. Abbot Joseph and his supporters, however, argued for a more communal and sensuous worship experience as a window through which the believer could glimpse the eternal glories of heaven.

The road to "Truth" is often precarious and bloody, and the conflict between Nil Sorsky and Joseph grew increasingly bitter. Then in 1525–26 the Non-Possessors attacked Tsar Basil III for unjustly divorcing his wife. The ruler's wrath forced the government to support the Possessors, driving the Non-Possessors underground and exposing them to persecution. Still, Nil Sorsky's position struck a sympathetic note among many believers, and he was eventually canonized along with his rival and persecutor, Abbot Joseph.

Joseph's victory in the Non-Possessor/Possessor controversy is important because it solidified the association between church and state. He and his followers may not have foreseen the dangers to the spiritual independence of the church that arose during the reign of Ivan the Terrible (1533–84). Metropolitan Philip of Moscow, who protested the tyrant's brutality, was arrested and strangled in 1569. Further clashes between the church and the tsar are prominent in the seventeenth century.

The belief that Moscow was the "Third Rome" was confirmed in 1589 when the Metropolitan of Moscow became the first Patriarch of Moscow and All Russia. Moscow thus took its place alongside the ancient Orthodox patriarchates of Constantinople, Alexandria, Antioch, and Jerusalem.

Tsar Peter's Vision

With the reign of Tsar Peter the Great (1682–1725), grandson of the founder of the Romanov dynasty (Tsar Michael) and great-grandson of Patriarch Philaret, a new period begins in the Russian Orthodox Church. Influenced strongly by Western European developments and examples, Peter decided to curtail drastically the power and influence of the church, molding it more in the manner of Protestant churches in the West.

During the seventeenth century, Russia was still a medieval society. The West had moved far ahead of it economically, militarily, and technologically. Peter's early contacts with the resident foreign community in Moscow and, later, his travels as a young tsar revealed to him the relative backwardness of his country. He knew that the future development of Russia depended on its ability to adopt the advances of the West.

The young, visionary ruler faced an immense task in getting the necessary support from the nobility and the church. The nobility remained steeped in a semi-barbarian frame of mind and style of life, while the church was xenophobic, convinced that it was God's only true church and that those affiliated with any other churches, particularly Westerners, were the devil's agents.

Peter's dream of making Russia into a modern nation along Western lines depended on his ability to create a new foundation. He took a bold step in 1703 by founding a new capital on the Gulf of Finland, in territory recently taken from the Swedes. Saint Petersburg (now Leningrad) remained Russia's capital city until 1917. It was considered Russia's window to the West. Important families had to join the imperial family there if they wanted access to power and influence. Peter also forced his subjects, particularly the nobility, to become "European" by adopting Western customs, dress, and education. Peter imported Westerners who served as teachers, as technical experts in various fields, and as examples of a more modern, enlightened way of life. None of this would have been possible without the support, or at least the acquiescence, of the church, which remained the center of Russian civilization.

Peter was rather critical of the church. Though not an agnostic, he did not assume the attitude of a "true believer": he did not look to the patriarch as the "other" head of Russia. For him, there could be only one ruler; the role of the church was to give spiritual guidance and encourage loyalty to the state. So when Patriarch Adrian died in 1700, Tsar Peter refused to permit the election of a new patriarch, and from 1700 to 1721 he appointed a "keeper and administrator of the Patriarchal See." The office was held first by Bishop Stefan Yavorsky and then, after his death, by Archbishop Theophan Prokopovich.

The Church's Loss of Autonomy

By 1721, Peter's effort to control the church was organizationally complete. The office of the patriarch was abolished, and a college of twelve spiritual leaders representing the bishops, the monasteries, and the married clergy was established. This "Holy Synod," kept under the tsar's close supervision, remained in charge of the hierarchy until the overthrow of the Romanov dynasty in 1917.

Peter outlined the new position of the church in the *Spiritual Regulation* of 1721, which completely subjected the interests of the church to those of the tsar and the state. The Russian Orthodox Church thus joined its Western—primarily Lutheran—cousins in losing its autonomy, and, as with the destruction of the city assemblies centuries before, a possible restraining force on absolute government was eliminated. If not in theory then at least in practice, the tsar became the ultimate authority in church affairs. This new reality was expressed clearly when Tsar Paul said in 1797 that "the tsar is the head of the church" (Vernadsky, *History of Russia*, 1961, p. 188). The clergy were made officials of the state. They were even required to report to the state authorities any act or consideration of sedition or treason that might have been admitted during confession.

The role of the powerful and wealthy monasteries was substantially diminished under Peter's policies. The number of monasteries, as well as their membership, was greatly curtailed, and a portion of their income was diverted into government hands, a practice that Peter's successors continued throughout the eighteenth century. One of the main motives for Peter's action against the monasteries was his conviction that the primarily contemplative monks and nuns made no contribution to society. He recommended that they should concern themselves with productive work for the poor, the aged, and orphans. A more active role in caring for the underprivileged would justify the monasteries' existence. Unfortunately, however, the tsar also removed the financial basis necessary for such work.

Opposition to these and other "Westernizing" policies of Peter and his successors was ruthlessly suppressed. The resistance found its most tragic expression in the fate of Peter's oldest son, Alexis. The young crown prince was drawn into a conspiracy against his own father; after it was discovered, the prince was tried and tortured to death. By not sparing his own son the tsar proved that no opposition to his plan to make Russia a modern Western power would be tolerated. In this respect, Peter's example had its imitators. When in 1762 Archbishop Arseni Matseevich protested Catherine the Great's confiscation of church land, he was arrested and imprisoned for life.

The reform measures of Peter and his successors alienated large segments of the population from their own government and church. Many of the educated among the nobility as well as commoners fell under the spell of modern ideas through Western education, travel, and association with resident foreigners. Among the rising intelligentsia, such Western movements as the Enlightenment, Romanticism, Darwinism, and Marxism took the place of Orthodox Christianity in providing insight and inspiration for Russia's modern development. Those who became supporters of these modern movements saw the church and its clergy largely as stagnant and irrelevant, a hindrance to Russia's becoming a—if not *the*—major European power.

Many of the less educated, too, especially among the commoners, were dissatisfied with the "new" church. They turned toward various sects or toward a more personal religion. Dissenting groups, such as the Old Believers, and sects, such as the Khlysty, Dukhobors, Molokanes, and Stundists, enjoyed a rapid increase of followers during the latter part of the nineteenth century. The approximately 9 million dissenting and sectarian believers in 1850 had more than doubled to some 20 million by 1905.

The Nineteenth Century: Religious Revival

While the Russian Orthodox Church was a convenient tool for the state to use in controlling the common people, the political use of the church did not spell a complete abandonment of its purpose or the end of its spiritual strength. In fact, after adjusting to the political realities of the eighteenth and nineteenth centuries, the church underwent a significant religious revival. The number of monastic institutions more than doubled during the nineteenth century, and the suppressed views of the Non-Possessors re-emerged within the monasteries.

One reflection of this religious revival and of the wellsprings of spirituality deep within the Russian Orthodox tradition is the rise and appeal of the *startsi*. Considered to be special conduits of God's grace to the faithful, the *startsi* were men who, through many years of strict asceticism and spiritual contemplation, had gained the reputation of extraordinary saintliness and wisdom. People from all corners of Russia made pilgrimages to their places of abode for spiritual guidance, practical advice, and physical healing. It is said that Saint Seraphim of Sarov, who lived from 1759 to 1833, would sometimes see hundreds of devout men and women in a single day. The influence of the *startsi* was pervasive, as those who sought their advice came from all walks of life. Even members of the Russian intelligentsia such as Tolstoy and Dostoevsky were influenced by them.

Russian Orthodoxy also exhibited its new dynamism in a revival of missionary activity. The collapse of the Mongol Empire and the development of a Russian Empire stimulated the desire of both church and state to expand the Russian Orthodox faith among pagan and Muslim subjects. While the attacks by the Romanov rulers on the monasteries during the eighteenth century slowed the missionary work of the monks, men like John Veniaminov (1797–1879)—later Metropolitan Innocent of Moscow—traveled through Siberia, to the Pacific, and even to Alaska to preach the gospel of the Russian Orthodox Church.

A further development was the appearance of a rather remarkable and influential group of intellectuals, some of whom had been admirers of Western ways and modes of thought but had become disillusioned with modernity and returned to the Orthodox fold. After being exposed to the best secular learning of the eighteenth and nineteenth centuries, these persons returned to the spiritual roots of their country and people, realizing that the character of Russia was deeply rooted in the church and that they could best serve the future of the nation by building on the ancient heritage of Russian religiosity. Such men as Alexis Khomyakov (1804–60), one of the greatest and most original Russian theologians, and Vladimir Solovyov (1853–1900), one of the greatest Russian philosophers, were the product of this movement. Indeed, the vitality of Russian religiosity can also be seen in the great masterpieces of literary geniuses like the radical dissenter Lev Tolstoy, and the devoutly Orthodox Fyodor Dostoevsky; thus it entered into the mainstream of world literature. Both of these writers had experienced a religious conversion that turned them away from nineteenth-century secularism and toward their country's spiritual foundations.

The Early Twentieth Century

The Russian Orthodox Church prior to the catastrophe of World War One had overcome the negative effects of Peter's reforms, had maintained the allegiance of the vast majority of the Russian people, and was experiencing what could be termed a revival or renaissance. At the same time, however, a growing number of religious groups such as Old Believers and what we today call evangelicals were not affiliated with the official church; clearly there was a significant amount of dissatisfaction. While many Russian intellectual leaders were proud and supportive of the Orthodox tradition, many of them saw a need for change within the church and in its relation to the government.

By 1900, both clergy and lay voices were calling for removal of the heavy hand of the state in church affairs and for the restoration of the patriarchate. But the latter goal was not to be accomplished during the peaceful days preceding the Great War. The synodal structure set up by Peter the Great was eliminated only after the turbulent and dark days of the Bolshevik *coup d'état* of 1917, which was followed by civil war. By this time, however, the church and the dissenters had to prepare to face the much more brutal and menacing force of Bolshevism. Had Romanov absolutism prepared the church to survive this challenge?

2

Church and State 1917–64

Andrew Sorokowski

THE RELIGIOUS picture in Russia and the Soviet Union between the 1917 revolution and the fall of Khrushchev in 1964 is varied and complex. Many branches of Christianity either existed in the Russian Empire or developed after the Soviets' rise to power, each with its own view of relating to the state. And as various lands and nations came to be incorporated into the expanding Soviet Union, each brought its own variants of the major religions as well as its own national church.

REVOLUTION AND CIVIL WAR, 1917–21

When Tsar Nicholas II abdicated in March 1917, control of the Russian Empire fell to a provisional government that sought to manage the country in a democratic manner until popular representatives could choose a permanent form of government. That empire comprised a host of nations and nationalities adhering to Christianity, Islam, Judaism, Buddhism, and other religions. All three major branches of Christianity—Orthodoxy, Catholicism, and Protestantism—were represented. The official state religion, however, was Russian Orthodoxy, whose 100 million nominal members made it by far the largest religious group in the empire.

Andrew Sorokowski, formerly a member of the research staff at Keston College, is currently a doctoral candidate in history at the University of London. He has an M.A. in Soviet studies from Harvard and a J.D. from the University of California.

Deprived of a patriarch since the eighteenth century, the Russian Orthodox Church was under the control of the state through the Holy Synod established by Tsar Peter in 1721. The Synod nevertheless supported the revolution and the provisional government and, after some change in its membership, came out in favor of liberal reform and democracy. On the whole, the Russian Orthodox clergy and laity supported the government's planned land and labor reforms. While Orthodoxy remained the state religion, complete religious toleration for all faiths was introduced.

The provisional government allowed the Russian Orthodox Church to begin preparations for a nationwide *sobor* (council) of bishops, clergy, and laity. A major question before the council was whether the patriarchate should be restored.

The Bolshevik Coup d'État

But the process of bringing reform and democracy to both the government and the Russian Orthodox Church was interrupted on November 7, 1917, when the Bolsheviks, a radical, conspiratorial, revolutionary party led by Vladimir Ilyich Ulyanov (Lenin), seized power in what is known—using the Julian calendar—as the October Revolution. Almost immediately this party's views on government and religion began to shape the fate of the Russian Orthodox Church and all other religious bodies.

As Marxists, the Bolsheviks believed that religion could be reduced to an illusion that served to deaden the pain of the oppressed class; it was the "opium of the people." Therefore, religion was necessary only as long as one class oppressed another; when socialism was finally achieved, there would be no more oppression and no need for religion. The people would abandon religion as naturally as they would stop using a drug once the discomfort of the disease was over.

Under Lenin's guidance, however, the Bolsheviks modified Marx's theory. They said that the oppressor classes used religion to keep the oppressed subservient. Therefore, as a tool of the capitalist bourgeoisie, religion had to be actively combatted. Perhaps even more significant was the Bolshevik belief that there is no absolute morality. Morality, being a function of society, is relative; there is no morality beyond class. This meant, first of all, that the morality of Communist society was fundamentally incompatible with religious morality, which was regarded as a fraud. Second, it meant that morality was to be subordinate to the class struggle, an inevitable development in which any or all means to obtain the desired end were justified.

Once they had seized power, the Bolsheviks quickly learned that there were different ways to combat religion. Sometimes peaceful persuasion was preferable to coercion, since to offend believers' feelings could be counterproductive. Although party members were by definition atheists, religious people could be used to support the Party. In fact, some Bolsheviks even presumed that a tolerant attitude toward religion might persuade believers to become Marxists under the assumption that Marxism and religion were not incompatible. In other situations, however, force would be required if there was to be progress against religious superstition. This duality was to remain a characteristic of Bolshevik religious policy.

It was not ideology alone that determined the Bolsheviks' attitude toward religion, though other factors were only implied, not explicitly stated. Because Marxism purports to answer all philosophical, social, economic, and political questions, it leaves no room for competing philosophies. Christianity, Islam, Judaism, and other religions offer alternative philosophies of life, alternative value systems for which there is no room in the water-tight Marxist view of the universe. On a psychological level, one may speculate that the committed Marxist of the Soviet variety sees every competing world view as a personal threat. On a political level, the Bolsheviks and their successors have seen religion as a dangerous competitor for the hearts and minds of the people.

For these reasons, there has been virtually nothing illogical or anomalous in Soviet religious policy since 1917.

The Russian vs. the American Revolution

Some commentators have found similarity between the American and Russian revolutions, pointing out that the former emphasized individual rights and that the latter was concerned with a different level of rights, group or collective ones. The comparison is not wholly inappropriate, since the Russian Empire did develop more slowly than the West and reached certain stages at a later time.

But the discussion is complicated by the fact that there were really three Russian revolutions. The aborted revolution of 1905 was continued in 1917 by the February Revolution (March on our calendar) in its striving toward a democratic, constitutional government with individual liberties. In its ideals this revolution resembled the American Revolution. If one wishes to see it as a "capitalist" revolution of the middle class, the comparison still holds inasmuch as capitalism reached Russia later than it reached America and Britain.

The third "revolution," however, the Bolshevik takeover in November, represented altogether different ideals. It was not really a revolution but a *coup d'état* in which a small, militant group was able to impose its ideology of collectivism, class interests, and class warfare "from above." Its power did not arise from the socio-economic conditions of the time: the peasants were interested in owning the land, not in giving it up to socialist collectives, and an essentially proletarian revolution could appeal to only a fraction of Russia's population. Nor had Marx predicted that the revolution would occur in such a backward country. But the weakness of the war-torn empire, combined with an autocratic and bureaucratic structure, played into the hands of the Bolshevik party.

In fact, the Bolshevik system can be seen as a transformation of some venerable tsarist traditions. Autocracy was transformed into the "dictatorship of the proletariat"—i.e., the dictatorship of Lenin exercised through the Party, which took over the old bureaucracy. Official Orthodoxy was converted into official atheism, as new ideological symbols were set up to represent the official faith. It can be argued that the main point of difference between the American and Russian revolutions is that the Russian revolution was never completed. Instead, certain elements of the old order, metamorphosed by Marxist ideology, were reimposed on society by an unrepresentative minority.

Another point of difference is that the American revolution

was also a war of independence. Several wars of independence did threaten the Russian Empire during the civil war, and Poland, Finland, and the Baltic states succeeded in freeing themselves. The effect of the Bolshevik takeover, however, was to reassert the Russian imperial structure in "Sovietized" form over the remaining rebellious colonies.

Revolutions in Russia and the Soviet Union, whether "from below" or "from above," were on occasion interrupted and continued later. Just as the popular revolution of 1905 was continued in the revolution of March 1917, so the Bolshevik "revolution from above," after the retreat known as the New Economic Policy in the 1920s, was completed by Stalin's forced collectivization in the 1930s. Similarly, the assault on religion during the 1920s and 1930s was interrupted during the 1940s and early 1950s by the state's need to use the churches in its war effort and in its foreign policy; then the assault was resumed in the anti-religious campaign of 1959–64. This pattern of stop and restart forms the background of the events that are the subject of this chapter.

The Russian Church and Autocephaly

As the Bolsheviks were consolidating their power in the midst of social chaos, the *sobor* (council) of the Russian Orthodox Church—convened before the October Revolution—continued with its primary goal: to re-establish the patriarchate. The structure of the church was to be conciliar, with the *sobor* as the supreme body. The patriarch would act as chairman of the Synod of Bishops, which would deal with purely religious and administrative matters, as well as of the Higher Church Council, which would be concerned with church-related social questions. The empire would be divided into five districts, presided over by metropolitans, and subdivided into dioceses, where bishops would be elected by diocesan councils of clergy and laity. In this early period of Soviet rule, however, the church still considered itself the national church, with legal status and a role in society, particularly in the schools. Among the church's demands were that the head of state and the ministers of education and religious affairs be Russian Orthodox.[1]

Among the pressing matters before the Moscow *sobor* were the claims of other Orthodox churches to autocephaly (self-government) and therefore independence from the Russian Orthodox Church. With the breakup of the Russian Empire, national churches as well as nations sought to free themselves from Russian control. The largest non-Russian Orthodox church was in Ukraine, followed by the Byelorussian, Georgian, and Armenian churches (although the Armenian Apostolic Church is theologically distinct from the Eastern Orthodox churches).

The proponents of a Ukrainian Autocephalous Orthodox Church sought to revive those church traditions that preceded its absorption by the Russian church in 1686. In addition, they wanted to replace the archaic church Slavonic language in the liturgy, and the Russian language in sermons, with modern Ukrainian. Favoring a conciliar system of administration, with lay participation along democratic lines, they rejected Russification, autocracy, and bureaucracy—characteristics of the Russian Orthodox Church of tsarist times—and sought the Christianization of all aspects of life, in harmony with the egalitarian social and political ideals of the Ukrainian revolution.[2]

An all-Ukrainian church *sobor* met in 1918. While the Moscow *sobor*, meeting at the same time, rejected Ukrainian demands for autocephaly, it offered autonomy, i.e., a more limited independence in which the Ukrainian church would remain under the Russian patriarch's authority. For their own reasons, however, the Bolsheviks tolerated Ukrainian autocephaly at least insofar as it tended to weaken the Russian church. Besides, the Ukrainian church was socially and politically "progressive," accepting the separation of church and state and registering its parishes with the Soviet authorities.

When in May 1920 the Ukrainian Orthodox Church proclaimed itself autocephalous, the Russian church defrocked the Ukrainian clergy and ordered the church dissolved under threat of anathema. Electing Archpriest Vasyl Lypkivsky as Metropolitan of Kiev and All Ukraine, the assembled clergy and laity consecrated him in October 1921 in the ancient apostolic (but uncanonical) manner of laying on hands. The Ukrainian Autocephalous Orthodox Church was not, however, recognized by other Orthodox communions.

Bolshevik Anti-Church Decrees

Shortly after seizing power, the Bolshevik government decreed in December 1917 that church marriages and divorces would not be recognized. The Commissariat of Justice, which until 1924 would deal with church affairs, ordered the "painless but complete liquidation" of monasteries, and decreed that churches could be put to other uses, as, for instance, cinemas, theaters, clubhouses, and storehouses. Clerics lost citizens' rights (often including even the right to have ration cards), could not be employed by state enterprises, and could not enroll their children in school beyond the elementary level. They were nonetheless required to pay higher rent and higher taxes than other citizens. In addition, the teaching of religion was banned from public and private general-education schools, and by 1921 religious instruction of those under eighteen was declared illegal. Thus the church was prohibited from exercising any educational role in society, even from teaching religious subjects to children in a Sunday-school setting. Only the strictly private teaching of religion to adults was permitted.

In 1918 a constitution was promulgated for the Russian Soviet Federated Socialist Republic, which today is the largest of the republics in the Soviet Union. Article 13 permitted both religious and anti-religious propaganda, establishing a precedent for other republics. On January 23 of that year, the most important Bolshevik legislation of this period was enacted: the Decree on the Separation of Church From State and School From Church. This decree nationalized church property; it also deprived the church of the rights of a "legal person," making it impossible for church bodies to acquire property again. Only individual parishes could obtain land and buildings, and that only by leasing them from the local authorities, albeit free of charge.

While some of the Bolshevik decrees were clearly anti-religious, or at least anti-church, others, such as the separation of the church from the state and school, and the freedom to engage in both religious and anti-religious propaganda (although the right to conduct religious propaganda would later be withdrawn), are similar to the law of the United States and other Western countries in treating religions in a relatively even-handed manner. But in Leninist theory, such "bourgeois rights" are only part of the *transition* to socialism. When the people's consciousness changes in line with new socio-economic and political conditions, bourgeois rights become unnecessary. With religion dying out, the Bolsheviks reasoned, freedom of religion would become irrelevant.

Yet the Bolsheviks would not wait for religion to die of its own accord; they believed it must be combatted. They therefore harassed believers, confiscated church property, and engaged in violence against the clergy. Tikhon Belavin, selected by lot from among three candidates to become patriarch in late 1917, issued an encyclical in January 1918 warning the government not to persecute the church and excommunicating those who had taken part, but this only excited more violence. Between 1918 and 1920, at least twenty-eight bishops were murdered, thousands of clerics were killed or imprisoned, and an estimated 12,000 laypersons were put to death for religious activities. Thousands suffered arrest, trial, and deportation to labor camps or exile. By 1920, some 673 monasteries had been liquidated—in what was hardly the "painless" process ordered by the Commissariat of Justice.[3]

In September 1919, the patriarch issued another encyclical ordering the clergy to refrain from political involvement and reminding the faithful that the church imposed upon them no political obligations. This was evidently in response to Bolshevik allegations, in part true, that Russian Orthodox priests were supporting the White armies struggling against the Bolshevik regime.

While gravely suspicious of Russian Orthodoxy, the Bolsheviks looked much more favorably upon the Protestants, of which the main groups were (and still are) Evangelical Christians and Baptists. As persecuted communities under the old regime, these groups were in some ways privileged under the Bolsheviks. Their lower-class origins and egalitarian ideas, as well as their potential as a counterweight to the Russian Orthodox

Church, stood them in good stead. The Bolsheviks were even prepared to overlook their pacifism, permitting Protestant conscientious objectors to serve in hospitals as an alternative to military service (from January 1919). Some Evangelical Christians even began Christian collective farms that year with official approval.

By contrast, the new regime was fundamentally hostile to Catholics, since they were loyal to a foreign power and thus not susceptible to total control. Undoubtedly, a centuries-old Catholic-Orthodox antipathy exacerbated the situation. Indeed, the Catholic Church in Russia, headed from July 1917 by Archbishop deRopp of Mogilev, openly opposed the nationalization of church property in its Instruction of December 1918. The archbishop was arrested the following year and replaced by Msgr. Cieplak.

In addition to the Latin-rite Catholic Church, there was an Eastern-rite church, the Russian Catholic Exarchate. (An Eastern-rite Catholic church, also called a Uniate church, uses the Orthodox liturgy but is in communion with Rome.) This church was founded by Metropolitan Andrei Sheptytsky in 1917 in Minsk, the capital of Byelorussia, which two years later was proclaimed a Soviet Socialist Republic.

Church-State Relations, 1921–29

By 1921, the devastation caused by the revolution and the ensuing civil war had brought on a famine. Patriarch Tikhon appealed for international aid and set up a church relief commission, which the government abolished. The following year, the patriarch appealed to the parish councils to donate church objects for famine aid, excluding articles required for sacramental use. The government, however, ordered state agents to collect all church valuables without exception.

The church resisted the confiscation of sacramental objects, and fifty-four Orthodox clerics and laymen were put on trial in Moscow in April and May 1922. Five were executed. In May, Patriarch Tikhon was put under house arrest. Between 1921 and 1923, 2,691 married priests, 1,962 monks, 3,447 nuns, and numerous laity were killed.[4] Meanwhile, a 1922 decree required religious associations to register with the authorities, but neither the individual associations nor the church body as a whole was granted legal recognition.

Despite the intense persecution, there was a remarkable revival of church life at this time. In 1925, for example, Orthodox membership grew by 9 per cent.[5] Choirs and youth groups flourished.

The government countered with a number of measures. It forbade the holding of religious services or ceremonies outside of churches without written permission, and it launched the aggressively atheistic League of Militant Godless.

After the death of Tikhon in April 1925, the authorities tried to prevent an orderly, canonical succession to the patriarchate by arresting some 117 of the church's 160 bishops. However, the Russian Orthodox hierarchy did manage to arrange a succession, though it was indeed uncanonical, as the state had desired. In his will, Tikhon nominated three temporary administrators (or *locum tenentes)* of the patriarchate. All were eventually imprisoned. The third, Metropolitan Peter Polyansky, designated in turn three *locum tenentes* to succeed him. The first of these was Metropolitan Sergei. When Peter died in exile in 1936, Sergei became the *locum tenens* in his place.[6]

Because of the highly irregular succession, Sergei's support and influence among both hierarchy and laity were never consolidated. Yet it would be during his years as administrator and later his brief tenure as patriarch (1943–44) that the church would develop its *modus vivendi* with the state, establishing a pattern that still prevails today.

Sergei's "Declaration of Loyalty"

As *locum tenens*, Metropolitan Sergei sought legalization of the Russian Orthodox Church in 1926, offering loyalty to the state but not political involvement with it. The government, however, demanded the power to dismiss bishops; when Sergei refused, he was arrested. During this time, as the number of Orthodox believers continued to grow, the authorities also sought to remove the church's material base through discriminatory taxation and other economic strictures.

Faced with an increasingly difficult situation, Metropolitan Sergei continued negotiations with the government after his arrest, and in March 1927 he was released. On July 20, he issued a declaration that said in part;

> It is . . . the more imperative for us now to show that we, the church functionaries, are not with the enemies of our Soviet state, and not with the senseless tools of their intrigues, but are with our people and our government. . . .
>
> We express, with all the people, our thanks to the Soviet government for such attention to the spiritual needs of the Orthodox inhabitants [permission to form a Temporary Synod], and we at the same time assure the government that we will not abuse the confidence shown us. . . .
>
> We wish to be Orthodox and at the same time to claim the Soviet Union as our civil motherland, the joys and successes of which are our joys and successes, the misfortunes of which are our misfortunes. . . . Remaining Orthodox, we remember our duty to be citizens of the union "not from fear, but from conscience," as the apostle has taught us.[7]

Metropolitan Sergei's "declaration of loyalty" produced few tangible concessions by the state. An Orthodox theological institute was opened in 1927 but closed two years later. Only a few exiled bishops were reinstated, and the arrests persisted. The government continued to close churches and to refuse legal recognition to the patriarchal administration or the church. A continuous work week, aimed at undermining the religious Sunday, was introduced in 1929. Also in 1929, the melting down of church bells was begun (allegedly by popular demand), 1,440 churches were closed, and a restrictive Law on Religious Associations was enacted. In 1933 the *Journal of the Moscow Patriarchate* was permitted to appear, but only until 1937.

To make matters worse, there was such a negative popular reaction to Sergei's declaration that many believers and clergy refused to offer prayers for him. What indeed had prompted the metropolitan to make his declaration of loyalty? Mass arrests, competition from the state-sponsored Renovationist Church (see below), and what may have been a GPU (secret police) threat to shoot all arrested clerics may simply have convinced him that there was no other way to save the religious body. Nevertheless, in the minds of many believers that declaration compromised the patriarchal church irrevocably.

It should be pointed out that Sergei did not declare total loyalty to the Bolsheviks; he pledged civic loyalty to the state, rather than an ideological loyalty to Communism. In fact, the wording of the declaration seems to indicate that his real loyalty was to Russia rather than to the current regime, and that he intended to retain a certain spiritual independence for his church.[8]

The Renovationist Church

One reason for the weakness of the patriarchal Russian Orthodox Church during this period was the rise of the Renovationist Church, which originated in a pre-revolutionary movement of leftist, socialist clerics along with secular intelligentsia who had turned from Marxism to religion while maintaining their social radicalism. Among other things, it opposed the monastic clergy, from among whom all bishops were chosen. After the revolution, the Bolsheviks succeeded in taking partial control of this movement and even turned over church buildings to the Renovationists. The three branches of the church—the Living Church, the Union for Church Renovation, and the Union of Communities of Ancient Apostolic Churches—in turn supported the Bolsheviks.

Operating from a position of relative security in relation to the state, Renovationist leaders in 1922 persuaded Patriarch Tikhon, who was under house arrest, to turn over temporary authority to them. The following year they held a *sobor* at which they set themselves up as the legitimate administration of the Russian church. The Renovationists never gained much popular support, however, and once Metropolitan Sergei had made his declaration of loyalty in 1927, the need for Renovationist pressure on the patriarchal church fell away and the Bolsheviks withdrew their support.

Schismatic and Catacomb Churches

The 1920s were ripe for the growth of schismatic churches. There was disarray in the administration of the Orthodox

Church, and Patriarch Tikhon in 1920 had ordered that temporary autocephalies be set up in case the central administration was paralyzed. Bishops like Teofil Buldovsky of Poltava took advantage of the situation and established autocephalous churches. When Bishop Buldovsky's church at Lubny held a *sobor* in 1925, however, Patriarch Tikhon was quick to excommunicate him. Other bishops formed churches with similar results.

The 1920s also saw the beginning of the "catacomb church." This general term refers to clergy and laypeople who, though they retained the dogma and ritual of the patriarchal church, either (1) wished to dissociate themselves from the administration of the Moscow patriarchate without denying its spiritual validity, or (2) felt that collaboration with the regime had deprived the established church of the divine gift of administering valid sacraments.

Underground believers of the first group, who had been *forced* underground, did not break completely with Sergei. They succeeded in operating unofficial seminaries and monasteries. This group includes what some authors perceive as three levels of alienation from the official church: (a) believers who wished to remain part of the church but were forced underground through persecution or refusal of registration; (b) those who maintained an underground existence as a "reserve" in case the official church should be destroyed (a parallel catacomb structure could also serve to keep up pressure on the authorities and thus secure better treatment for the mainstream church); and (c) those who rejected the official policies of the church hierarchy outright but still recognized its sacramental validity.

Among members of the second group, those who believed the patriarchate had lost its spiritual validity by collaborating, were the "Non-commemorators," who refused to mention Sergei in liturgical prayers after his declaration of loyalty to the state. Also in this group were the "True Orthodox Church" and the "True Orthodox Christians," the latter probably being a priestless version of the former.

Other Orthodox Churches

During this time the other national churches of the USSR flourished briefly before succumbing to the general onslaught against religion. In the Ukrainian Soviet Socialist Republic, where a kind of "national communism" and a process of "Ukrainization" was permitted for several years, the Ukrainian Autocephalous Orthodox Church thrived. By early 1924 it had 30 bishops, some 1,500 priests and deacons, and nearly 1,100 parishes. At its peak it may have had from three to six million followers.[9] As early as 1922, however, it came under pressure because of suspected nationalistic tendencies, and in 1923–25 the regime tried to split the church by favoring one faction over another. Arrests of clergy began about 1923, and Metropolitan Lypkivsky was arrested in 1926. The second all-Ukrainian church *rada,* the council set up to head the church between *sobors*, was ordered dissolved. In 1927 Metropolitan Lypkivsky was dismissed. Mass repression began two years later, simultaneously with collectivization, and most of the Ukrainian Orthodox parishes were closed.

Like the Ukrainian church, the Byelorussian Orthodox Church had lost its independence in the seventeenth century and hoped to recover it under the new government. In July 1922 in Minsk, a Byelorussian *sobor* declared the autocephaly of the Byelorussian church and elected Melkhisedek Paevsky as metropolitan. He later renounced the title. In 1927, following the arrest and deportation of the metropolitan for allegedly concealing church valuables, a *sobor* promulgated new statutes and reasserted autocephaly, declaring the church's right to be free of interference from the Russian Orthodox hierarchy. Three bishops were eventually arrested and died in prison. According to one source, some 3,600 priests were removed and 2,800 parishes dissolved.[10]

Upon taking over Georgia in 1921, the Bolsheviks deeply offended the nation's cultural and religious pride: they confiscated valuables and land of the Georgian Orthodox Church, exhumed the relics of the martyrs David and Constantine, and closed church buildings or converted them into secular facilities for theaters, clubs, and the like. Religious holidays were abolished and theological schools were closed. By 1923 the authorities had closed 2,355 churches, 27 monasteries, and seven convents. When the Kutaisi Cathedral was demolished, the government erected a statue of Lenin in its place.[11] Naturally, all this elicited popular discontent, and in February 1922 Ambrosius, the *catholicos* or head of the Georgian church, issued a protest to the Genoa international conference at which Soviet Russia was establishing relations with the European states. Although during the next year church closings ceased, there were no reopenings, and in March 1924 Catholicos Ambrosius was tried in Tbilisi and convicted of treason. He received a sentence of eight years.

The Armenian Apostolic Church (which, as mentioned before, is not strictly speaking Orthodox) had to compete with a Renovationist-style "Free Church" sponsored by the authorities during 1924–25. Although the Free Church failed—as had similar experiments elsewhere—the clergy of the Apostolic Church were persecuted, church buildings were closed or destroyed, theological schools were shut, and ordinations ceased. The League of Militant Godless was particularly active here, while the GPU (secret police) penetrated the church's clerical ranks.

The Protestant Churches

The relatively favorable treatment experienced by the Protestants after the Revolution was reinforced by the New Economic Policy of 1921, benefiting small farmers, who made up the bulk of the Protestant groups. In April 1923, however, the Twelfth Party Congress, noting the growth of "sects" with European and American "bourgeois" ties, called for counteracting propaganda. The Party Congress of the following year again recommended attention to these groups, whose economic and cultural activity was to be steered into officially approved channels. The Bolsheviks respected the industry and moral strength of the Protestants, and sought to harness their energy while striking at the roots of their faith. The 1928 "trial" of the Bible itself exemplifies the regime's attempts to discredit the scriptural basis of Protestantism.

The toleration in practical affairs of the Evangelical Christians and the Baptists was conditional upon their accommodating to state interests. In 1923, for example, when exemption from military service was no longer allowed, the Evangelical Christian

Union changed its stand against military duty, declaring that it was a believer's obligation. In return for such cooperation, an Evangelical Christian Bible school was permitted to open in Leningrad in 1924, and in 1927 a theological college was founded in Moscow. By 1928 Evangelical Christians numbered 3,219 congregations with around four million followers, mostly well-to-do peasants, Cossacks, tradespersons, and artisans, with heavy concentrations in Ukraine and Siberia.[12]

At their congress in 1927, the Baptists followed the Evangelical Christians in supporting military conscription, as well as declaring that the government allowed complete freedom of conscience. That same year the state permitted a Baptist preachers' school to be opened in Moscow. By treading a careful path in relation to the Soviet authorities, Evangelicals and Baptists together were able to carry out considerable evangelization in Siberia and the Far East in the 1920s, as well as translating, printing, and distributing the Bible in various languages of the USSR. The two groups did not, however, unite at this time.

Lutherans in the Soviet Union—mostly German colonists—shared the principal difficulties of all religious groups in the 1920s. By June 1924, when they held a General Synod, the Lutherans had fewer than half the clerics they had had in 1917. In September 1925, however, they were allowed to open a seminary for training ministers in Leningrad, and in 1927 a German Lutheran newspaper was established. But the following year saw their second and last General Synod, as the church suffered from a shortage of pastors and competition from the Renovationist-like "German Living Church."

In contrast, both Pentecostals and Seventh-day Adventists enjoyed relative prosperity in the 1920s. In 1921 a Pentecostal missionary named Ivan Voronaev entered the Ukraine, and by 1926 there were 350 Pentecostal congregations in the Soviet Union with some 17,000 followers. The Pentecostals founded the All-Ukrainian Council of Christians of the Evangelical Faith, based in Odessa, and launched the short-lived journal *Evangelist* in 1928. Seventh-day Adventists were also allowed to publish, editing newspapers for Russian- , Ukrainian- , and German-speaking readers. With some 600 congregations in 1928, they numbered 12,405 baptized believers.

The Catholic Church

While church-state relations for Protestants in the 1920s could be described as relatively calm, the situation for Catholics was grim. Many priests were arrested during this period over the church-valuables affair, and in March 1923 Archbishop Cieplak, fourteen priests, and one layman were put on trial. Some were accused of opposition to government measures, others of treasonable contacts with Poland. One of the defendants, Monsignor Budkiewicz, was executed; Archbishop Cieplak was given a life sentence but was later returned to Poland in a prisoner exchange. In the Byelorussian SSR there was no Catholic hierarchy at all between the arrest of Archbishop Cieplak in 1923 and 1926, when Msgr. Boleslas Sloskans was secretly appointed apostolic administrator for the Mogilev and Minsk dioceses. Predictably, however, Monsignor Sloskans was arrested in 1927 and sentenced to three years in a labor camp.

In a bold attempt to strengthen the Christian community as a Catholic-Orthodox whole, the Russian Catholic Exarchate—the Eastern-rite church set up in Byelorussia by Metropolitan Sheptytsky in 1917 under Exarch Leonid Fyodorov—directed its efforts toward a union of the Western and Eastern churches. Exarch Fyodorov's activity excited hope among some Byelorussians for a revival of their forebears' Uniate church, Catholic in theology and Orthodox in liturgy. Byelorussian intellectuals in particular saw the possibility of forming a Byelorussian national Catholic church, and Exarch Fyodorov supported this idea. But when the exarch was made a defendant in the 1923 Cieplak-Budkiewicz trial, the prosecutor stated that Fyodorov must be judged not only for what he had done but also for what he might do. Evidently, the authorities feared the prospect of a Catholic-Orthodox front arising from Fyodorov's ecumenical activity. He received a ten-year sentence but was released in an amnesty after three years.[13]

The Law on Religious Associations

A law passed in 1929 defined the status and rights of religious associations in the Soviet Union, as well as prescribing the way in which these associations were to be governed. It has remained in effect, with some amendments, until the present day, though a draft replacement law was under consideration in 1988–89. The Law on Religious Associations of April 8, 1929, addresses itself to groups of twenty or more persons ("religious associations") rather than to entire church or denominational bodies. It requires such groups of believers to apply to the authorities for registration but does not require the authorities to register them, even if they meet all the conditions. Of course, the law permits only registered groups to exist.

The law also defines what activities a religious association may and may not carry out. It may not operate schools (including Sunday schools), discussion groups, self-help organizations, libraries and reading rooms, youth groups, leisure activities, and so on. Charitable activity is forbidden. Religious rites outside church buildings (for example, in cemeteries or private homes) are forbidden without special permission. Following the 1918 Decree on the Separation of Church From State, the law specifies that church property belongs to the state but may be leased to religious associations free of charge. Procedures are also set out by which the authorities may close or destroy places of worship or convert them to other uses.[14] What were the principal effects of this law? First, church bodies—including the Russian Orthodox Church—continued to remain without juridical personality: only individual parishes were recognized by the state as legal entities. Second, the authorities gained a significant degree of control over religious associations inasmuch as they could veto membership in the lay councils governing them. Third, the law virtually confined the permissible activity of a religious group to religious ceremonies performed within a place of worship, excluding any activity through which a group might have an effect on society. The prohibition against teaching religion in schools (except in seminaries) was particularly hard on evangelical groups, whose faith required spreading the message of Christ. Indeed, Article 17 of the law, describing prohibited conduct, is virtually a catalogue of typical evangelical activities.

Since it was first introduced in 1929, the Law on Religious

Associations has been amended, as well as supplemented and apparently superseded in part at various times by administrative regulations and instructions, often unpublished. The law has also been enforced selectively, and at times its strictures have been deliberately suspended to allow a temporary freedom. Indeed, while the law itself has remained relatively constant, its application has been subject to the dictates of perceived government interests. (A detailed analysis of this law appears in chapter three.) In May 1929, the constitutional right of religious propaganda was suspended.

Church-State Relations, 1929–39

After Lenin's temporary ideological retreat in the New Economic Policy of the 1920s, Stalin and his Communist Party supporters completed the Bolshevik "revolution from above" through the breakneck industrialization and collectivization of the 1930s. They crushed opposition to the first Five-Year Plan (1928–32) and subsequent measures by starving several million farmers in the Ukraine and adjacent areas in 1932–33, and by sending millions of citizens to their deaths in labor camps or before firing squads in the terror of the middle and late 1930s. Simultaneously, they began an all-out attack, interrupted only by tactical retreats, on all forms of religion.

Attempted Destruction of the Russian Orthodox Church

According to Metropolitan Sergei, in 1930 the patriarchal Russian Orthodox Church still had 30,000 churches, 163 bishops, 60,000 active clergy, and tens of millions of believers. Mass church closings soon began, however, and in 1931 the number of open churches had dropped to between 20,000 and 25,000. In Moscow, the number had been halved since 1917. After this initial campaign, the party Central Committee in 1930 forbade further church closings without majority consent. Excessive discrimination against priests, such as eviction from state and nationalized housing, was also prohibited, but priests continued to suffer from higher taxes.

In 1932 a new offensive against the church began, marked by

the continuation of anti-Christmas and anti-Easter campaigns (until 1935). The League of Militant Godless reached its peak membership of a reported 5.5 million. By 1933, the number of open Orthodox churches in Moscow had again been halved. Throughout the entire country, only some 15–25 per cent of the churches functioning before the revolution remained open in 1933. By 1939, possibly only a few hundred Russian Orthodox parishes remained.

In addition, various estimates are that some 30,000 to 42,000 Orthodox clerics were shot or imprisoned in the 1930s. Many Orthodox monastic communities were disbanded in this decade as well, and dispersed monks and nuns were often exiled, imprisoned, or shot. Mass "show trials" were held in 1937–38—farcical judicial proceedings for anti-religious propaganda effect. A story told by a Soviet Christian to Dimitry Pospielovsky (author of *The Russian Church Under the Soviet Regime, 1917–1982*, to which I am indebted for information used in this chapter) illustrates the atmosphere of those times. At the request of Stalin's ophthalmologist, one Orthodox church had been left open in Odessa, a city of some 500,000 at the time. Every Sunday a different priest would come forward from the congregation of the church to say Mass, only to be arrested by the police. When there were no more priests, deacons began to appear; when there were no more deacons, psalmists. This went on for some months, until finally the believers were left to worship by themselves.[15]

In 1936, in the midst of all this brutality, a new Constitution was promulgated guaranteeing all citizens equal rights. Clergy and their families were no longer officially subject to special discrimination, and priests' children were no longer officially prohibited from entering universities (though it is doubtful whether this had a practical effect). But when some interpreted a constitutional provision on "social organizations" as permitting the church to nominate candidates for political office, state officials responded by asserting that the church could have no role in Soviet society. Indeed, in 1937 the Party called for a renewed anti-religious propaganda offensive.

Yet between 1937 and 1940, according to state officials, some

80 to 90 million people—that is, 40–45 per cent of the population—were still "religious." Orthodox churches that would not or could not register their parishes under the 1929 Law on Religious Associations carried on as catacomb churches. The Fedorovites and similar movements flourished under these conditions. So did the True Orthodox, who in 1937 even managed to hold a chance *sobor* in a detention center, attended by two metropolitans and four bishops! Agreeing to prayer and liturgical intercommunion with the legal, registered church, they nevertheless decided against sacramental contact with its clergy.

Other Orthodox Churches

In January 1930 the Ukrainian Autocephalous Orthodox Church was pressured by the authorities to hold an extraordinary *sobor* at which it announced its own dissolution. Several of its leaders were implicated in the show trial of the "League for the Liberation of Ukraine," staged a few months later. Metropolitan Boretsky and Volodymyr Chekhivsky, the church's chief ideologist, were among those sent to prison or exile. The remaining clergy were permitted to form a new "Ukrainian Orthodox Church" under Metropolitan Ivan Pavlovsky, but only after modifying their principles and promising loyalty to the Soviet regime. This apparent détente did not last long, however, and the last parish was liquidated as early as 1936. Meanwhile, the majority of the bishops and clergy of the Ukrainian Autocephalous Orthodox Church and thousands of its lay activists died in the terror.

The Ukrainian churches were seen as repositories of Ukrainian nationalism, which the Soviet regime considered more threatening to the stability and unity of the state than religious faith as such. Indeed, some churches in the Ukrainian capital city of Kiev were dynamited in the 1930s and in the wake of the Soviet retreat before the advancing German armies in the autumn of 1941.[16] The Soviets may have feared that the Germans would open the churches, thereby stimulating Ukrainian national feelings that would weaken the Soviet regime.

In Armenia, national feelings were likewise considered more dangerous to the state than religious faith itself, but here the authorities' treatment of the church was relatively mild. The potential role of the Armenian Apostolic Church in mobilizing the opinion of the large Armenian diaspora in favor of the USSR, or at least in neutralizing that opinion, was probably a factor in the authorities' behavior. Elected catholicos in November 1932, Khoren I succeeded in opening closed churches and recovering other property before he was murdered five years later. Thereafter, no catholicos could be elected until 1945, while Kevork Cheorekchian as *locum tenens* (temporary administrator) pursued a policy of reconciliation with the state.

The Georgian Orthodox Church was headed from 1932 by Catholicos and Patriarch Kallistrat Tsintsadze, who maintained that Christianity and Communism could co-exist. Still, the Georgian Orthodox Church suffered heavily from a particularly energetic League of Militant Godless, which claimed over 4 per cent of the Georgian population in 1938—a time when it was relatively weak elsewhere in the USSR. The authorities encouraged a revival of paganism in certain remote areas of the region, while the notorious Lavrenti Beria, head of the Georgian GPU and later Stalin's chief of security, contributed to the atheistic campaign as party chief 1931–38.

The Protestant Churches

The Evangelical Christians and the Baptists were particularly hard hit by the collectivization of agriculture and the artificially induced famine of 1932–33, as the small, independent farmers were the socio-economic base of these religious groups. In addition, Protestant collectives were disbanded. Church activities were curtailed by the 1929 Law on Religious Associations, doubtless directed in part at evangelical traditions. Beginning in 1929, the authorities invented criminal charges on which to prosecute believers: in the Volhynia region, in Kiev, and in Minsk, believers were tried for conducting espionage on behalf of Poland; in Leningrad and Moscow they were accused of spying for Germany; in Siberia they were indicted as spies for Japan.

In addition, Bibles could no longer be printed, and the journals *Baptist*, *Baptist Ukrainy*, and *Khristianin* were shut down. In

1929 the authorities forced closure of the Baptist preachers' school and the Evangelical Christian Bible school, and in the following year youth clubs were proscribed, although youth work and evangelization did continue informally. The year 1929 also witnessed the last Evangelical Christian congress. By 1935, the Baptist central organization had ceased functioning, and the following year its Moscow branch closed its doors. Here, as in other areas, some Baptists transferred to Evangelical Christian groups, effecting a practical if unofficial ecumenical alliance that periods of greater freedom and stability had not fostered. As anti-Protestant propaganda gained in intensity, Baptists and Evangelical Christians alike were branded as American or West European spies.

Lutherans were victims of the same type of propaganda, and some were arrested on charges of treason. By the early part of the thirties, so many Lutheran ministers had been imprisoned, exiled, or otherwise prevented from fulfilling their duties that by 1936 only eight were active, and by the end of 1937 none remained in place. In 1938 the Moscow Church of Peter and Paul closed its doors.

The pacifist and German-speaking Mennonites, who had settled in southern Ukraine in the late eighteenth and early nineteenth centuries, emigrated to Canada in considerable numbers in 1923–30 seeking religious tolerance. Many of those who remained in Ukraine, however, sought to reconstruct Mennonite economic and social life, as well as to defend against anti-German administrative discrimination, by forming an "Association of Citizens of Dutch Descent in Ukraine."

The Catholic Church

In an outcome consistent with the state's longstanding anti-Catholic bias, the Catholic Church became all but extinct in many parts of the USSR. By 1931 there were only forty-six Catholic priests in the whole country, most of them in Byelorussia. The government's anti-Vatican propaganda was certainly out of proportion to the size of the church's presence, and may have had entirely different motives.

In 1937 the NKVD (the bureau in charge of the secret police) purported to find nests of spies directed by Catholic priests. Monsignor Sloskans, apostolic administrator for the Mogilev and Minsk dioceses, was rearrested in 1930 and deported without trial to Siberia, but was released in 1933 in a prisoner exchange. By 1936, not one open Catholic church or one active Catholic priest remained in the entire Byelorussian SSR.

World War II, 1939–45

A variety of churches and religious groups came under Soviet rule between 1939 and 1941, after the USSR occupied several countries by agreement with Nazi Germany, only to come under Nazi occupation in 1941. The church in the Soviet Union had been living on the edge of extinction in recent years, and the tragedy of the "Great Patriotic War" contained, paradoxically, the seeds of religious rebirth—within both Soviet-controlled and Nazi-occupied areas.

Soviet-Occupied Lands, 1939–41

Most of the population that came under Soviet rule in 1939 was Catholic. The Soviet regime saw the church in these countries, not only as a bastion of archaic superstition and allegiance to a Western authority, but also as a depository of national culture, nationalism, and resistance (as in Catholic Poland today). Hence, Soviet policy attempted to navigate a narrow passage between repression—both to foster its own ideology and to suppress nationalist feelings in the invaded lands—and accommodation, to pacify the population.

In the western Ukrainian lands that had been under Polish administration, the Soviet authorities tried in vain to persuade the scholar-priest Havryil Kostelnyk to head the Ukrainian Greek Catholic Church (an Eastern-rite or Uniate church) in place of the popular and anti-Communist Metropolitan Andrei Sheptytsky. The authorities did succeed in closing church schools and in intimidating the religious community by executing, imprisoning, or deporting a number of priests. The mostly Polish Latin-rite Catholics of this and other areas annexed from eastern Poland suffered as well in the massive deportation conducted in 1939–40.

Lithuania, with 81.2 per cent of its population Roman Catholic, was invaded by the Soviet Union in June 1940. Mass deportations followed; during the week of June 14–21, for example, more than 34,000 persons were deported to Siberia and elsewhere in the Soviet Union. The Soviet authorities forbade the clergy to instruct children, introduced anti-religious propaganda in the schools, destroyed religious books, suppressed publications, introduced new secular holidays to supplant Christian ones, and closed monasteries as well as theological seminaries. They seized church-owned lands, though not the churches themselves, arrested some priests, and placed others under surveillance. Popular and official protests only elicited further repression. In the summer of 1941, the Red Army, retreating before the German invaders, carried out large-scale massacres of the civilian population.

In the annexed lands of western Ukraine, eastern Poland, and western Byelorussia, the Soviet occupiers confronted a sizable Orthodox population. A number of priests in western Byelorussia were deported, the Orthodox seminary was closed, and burdensome taxes were imposed, but the Soviet occupation authorities tended to avoid severe persecution in order not to alienate the population further. In addition, the Moscow patriarchate appointed Metropolitan Nikolai Yarushevich as exarch for this area, in order to control and absorb the national churches. The Orthodox churches of Latvia and Estonia were similarly taken over by the Moscow patriarchate during this time, with Metropolitan Sergei Voskresensky as overseer and later exarch.

Most Estonians and Latvians, however, were Protestants. In Estonia some 800,000 Lutherans constituted over three-quarters of the population, while some 1,094,000 Lutherans made up 56.6 per cent of Latvia's population. In addition to these nearly two million Lutherans there were tens of thousands more in Lithuania. All three groups suffered in the arrests, repression, and deportations carried out by the Soviet occupiers.

Nazi-Occupied Lands, 1941–44

On June 22, 1941, Nazi Germany launched an attack on the Soviet Union. The invasion ultimately swept over the Baltic states, all of Byelorussia and Ukraine, as well as the adjacent portions of Russia. Freed from overt, state-imposed anti-religious pressure, churches were reopened *en masse*. In a move calculated to win local support, the Nazis allowed a greater degree of religious freedom than the Soviets had allowed. As a result, a pervasive religious revival took place in these areas. In August 1941, when Metropolitan Sergei Voskresensky undertook a mission to the Pskov region of German-occupied Russia—accompanied by fifteen Orthodox priests—the popular response in this area (to the west and south of Leningrad) was immense: churches were reopened, services began, and soon there were some 200 functioning parishes with 175 priests. In January 1942, approximately 40 per cent of the population of Pskov participated in the traditional blessing of the water at Epiphany.[17] In addition, nearly all the secondary school teachers of that city—ostensibly atheists—returned to the church, while religious instruction and publishing resumed.

The church revival, however, was short-lived. On April 28, 1944, Metropolitan Sergei (not Patriarch Sergei, who died the same year), traveling by automobile between Riga and Vilnius, was gunned down by persons in Nazi uniforms. It is not known whether Nazis, Soviet partisans, or the NKVD was responsible. Both Nazis and Soviets would have had a motive to eliminate the metropolitan. While he had remained loyal to the Moscow patriarchate and was clearly popular with the Russian people, he had chosen to remain under German occupation and had encouraged a religious revival that threatened Communist psychological control over the masses.

In Byelorussia, the Nazi authorities supported the rebirth of the Byelorussian Orthodox Church as a counterweight to Russian Orthodoxy. By September 1941 Metropolitan Dionisi of the Polish Orthodox Church was able to call a Byelorussian church council. Between 1941 and 1942 three Byelorussian Orthodox bishops were appointed, and in August-September 1942 a council in Minsk established the Byelorussian Autocephalous Orthodox National Church. The church as an institution gained little popular support; at the same time, as in neighboring Russia, the Byelorussian religious revival was overwhelming. Churches were rebuilt, priests were ordained, and religious education commenced. At one point, as many as 10,000 young people per day were reportedly being baptized in Minsk.[18] In January 1944, around 30 to 40 per cent of the city's population took part in the Epiphany procession. In a survey taken by the Germans in Smolensk, only 1 per cent of the inhabitants declared themselves atheists.[19]

Mass baptisms and weddings also took place in Ukraine, where an estimated 70 to 95 per cent of the people turned to the church. Here, however, two rival Orthodox churches sprang up in the wake of the Soviet retreat: the Autonomous Orthodox Church of the Ukraine and the Ukrainian Autocephalous Orthodox Church. The former remained loyal to the Moscow hierarchy in principle but kept relations in abeyance until such time as the patriarchate should free itself from Soviet control. Based on a decision of the 1918 Moscow *sobor* permitting Ukrainian Orthodox autonomy but not autocephaly, the Autonomous Orthodox Church enjoyed canonical status as well as the support of the conservative, Russian-oriented clergy. Taking a more independent stance, the competing Ukrainian Autocephalous Orthodox Church was a reincarnation of the Autocephalous Church of the 1920s but with traditional episcopal orders; it had to struggle against the pro-Russian pre-revolutionary tradition.

The situation was ripe for exploitation by the German occupation forces. At various times the Nazi authorities favored each of these churches, persecuting the other; they helped prevent the two churches' union—agreed upon in October 1942 at Pochaiv (Pochaev)—from materializing.

Some 30,000 Byelorussian Uniates (Eastern-rite Catholics) also found themselves under German occupation. In March 1942 they organized an exarchate under Father Anton Nemantsevich. In November, Father Nemantsevich was arrested by the Gestapo; he was probably executed. With his death, the Byelorussian Uniates disappeared as an organized body.[20]

Although based on race rather than religion, the persecution of the Jews was of course the most devastating part of the Nazi occupation. Tragically, it was those parts of the Soviet Union with the heaviest Jewish concentrations—Byelorussia and Ukraine—that bore the brunt of the German invasion and occupation.

Russian Orthodox Church, 1941–45: Rehabilitation

As soon as news of the Nazi invasion reached Metropolitan Sergei Stragorodsky in June 1941, he issued a pastoral letter appealing to all his parishioners for the defense of the motherland:

> Our Orthodox church has always shared the fate of the people. It has always borne their trials and cherished their successes. It will not desert the people now. . . . The Church of Christ blesses all the Orthodox defending the sacred frontiers of our motherland. The Lord will grant us victory.[21]

Later, in November, Metropolitan Sergei called for a "holy war" against Hitler on behalf of Christian civilization and for freedom of conscience and religion. In addition, metropolitans Sergei, Alexei, and Nikolai—the only remaining Russian Orthodox metropolitans in the country—remained active in supporting the war effort. Sergei issued appeals, set up a defense fund, and provided for a tank column; Alexei organized church collections; Nikolai even co-signed a document falsely alleging that the Germans, not the Soviets, had murdered thousands of Polish officers at Katyn.

Impressed with their patriotic activity, Stalin invited the three metropolitans to meet with him on September 4, 1943. Four days later, nineteen bishops appeared for a *sobor* that promptly elected Sergei patriarch—the first since Tikhon's death in 1925. By October, the government had established the Council for the Affairs of the Russian Orthodox Church.

Why did Stalin permit the revival of the Moscow patriarchate and of the church as a whole? One reason may have been the spontaneous and largely tolerated revival of the church in Soviet territories under Nazi occupation. This damaged Soviet propaganda and could have become a problem once those regions were rejoined to the religiously repressed Soviet heartland. Second, perhaps Stalin wished to reward—and, more importantly, to ensure for the future—the church's loyalty to the regime.

A third and related reason for easing state pressure on the church must have been the church's mobilizational and political potential. The church had proved it could draw on the loyalty of its faithful to raise money and generate moral support for the regime's war effort. Clearly it could mobilize similar support in the future. Furthermore, the church hierarchy could serve the state's political interests by representing a new policy of toleration abroad; by calling for pan-Orthodox unity, it could also reinforce the government's foreign-policy ambitions to become protector of Eastern Europe and the Balkans. Metropolitan Nikolai, who became head of the church's Department of External Church Relations, issued an appeal for unity to the Orthodox communities of Romania, Greece, Yugoslavia, and Czechoslovakia.

And why did the Russian Orthodox Church rally so decisively in defense of the atheistic Soviet state? Reduced to a minimal existence, the church probably saw no other way to survive. Besides, there are ample indications that the leaders of this traditionally patriotic institution were defending not the USSR but Mother Russia.

Indeed, the tangible results of the church's wartime loyalty in defense of Russia were much more positive than those of Metropolitan Sergei's 1927 declaration of loyalty to the Soviet regime. In 1943 a church was opened in Krasnoyarsk, and church openings would continue—though they would never equal the number of reopenings under the German occupation. The greatest number of reopened churches in the closing years of the war were in formerly German-occupied lands and near the front lines (in the latter instance, apparently, to avoid invidious comparisons); relatively few were opened in the more remote regions. By June 1945, some 16,000 Orthodox churches were in operation.

Another important effect of the wartime *modus vivendi*

worked out by the church during the period was the restoration of an orderly, canonical succession to the patriarchate. After Sergei died in May 1944, a *sobor* held at the end of January 1945 elected Metropolitan Alexii Simansky as patriarch. Forty-one Russian Orthodox bishops and several foreign guests attended the *sobor*, which also adopted a new statute strengthening the patriarch's role and providing for a highly authoritarian and centralized church organization. The statute did not provide for regular subsequent *sobors* but left the patriarch responsible for convening them when necessary. In addition, the establishment of a theological institute at the former Novodevichy convent (later moved to Zagorsk near Moscow) in June 1944 ensured the survival of the church's clergy.

Despite such accommodations, the government's overall policy toward religion did not change. Although anti-religious propaganda had stopped in 1941, as early as September 1944 a party Central Committee decree called for renewed efforts in this direction.

The government's outwardly more accommodating treatment of religious groups also touched the loyal hierarchies in Armenia and Georgia. In Armenia, war-time loyalty apparently made possible the election of Kevork as catholicos in 1945. In October-November 1943, the just revived Moscow patriarchate recognized the autocephaly of the Georgian Orthodox Church, no doubt with prior government approval. The Synod of the Russian Orthodox Church pointed out that autocephaly in this case was canonically proper because Georgia had its own state territory and administration, and ecclesiastical boundaries should follow state boundaries. (Of course, the same analysis could have dictated autocephaly for the Byelorussian and Ukrainian Orthodox churches.)

The Protestant Churches, 1941–45

The deportation of the Germans in the Soviet Union after the outbreak of war with Nazi Germany affected the predominantly German Lutherans and Mennonites most severely. Yet many new congregations eventually sprang up in Central Asia, particularly in Kazakhstan. The Evangelical Christians and the Baptists, though greatly weakened in the preceding decades, supported the Soviet war effort; their leaders sent a message to believers in Nazi-occupied lands urging them to aid in the anti-Fascist struggle. An important side benefit of this loyalty seems to have been the government's amenability to a union of the two groups, though it was also in the government's interest to have them in a single, more manageable unit. The state council for the affairs of non-Orthodox "cults," organized in July 1944 to parallel the Council for the Affairs of the Russian Orthodox Church, permitted the surviving Evangelical Christian and Baptist leaders to meet in Moscow in October to form the All-Union Council of Evangelical Christians–Baptists.

For some, this new body was an important and welcome step toward consolidating the position of the two groups; for others, it was but another step in submission to an unholy alliance with an atheistic regime. Headed primarily by Evangelical Christians (since these tended to be of Russian nationality), under the chairmanship of Yakov Zhidkov, the All-Union Council of Evangelical Christians–Baptists (AUCECB) organized its adherents into seventy districts presided over by seventy senior presbyters. In August 1945 the organization was joined by some 400 Pentecostal congregations, primarily from Ukraine and Byelorussia (some Pentecostal groups, however, declined membership).

Reflection: The Great Compromise

William C. Fletcher has commented that the years 1927–43, when Sergei was metropolitan, *locum tenens,* and finally patriarch, were "the crucial period in the history of the Russian Orthodox Church under the Soviets."[22] It was then that the church formulated its attitude toward the state and worked out a *modus vivendi.* Indeed, this was an important development in religious history in general, for it was the first time a major church had learned to survive within a modern totalitarian state. The arrangement arrived at in 1943 has become a model for church-state relations in the Soviet Union, and to some extent in other Marxist states: The hierarchy or other leadership of a church is granted privileges in return for loyal service to the state, which usually includes propaganda service; meanwhile, the state attempts—with varying degrees of determination—gradual reduction of the body of believers through atheistic propaganda, administrative pressure, and outright persecution. Under Stalin, the state tolerated the church only as long as it could be exploited for the war effort and for foreign-policy propaganda. In 1959 Khrushchev took up—though by other means—where Stalin left off in the persecution of religion.

The idea persists within Soviet ideology that sooner or later all religion must disappear. Does this make a permanent accommodation with any church both logically and practically impossible? Soviet practice has indeed borne this out, though not without seeming inconsistencies.

Post-War Developments, 1945–59

After World War II, the Soviet authorities did not renew their pre-war frontal assault on religion by the massive application of force and terror, with a few notable exceptions. The anti-religious campaign now took a more subtle form, focusing on propaganda, subversion and control of established churches, and a system of incentives and disincentives. The failure of these methods to eradicate religious belief led ultimately to another confrontation between state and believers.

The Russian Orthodox Church

World War II left the Russian Orthodox Church not only with a restored patriarchate but also with an expanded jurisdiction. The Orthodox of northern Bukovina had come under its rule during the war; in 1945 the Orthodox Church of Transcarpathia was transferred to it; the Orthodox of western Byelorussia and western Ukraine and, in 1946, the Eastern-rite Ukrainian Catholics were joined to it; finally, in 1945–46 the Baltic Orthodox churches were reintegrated with the Russian church.

The church developed internally as well. In April 1945, Foreign Minister Vyacheslav Molotov promised Patriarch Alexii the establishment of eight seminaries in addition to the Moscow seminary, as well as a printing press. (By 1947 the seminaries and two academies had been established, but no press.) The Trinity–St. Sergius Monastery at Zagorsk was returned to the church, and from 1946 it housed the Moscow theological schools. Although the shortage of priests and the low level of their education reflected the dire conditions of the 1930s, the number of applicants to the seminaries grew in the early 1950s. By 1953 there were 30,000 Russian Orthodox priests and between 20,000 and 25,000 parishes. In 1954–58 a number of churches were reopened or rebuilt; a few churches were newly constructed as well.[23]

Still a catacomb Russian Orthodox Church lived on. For although many believers returned to the official church once a patriarch had been canonically elected in 1945, others chose to remain underground.

While the rapid growth of the Orthodox Church must have alarmed some party functionaries, the government showed a degree of caution in its response. Thus, while by 1947 the anti-religious campaign had been escalated, the League of Militant Godless was replaced by the *Znanie* (knowledge) society to offer a more sophisticated approach to combatting religion. From January 1950 to Stalin's death in March 1953, only two Russian Orthodox bishops were consecrated; there were also arrests and forced retirements. In 1954 the party Central Committee noted the attraction of youth to the church as well as to non-Orthodox "sects" and called for an intensification of the anti-religious campaign. Later the same year, however, a resolution condemned arbitrary and defamatory attacks on clergy and believers. By 1955 atheistic education had been introduced into the armed forces, and both Znanie and Komsomol (the Communist youth organization) had been reactivated. When defectors from the church joined the anti-religious campaign, the patriarchate publicly excommunicated them.

In the post-war years, the Orthodox hierarchy actively supported Soviet foreign policy. As early as May 1945, Patriarch Alexii made an official visit to the Holy Land, stopping in several Middle Eastern countries along the way. It was Metropolitan Nikolai, however, who took charge of the church's foreign-policy activity, visiting Great Britain in 1945 and vigorously supporting the regime's "peace policy." Still, the hierarchs were not simply acting as Soviet state functionaries; it is clear that they also took the opportunity to offer pastoral care among believers as well as to give instruction in Christian morality and Orthodox theology through sermons, encyclicals, and other messages.

Other Orthodox Churches

While the Russian Orthodox Church was enjoying better relations with the state authorities than it had had in the earlier years of Soviet rule, this easing of tensions did not affect the fate of other national Orthodox churches. The remaining clergy and parishioners of the Byelorussian church and the Ukrainian Autocephalous and Autonomous churches were absorbed into the Russian church. Although the autocephaly of the Georgian Orthodox Church was recognized, it could count a mere 100 open churches in 1951 (before 1917 there had been 2,455), with about as many priests.

Despite the efforts of Catholicos Kevork of the Armenian Apostolic Church in the "peace" and anti-Vatican campaigns of 1945–49, a decade later only two out of thirty church buildings remained in the Armenian capital of Yerevan. Throughout the republic, many churches and monasteries remained closed and in disrepair; altogether, only ten or fifteen churches out of 1,250 were opened. But the year of Kevork's death, 1954, witnessed the opening of a reported total of eighty-nine churches and the publication of the church journal *Echmiadzin*.

In October 1955, Vazgen I was elected catholicos, and the following year he toured the Armenian diaspora, shoring up the Soviet Union's foreign image. After a meeting with Premier Bulganin, he was able to direct funds collected abroad toward restoring churches, expanding the seminary, and purchasing a press. Additional churches were opened, while some monasteries were returned by the government.[24]

The Protestant Churches

Protestants enjoyed relative tolerance in the post-war years, followed by a certain relaxation of controls in 1954–58—a respite that permitted considerable growth. As with the Orthodox, the early post-war years provided an opportunity for the Protestant churches to define their positions relative to the ideologically jealous state. The All-Union Council of Evangelical Christians–Baptists (AUCECB) firmly declared its political loyalty to the regime; in a letter sent to the 1947 Baptist World Alliance congress in Copenhagen, it asserted that Communist social and economic principles were not in contradiction to Christian teaching.[25] The AUCECB leadership also confined the pacifist doctrine to personal as opposed to social interaction, and accepted military conscription. Not surprisingly, some believers refused to accept the compromises involved in the founding of the AUCECB and later declarations. When in 1953–54 many Baptists returned from the camps, and when the 1955 amnesty for Germans swelled the ranks even further, some were appalled at the accommodations that had been made to the atheistic regime. They formed groups of "Pure Baptists."

The AUCECB's accommodations could not protect the community from the onslaughts of Soviet propaganda that insisted on the Baptists' connection with American "imperialists" and "war-mongers." Still, the state's official sanction offered advantages. In 1955 the AUCECB sent representatives to the London congress of the Baptist World Alliance, at which Yakov Zhidkov, AUCECB chairman, was elected a vice-president. In 1956–58 a few ministers were permitted to study in England. In the USSR, however, ministerial training remained unavailable. In 1956 the AUCECB was allowed to publish 15,000 copies of a hymnal, and in the following year some 10,000 copies of the Bible.

Church-state tensions were not the only difficulties for the AUCECB during this period. Friction with the Pentecostals plagued it as well. Having spread beyond their Ukrainian base, the Pentecostals often chose a near-nomadic life, wandering from place to place in an effort both to escape persecution and to live by their principles. Indifferent or even hostile to the state, the Pentecostals in the AUCECB caused the registered Baptists some discomfort.

There were at least 26,000 members of registered Seventh-

Day Adventist congregations in the Soviet Union in the 1950s. Like the AUCECB, the All-Union Council of Seventh-Day Adventists accommodated to state interests and took part in Soviet propaganda initiatives, especially in foreign policy. Also, their anti-Catholic bias was appreciated. Nevertheless, Adventist believers were the object of a strident internal propaganda effort, not least because of the practical problems they caused the authorities with their beliefs in the Saturday sabbath and the imminent end of the world.

In contrast with those Protestants who progressed by tempering valor with discretion, the Jehovah's Witnesses never compromised with the Soviet state. Coming under Soviet rule in eastern Poland during the war, they remained illegal throughout the 1950s and continue so today. Though subjected to trials and stiff sentencing, they continued to operate presses, proselytize, and distribute copies of *The Watchtower*.

The Catholic Church

Other than in recently occupied Lithuania and Latvia, the Catholic Church by the 1950s was left with only minimal formal existence in the USSR. In 1946 two of three seminaries were reportedly closed, although from at least 1959 the Kaunas seminary in Lithuania and the Riga seminary in Latvia were functioning. Because of the threat to Soviet hegemony posed by the strength and cohesion of Catholicism in Lithuania, around 1952 the regime tried to foment a Lithuanian "national church" under its control, but the effort failed. The regime did succeed, however, in persuading Lithuanian and Latvian hierarchs to support its propaganda efforts, and in 1955 two Lithuanian bishops were consecrated while a number of priests returned from exile. Still, Lithuanian clergy were subjected to economic and administrative pressure such as higher rent and electricity rates, and, as elsewhere in the Soviet Union, anti-Catholic propaganda continued apace. By January 1954 in Lithuania, there were 741 Catholic priests, 688 open churches, and 75 theology students—serving an estimated Catholic population of more than two million.[26]

The regime had earlier, in 1949, attempted to form an anti-

Vatican "national" Catholic church in Byelorussia. Here, too, the attempt had failed, partly because Archimandrite Andrej Cikota, though kept in solitary confinement, refused the state's offer to become head of such a church; he died in Siberia in 1952. Statistics from 1956 show that there were between 30 and 35 Catholic priests in the republic, 30 parishes, and perhaps 800,000 faithful. In Minsk, the capital, however, there was not a single Catholic church.[27]

The Soviet occupation authorities in the western Ukraine moved cautiously regarding the Ukrainian Greek Catholic (or Uniate) Church until after the death of Metropolitan Sheptytsky in November 1944. Then, despite friendly gestures by his successor, Josyf Slipyj, the government went ahead with what appears to have been a carefully crafted plan to liquidate the church. In early 1945 the newly installed Russian Orthodox Patriarch Alexii publicly and falsely denounced the deceased metropolitan and the Uniate church as traitors and Nazi collaborators, calling on Ukrainian Eastern-rite Catholics to "return" to the Russian Orthodox fold. In April, Metropolitan Slipyj and four of the five Ukrainian Catholic bishops on Soviet territory were arrested; in May an "Initiative Group" surfaced to promote "reunion" with Russian Orthodoxy. Over the next year numerous clergy who would not convert were arrested, and in March 1946 the arrested bishops were publicly indicted. Several days later a *sobor* in Lviv proclaimed the dissolution of the four-million-strong Ukrainian Greek Catholic Church and the transfer of its faithful to the Russian Orthodox Church.

Ultimately, Metropolitan Slipyj and eight of the nine Ukrainian bishops, as well as hundreds of priests, religious, and laity, were sentenced and deported for their refusal to abandon the church. In 1949, two years after the murder of Bishop Teodor Romzha, the liquidation of the church in the Transcarpathian region was formally announced, and throughout the 1950s the Ukrainian Greek Catholic Church survived only underground, as it does today. Priests returning from exile in the mid-1950s probably increased its size, and one may speculate that many formally and ostensibly Russian Orthodox priests and parishes remained Ukrainian Catholic at heart.[28]

KHRUSHCHEV'S ANTI-RELIGIOUS CAMPAIGN, 1959–64

Starting in 1959, the Soviet government under Premier Nikita S. Khrushchev undertook a series of measures to eliminate or at least reduce the influence of religion in society. The campaign was more intense than any other since the Stalinist terror of the 1930s. On the propaganda front, the atheistic journal *Nauka i religiya* (Science and religion) made its debut in 1959. In January 1960 the party Central Committee called for intensification of anti-religious propaganda, and by 1964 anti-religious publications had reached a total circulation of six million copies. On the administrative level, tax exemptions on monastic lands and buildings that had been granted in 1945 were revoked, while some monasteries opened under the Nazi occupation were closed. On an informal level, pressure was applied to families to prevent minors from attending religious services. Some believers were beaten. Church property was damaged on various pretexts. Finally, an unpublished decree of the Supreme Soviet of the Russian Republic, dated October 19, 1962, amended the Law on Religious Associations to create serious inconveniences for religious groups.

The Russian Orthodox Church

By the mid-1960s, only 17 or 18 of the 90 Russian Orthodox monastic institutions that had survived since 1917 remained open. In 1960–61 some 10,000 Russian Orthodox churches were closed, and another 5,000 were shut during the next few years. The number of monks and nuns was likewise dramatically reduced, from around 10,000 to some 5,000.[29] By 1965, the 20,000 to 25,000 churches open in 1958 had been reduced to fewer than 8,000. Between the mid-1950s and 1962, the number of diocesan bishops fell from 74 to 63, parish clergy from around 20,000 to about 14,000. The eight seminaries operating in the 1950s were reduced to five by 1962; later, there would be only three.

Just as significant as the active repression, however, was the movement of the Council for the Affairs of the Russian Orthodox Church away from church-state mediation toward being an organ of government control over the patriarchate. Hence by 1960

Metropolitan Nikolai, who had stoutly defended the church against government incursion, had been dismissed. In 1961 the church statute was amended to reorganize the parishes in such a way that the priests were left with no administrative power; decisions were in the hands of a three-person executive committee of the parish council. The result was an increased possibility of government interference in church affairs.

Other Orthodox Churches

The situation of the Orthodox churches of Georgia and Armenia also deteriorated. By 1960 only three of fifteen Georgian Orthodox dioceses remained, with no more than 100 churches, one seminary, and eight bishops. It is said that because of the shortage of priests, on holy days believers would simply gather about the ruins of their churches for informal worship. Nevertheless, the Georgian hierarchy continued its propaganda role for the regime.

While the Georgian church's situation was difficult, it appeared better than that of the Armenian Apostolic Church. By 1960, all that remained of the official church structure in Armenia was the catholicos and several monks living at the monastery of Echmiadzin.[30]

The AUCECB : A Split

The Khrushchev years were a time of great upheaval for Evangelical Christians and Baptists. New statutes imposed secretly on the AUCECB in 1960 were revealed in a letter of instructions written by church officials and dispersed to senior presbyters. The letter said in part:

> The senior presbyter should understand thoroughly and remember that the chief goal of religious services at the present time is not the attraction of new members but satisfaction of the spiritual needs of believers. . . . It is the duty of the senior presbyter to check unhealthy missionary manifestations, called by the Apostle Paul "zeal for God without judgment." . . .
>
> Every presbyter is a minister only of his own church and should not carry on any spiritual work outside its borders, and he should not permit such activity on the part of other members of the church. On occasions when baptism does not take place in a pool or prayer

building but outdoors in a river, sea, or some other body of water, it is necessary to insure that large crowds do not gather around the baptism and that everything be carried out in calm and quiet. . . .

The number of services (worship meetings) in churches should not as a rule exceed two or three meetings per week. . . .

In the past, with insufficient observance of Soviet legislation on cults in some of our churches, violations of it have taken place. . . . It is necessary to remove all of this in our churches, and to bring our activities into line with the existing legislation.[31]

Among the "violations" mentioned in the letter of instructions were baptisms of persons under eighteen, Bible-study meetings, mutual-aid funds, meetings for preachers and choir directors, and preaching by ministers or lay preachers from other churches.

Not surprisingly, the letter resulted in a split in the AUCECB. The *Initsiativniki* (Action Group), led by A. F. Prokofiev and G. K. Kryuchkov, refused to submit to the restrictive new regulations. They wrote to the AUCECB leaders:

In your New Statutes and particularly in your Letter of Instructions you disobeyed the commandment of Christ by prescribing the following:

Sec. 4. At services a presbyter must not allow digressions which tend to become appeals. . . .

Sec. 5. Zealous proselytization in our communities must definitely stop . . . and an effort must be made to reduce the baptism of young people between the ages of 18 and 30 to a minimum.

Disobeying the commandment of Christ ("Suffer little children and forbid them not to come unto me," Matt. 19:14) you prescribed that:

Sec. 6. Children . . . should not be allowed to attend services.

You have also issued many other similar instructions. With these "documents" and "statutes" you have denied salvation to the sinner; when salvation is denied, then it follows there is no need for a Savior. Through this, then, you have rejected even the Savior himself.

And all this has been done to pander to atheism and to the world![32]

The *Initsiativniki* accused the AUCECB leadership of opposing the convocation of a new congress. Although in October 1963 a congress was convoked and the instructions were recalled, these and other concessions came too late for Prokofiev and some of his supporters, who by this time were in prison. The definitive break between the AUCECB and the congregations that refused to register under the restrictive laws took place with the founding of the unofficial Council of Churches of Evangelical Christians–Baptists in 1965.

During these years, the entire Evangelical-Baptist community was the object of propaganda that labeled it a nest of American spies and hypocrites and ridiculed its beliefs. For the AUCECB, difficulties in registration prompted believers to combine congregations, thus shrinking the church's administrative scope and most probably its ability for influence within a given area. Still, in 1963, the AUCECB was allowed to join the World Council of Churches and later was itself joined by some 18,000 Mennonite Brethren. The 1962 records show that the AUCECB counted 5,545 congregations with 545,000 faithful; there were 32,370 preachers, in addition to local ministers.[33]

The Catholic Church

In 1962–63 Pope John XXIII departed from the firm anti-Soviet line of his predecessors; in response, the Soviet Union, although in the midst of an anti-religious campaign, allowed Russian Orthodox observers to attend the Second Vatican Council. The aim of the new Vatican *Ostpolitik* was evidently to improve the lot of Catholics in the USSR—primarily in Lithuania and Latvia—through dialogue with the Soviet government and the Russian Orthodox Church. Indeed, in 1963 Metropolitan Slipyj of the Ukrainian Catholic Church was released from confinement and allowed to go to Rome, where he was made a cardinal two years later.

There were clear limits, however, on how much could be achieved. The catacomb church in western Ukraine, for example, remained persecuted. Naturally, the long-term goal of the Soviet regime was still the eradication of religion, and a deeply ingrained suspicion of the Catholic Church remained.

Reflection: Why the Campaign?

Did the anti-religious drive of 1959–64 merely reflect Khrushchev's personal prejudices, or were there deeper reasons for it? A likely answer would be found in the general demoralization of the population and government in the wake of Khrushchev's "de-Stalinization" of 1956. With the god of Stalin demythologized and discredited, devout Communists became disoriented and lax in their principles. A new ideal was needed to galvanize public morale. This ideal was to be atheism.

The campaign may also have been a reaction to the perceived threat of growing religiosity among the new generation. Unlike the older generation, many of whom had discarded their religious heritage along with all other "survivals of the past," many from the new generation, which had grown up under atheism, found it impotent and hollow. They were eager to discard it for something that could give more meaning to their lives.

A third reason for the anti-religious drive may have been the delayed effect of the re-establishment of the Moscow patriarchate in 1943. In a decade and a half, the Russian Orthodox Church had trained priests, opened churches, and begun once again to exert an influence within society. As in the past, the regime felt threatened by established religion. Also, through the territorial annexations of World War II, Catholic, Protestant, and Orthodox churches of the occupied lands brought new blood to the religious groups already in the USSR. These two factors could well have convinced the regime that the specter of religion would continue to haunt it until it took the appropriate actions.

After Khrushchev's ouster in 1964, it was recognized that the excesses of the anti-religious campaign had not produced the intended effects. A party Central Committee declaration of November 10, 1964, entitled "On Errors Committed in the Conduct of Atheistic Propaganda" rejected administrative interference in church affairs.

Concluding Observations

While this chapter has focused on church-state relations, there is of course much more to be said about church life in Russia and the Soviet Union in the period 1917–64. But because of the determined anti-religious policy of the Communist regime, religious life could never remain an altogether private matter for either individuals or churches. The state constantly impinged on the church.

The historical record suggests, however, that the state authorities were not at all times and in all situations bent on the destruction of religion. In at least some cases they seemed willing to allow believers to practice their traditions as long as they did not interfere in what the state considered its domain. While this may appear often to have been merely a temporary, tactical arrangement—subject to a long-term strategic goal of liquidation—it is conceivable that some Communist leaders were willing to tolerate religion indefinitely if it did not threaten their power.

Indeed, some Western commentators read Soviet history as showing that the kind of loyalty demanded by the Soviet state and the loyalty demanded by the Russian Orthodox Church are not mutually exclusive. They argue that as the Soviet Union is not truly an ideologically fixed Marxist-Leninist state—the Party is more interested in maintaining power than in enforcing Marxist doctrine—the existence of a non-Marxist ideology is acceptable if it helps keep the Party in power by, for example, lending it legitimacy. Russian nationalism has been such an ideology. As a "legitimizing" ideology for the Party, Russian nationalism dovetails neatly with its traditional partner, Russian Orthodoxy. This is an obvious advantage for the Russian Orthodox Church. Certainly the combination of Russian nationalism and Orthodoxy helped Stalin in 1943. Yet, as the waning Russian component of the population nears 50 per cent, it is not certain that this combination will work in the future.

Is a "live and let live" arrangement really possible? Can the Marxist-Leninist state and the church operate in truly separate spheres? The answer depends on how one perceives the nature of the state and of the given religious group. Some might argue that in a practical, limited way (though not in any ultimate sense), the domains of church and state can be separated. This has certainly been the position of official Soviet church leaders and the basis of church-state relations since 1943. But can a government that aims at total ideological control co-exist peacefully with an organization based on a theistic world view, one that cherishes the spiritual loyalty of the individual to God above all else? The future of church-state relations in the USSR will depend on the answer to this question.

3

Legislative and Administrative Control of Religious Bodies

John Anderson

SINCE THE October (1917) Revolution, Soviet policy has embodied a continuing theoretical and practical hostility toward religious belief. Nevertheless, the 1930s and early 1960s represent peak periods in the government's religious repression.

Following Stalin's death in 1953, his successors chose to renounce mass terror as a means of rule. In 1956 Khrushchev astonished delegates to the Twentieth Party Congress with an attack on the dictator's crimes, leading to a certain thaw in many areas of Soviet life. Although in comparison with liberal democracies the political system remained highly repressive, the new atmosphere made it possible for many groups to expand the scope of their legitimate activities. As Soviet authorities were soon to find out, however, this also meant that some members and groups in the society would no longer acquiesce quietly to policies that subverted their interests. When Khrushchev launched his campaign against religion, he discovered that many believers were prepared to fight for what they believed to be their natural and constitutional rights.

John Anderson is a Soviet researcher at Keston College. He also teaches Russian history and Soviet politics at the London School of Economics and Political Science, from which he holds a doctoral degree.

Khrushchev's fall in October 1964 brought an end to militant anti-religious campaigning. Religious arrests virtually ceased in 1965, and the rate of church closures slowed dramatically—although the 10,000 or more closed under the deposed first secretary were not reopened. Equally significant was the limited reassessment of religious policy to be found in the press, including implicit criticism of the brutality of Khrushchev's policies and a greater awareness of the complexity of the religious issue. Moreover, some concessions were made to officially recognized religious bodies in the form of registering more churches and permitting the publication of some religious literature. Yet the basically anti-religious tenets of Soviet ideology were not questioned.

The Beginning of Religious Dissent

One product of the Khrushchev era was religious dissent, initially by Baptists and Orthodox but from the late 1960s drawing in many other groups as well. The result was a return to harsher policies. In February 1966, a crude press assault on dissident Baptists was launched, followed in March by amendments to the criminal code aimed specifically at identifying certain of their activities as "crimes." Over the next twelve months nearly 200 dissident Baptists were arrested. Further campaigns against all forms of political and religious dissent occurred in 1971–73—the end coincided with the start of détente—and from 1979.[1] By early 1986 there were more than 400 known religious prisoners in the Soviet Union, though many of them were to be released in 1987–88.

While Brezhnev and his immediate successors proved more than willing to imprison religious activists, they sought to avoid the return to mass terror that complete elimination of nonconformity would probably require. Instead, they devised policies aimed at isolating "religious extremists" from the mass of believers and bringing religious institutions under tight state control. At the same time, they were cautious of pressuring the religious communities to the extent that still more groups would feel obliged to enter the less controllable realm of underground activity. Avoiding an increase of the underground seems to have been a dominant concern of the authorities since 1964.

Although post-Khrushchev religious policy has been relatively flexible and some concessions have been made, flexibility and moderation have not become that policy's salient features. The central questions we shall deal with in this chapter are, Why does the Soviet regime continue to pursue fundamentally anti-religious policies? How is this done within the framework of a professed freedom of conscience?

Theoretical Basis for Opposing Religion

Despite the frequent use of Marxist-Leninist rhetoric, in many areas of both domestic and foreign policy Soviet leaders increasingly appear to be motivated mainly by pragmatic considerations. Yet at the same time the official ideology continues to proclaim as its goal the full achievement of Communism—a precondition of which is said to be the elimination of religion.

The Ideological Components

Philosophically, Marxism is clearly atheistic. Marx followed the German thinker Feuerbach in depicting religious ideas as essentially a human creation and thus illusory. More practically, he described religion as something easily used by the exploiting elements in the society of his day. In his own rather caustic words:

> The classical saint of Christianity mortified his body for the salvation of the soul of the masses; the modern, educated saint mortifies the masses for the salvation of his own soul.

Nevertheless, Marx realized that the "opium of the people" met a real human need within an oppressive society.

Lenin followed Marx's analysis of religion, though the tone of his critique was often less refined—witness his description of religion as "spiritual booze." In a 1905 article, Lenin argued that religion would gradually disappear from human society as economic exploitation ended and scientific knowledge spread. Of course, some provision had to be made for the "transition period," that time when capitalism had been abolished but full Communism had not yet been achieved. In practical terms:

> Religion must be a private affair . . . so far as the *state* is concerned. . . . So far as the *Party* of the socialist proletariat is concerned, religion cannot be a private affair. . . . Our propaganda necessarily includes the propaganda of atheism [italics added].[2]

There is, then, in Soviet ideology a theoretical opposition to religion. But this in itself does not explain the harsh attacks on religious institutions, for Lenin in his pre-Revolutionary writings stressed the centrality of socio-economic change and education as opposed to coercion. For further light we must go beyond the materialistic basis of Soviet ideology to what might be called its "totalist" aspect: that is, the proclaimed belief that in Marxism-Leninism the Communist Party of the Soviet Union alone holds the key both to a proper understanding of the laws of social development and to the means of establishing the first truly communist society. This idea was reaffirmed in the new Constitution of the USSR in 1977.[3]

Belief in the total sufficiency of Marxism-Leninism leads the Soviet regime to deny legitimacy to alternative belief systems, such as religion. While practical considerations might dictate some concessions to institutional religion, the struggle against religious ideology is still the duty of every Communist and all party, state, and social organizations.

Other more pragmatic considerations support the continued official promotion of anti-religion. Some religious practices are considered to be incompatible with healthful living (for example, the baptism or circumcision of babies) or with the dignity of the individual (the payment of *kalym*, bride price, in Islamic areas). More important, a vast network of institutions and individuals involved in the promotion of atheism have a vested interest in continuing the ideological commitment.

An Ambiguous Freedom

Freedom of conscience (*svoboda sovesti*) is one of the numerous rights granted to citizens by the Soviet Constitution. It is a right, however, that even in its theoretical formulation is extremely ambiguous. In part this stems from the way "rights" are understood in the USSR. For Soviet writers, human rights do not have the absolute quality that they have in the West, in the sense of being God-given or inalienable and inherent in the individual—though at the Nineteenth Party Conference held in June 1988 Gorbachev denied that human rights were "a gift from the state" and suggested that they were "an inalienable characteristic of socialism."[4] In the Soviet view, "bourgeois societies" permit only *civil* rights, such as freedom of association and the right to vote, arranged so as not to threaten the dominant position of the exploiting classes. Contrasted with this in the Soviet view are socialist societies, which provide the more important rights, such as full employment and abolition of poverty.

The Party, we have seen, makes monopolistic claims to understanding the laws of social development. As a result, it claims the power to decide which rights are appropriate for the citizens of the socialist society and to what extent they may be exercised. The preamble to the 1977 Constitution defines the supreme goal of Soviet-style socialism as "the construction of a classless communist society," and all rights granted to the citizen must be conducive to that end. Article 39 of the Constitution states:

> In exercising their rights and freedoms citizens may not injure the interest of society and the state or the rights of other citizens.

In reality these "interests" of society and the state are defined by and coterminous with the interests of the Party.[5]

A Changed Understanding

The 1918 Constitution of the Russian republic stated:

> To secure for the working man true freedom of conscience, the church is separated from the state and the school from the church, and freedom of religious and anti-religious propaganda is recognized as the right of every citizen.

(In 1929 "freedom of religious . . . propaganda" was changed to the right "to profess religion.") For Soviet jurists, this definition of freedom of conscience surpassed that of bourgeois states in that it explicitly allowed for unbelief while protecting the legitimate rights of believers. Nevertheless, in some Soviet writing on the religious question there is to be found, explicitly or implicitly, the notion that true freedom of conscience also entails the liberation of believers from their religious illusions.[6]

Article 52 of the 1977 Soviet Constitution begins with these words:

> Freedom of conscience is guaranteed for citizens of the USSR, that is, the right to confess any religion or no religion, to carry out religious worship or to conduct atheistic propaganda.

Apart from a new clause prohibiting the incitement of hostility or hatred on religious grounds, the most notable features of this article were (1) its "guarantee" rather than simple "recognition" of freedom of conscience and (2) the replacement of "anti-religious propaganda" by the more neutral "atheistic propaganda." Just as significant, at least on paper, was the fact that Article 34 of the new Constitution declared all citizens to be equal before the law, regardless of "origin, social and property status, race or nationality, sex, education, language, attitude towards religion." This contrasted with the old Article 123, which simply guaranteed equality of rights to all citizens, without specification.

But for religious critics it was less the phrasing of Article 52 than its context that mattered. A document from the Soviet Union produced by the Christian Committee for the Defense of Believers' Rights noted the confusion of party and state built into the new Constitution. Although Lenin spoke of the *Party* as carrying out atheistic education (with the state officially neutral), the new Constitution speaks of "the education of the citizen of a communist society" as a major task of the state. According to the official ideology, this citizen could only be an atheist. Moreover, the new document binds all citizens, including believers, to building a "classless communist society," i.e., an atheistic one.[7]

Official interpretations of freedom of conscience are generally restrictive. Vladimir Kuroyedov, from 1965 to 1984 chairman of the government's Council for Religious Affairs, noted:

> The church is purely concerned with the performance of religious worship. Any propagandist or educational activity is not within the sphere of the church, which is an association of believers existing only for the satisfaction of people's religious needs.

These "needs" were narrowly defined so as to require simply acts of worship.[8]

Even the Soviet theoretical understanding of freedom of conscience, then, is rather narrow, limited to the right to confess any religion and to engage in worship. As Soviet commentators themselves make clear, this rules out charitable and educational activities taken for granted by religious organizations in many other parts of the world.

The 1918 Decree and 1929 Law

Soviet writers point to the 1918 Decree on the Separation of Church From State and School From Church as enshrining the basic guarantee of freedom of conscience. This decree abolishes all special privileges associated with religious adherence, bans religious services from state institutions, and bans religious teaching from state schools. It also denies to religious organizations the juridical status of a person-at-law; the church could not, for example, sue for slander or own property. (There is evidence to suggest that this position changed in 1985,[9] and the change will perhaps be codified in the revised religious law drafted in 1988.)

In the decade following the 1918 decree, the status of religious organizations was spelled out more precisely in a series of laws and instructions brought together in the 1929 Law on Religious Associations. This law has regulated institutional religious life ever since, though in 1988 a revision was under consideration. Before examining it, however, we need to look at some agencies involved in carrying out Soviet religious policy, in particular the Council for Religious Affairs.

Agencies of Control

After the October Revolution, control over religious affairs passed almost immediately into state hands. Although the Russian Orthodox Church had in effect been governed from within the tsarist bureaucracy for two centuries, the Bolsheviks were probably the first rulers in history to combine explicit unbelief as official ideology with the exercise of control over religious organizations.

Initially the task of supervising religious institutions fell to the Justice Commissariat, but it soon passed on to other government bodies before, in the 1930s, ending up in the hands of the secret police (NKVD) and its Commission for Cults (*Kultkomissiya*). One of the results of the wartime *modus vivendi* between church and state was the creation of the Council for the Affairs of the Russian Orthodox Church (CAROC) and the Council for the Affairs of Religious Cults (CARC). Although CAROC was headed by *Kultkomissiya* chairman Georgi Karpov, the two new bodies did appear to view their roles as primarily mediatory. All this changed with the Khrushchev anti-religious campaign, when, in the words of one Orthodox critic, CAROC became "an organ for exercising unofficial and illegal control" over the church.

Council for Religious Affairs

After Khrushchev's fall, CAROC and CARC merged to become the Council for Religious Affairs (CRA), attached to the USSR Council of Ministers and headed by CAROC chairman V. A. Kuroyedov. The primary role of the CRA is said to be mediation between church and state. It decides whether particular religious "associations" (groups of twenty or more believers) have the right to exist. It exercises *kontrol* over the observance by religious associations of the relevant laws, and explains these laws to state and social organizations that come into contact with religious bodies. (The Russian *kontrol* differs from "control" in that it means checking whether laws or economic plans are being fulfilled, rather than dominating the way people act or think.)

Structurally, the Council for Religious Affairs consists of seven departments concerned either with specific religious groups or with functional aspects of its work, such as law or international affairs. Researchers in the West have only limited information on the men who head the CRA. Kuroyedov, who was chairman 1965–84, had earlier worked in the Central Committee's Department of Agitation and Propaganda, whereas his predecessor at CAROC had come from the ranks of the secret police. The current CRA chairman, Konstantin Kharchev, has a more obscure biography; his previous post was ambassador to Guyana. It appears that most CRA officials come from a police or propaganda background and that at least one of the deputy chairmen is usually a KGB officer.

Outside Moscow, CRA officials are to be found at both the republican and the regional level. In some of the fifteen republics that make up the USSR—Ukraine, Armenia, and, since 1986, the Russian republic—there is a separate CRA council attached to the government of the area; in others; a single commissioner is directly responsible to the Moscow office. Each region (*oblast*), of which there are nearly 130, also has its own commissioner. Upon these men—and there appear to be no women—the everyday life of religious communities depends. Commissioners monitor religious situations in their areas, keep detailed statistics on official and unofficial religious activities, make recommendations about the opening and closing of churches, and instruct local officials in current religious policies.

For both institutional and personal reasons, the application of Soviet religious policy by CRA commissioners can vary considerably. As a bureaucrat, the commissioner has a dual loyalty: an institutional allegiance to the Moscow CRA, as well as a *nomenklatura* allegiance to the local party organization that recommended his appointment. (*Nomenklatura* posts are those that require the approval of party organizations; they include hundreds of jobs in every *oblast* or major town, such as directors of factories and heads of hospitals and schools.) If Moscow's assessment of policies differs from that of the local elite, the commissioner may feel obliged to follow central directions, yet be painfully aware that his future employment will, in most cases, depend upon the local bosses.

In addition, the individual characters of commissioners influence the implementation of policy. Some appear to take their work very seriously and to delight in humiliating believers;

others, especially those "put out to pasture" prior to retirement, may be rather lethargic in dealing with religious communities. Some even appear to have little idea of their responsibilities; a party official in the republic of Kazakh got a laugh at the usually rather humorless party congress in 1981 by telling of an *oblast* CRA official who wrote asking his superiors to send a *mullah* (Muslim religious leader) to bury a relative of his!

Despite these variations, however, Soviet religious policy is basically formulated and implemented from Moscow. Over the last three decades, when Moscow has decreed concessions or increased repression for particular groups, in all but a few cases the treatment appears to have been extended to like religious groups throughout the country.[10]

Other Agencies of Control

The Committee for State Security (KGB) has officers working within the CRA apparatus. Aside from these, the secret police maintains its own network of informers within religious organizations. Often these informers duplicate the work of CRA officials, though they are concerned less with the administration of religious life than with preventing the emergence of religious dissent. Within the KGB, a special Fifth Directorate created in 1970 to deal with dissent in general has a section responsible for religious dissent.

Local *soviets* (administrative councils) also have a general responsibility for ensuring that the laws are observed. Attached to most are voluntary commissions for checking on local religious associations. While these commissions do not have the right to punish breaches of the regulations and may only report them to other bodies, they often take an active part in the struggle against religion. For instance, in the Ukrainian city of Kharkov, the local commission sent a questionnaire to factories in the area asking for data on their workers' level of religiosity. A CRA instruction to local commissioners stated pointedly:

> One of the most important aims of the commissions for assistance should be to discover means of limiting and weakening the activities of religious associations.

The Law on Religious Associations

The major legislation governing Soviet religious life was first issued in 1929 and amended secretly in 1962 and publicly in 1975. This Law on Religious Associations sets out the procedure for opening or closing associations and outlines their *modus operandi*.[11]

The Registration Process

The most basic requirement of the 1929 law is that religious associations must register with state authorities before they begin their activities. According to at least some Soviet commentators, the lack of registration does not render them illegal but merely deprives them of legal protection.[12] Against this, however, one should note the harsh treatment meted out to non-registered groups and the fact that to encourage religious communities not to register is a criminal offense.

To register, a minimum of twenty believers eighteen and older must submit an application to the executive committee of the local *soviet*. This body's recommendation eventually reaches CRA headquarters in Moscow, where the final decision is made. Such centralization, which is said to protect believers from the whims of local officials, also enables the Council for Religious Affairs to enforce some uniformity in the implementation of policy.

Assuming all paperwork is in order, registration would appear to be a simple formality, were it not for the fundamentally anti-religious stance of the state bodies that supervise religious life. A number of unpublished instructions interpret registration as *sanctioning*, rather than simply *noting*, the existence of religious communities. Therefore, the registration of groups whose members have been guilty of "illegal" or "anti-social" activity or whose teachings have a "superstitious character"—a phrase covering anything from allegations of ritual murder to speaking in tongues—is strictly forbidden. Among the groups included in these categories are Jehovah's Witnesses.

One of the earliest pieces of Orthodox *samizdat* (covertly reproduced and distributed documents) to reach the West concerned attempts by believers in the town of Gorky to register religious associations. In 1968 the town had only three small registered churches to meet the needs of an estimated 100,000 believers. Repeated appeals to the authorities brought only job dismissals, threats of psychiatric internment for the petition signatories, and refusals. The grounds for the negative decisions included the fact that repairs on one church building would cost one million rubles, while another was "too near a school." Orthodoxy apparently shared with Socrates the capacity to corrupt the young.

In other cases, persistence has paid off. In 1957, a small group of Church Mennonites began to gather in private homes in the Kazakh city of Karaganda. After Khrushchev's fall in 1964, they began applying for registration and for permission to build a church. The authorities refused to register them and attempted to unite them with a local Mennonite Brethren community. But the congregation continued to meet, and in 1975, more than a decade after they began seeking registration, they received it.

More Flexibility in Registration

In the early 1970s the CRA began to adopt a more flexible approach toward registration. The policy change mainly benefited Protestant groups. In the case of the Baptists, the new flexibility apparently was motivated by the emergence of a strong underground dissent movement in response to Khrushchev's attempts to increase the level of state control. Under the influence of the dissenters, many congregations left the registered All-Union Council of Evangelical Christians–Baptists (AUCECB), which they thought was too much under the thumb of the state. From the state's perspective, this put hundreds of congregations in a situation much less amenable to control. Consequently the authorities decided to permit Baptist and Evangelical groups to register independently of the AUCECB with promises—and often nothing more—of less state intervention in their internal affairs. More than 500 such congregations had been registered by 1985.

Other groups that have benefited from this more flexible approach to registration are the Lutherans, Mennonites, Pentecostals, and Muslims. In the case of the Muslims, the state's greater willingness to register them appeared to stem from their higher birth rate, a rise in the level of conservative, unofficial Islamic activity (similar in some ways to that of the Baptists), and a concern over the possible consequences of Islamic "revivalism" along the Soviet Union's southern borders.

This new "liberalism" has not extended to those groups that continue to refuse registration. Also, the increase in registration for some religious communities masks the fact that over the same period others, most notably the Russian Orthodox Church, lost a considerable number of their churches through closure in primarily rural areas.

Declining Number of Registered Groups

Registration provides only limited security. Religious communities can lose their registration if they are found to have transgressed the law, if they fail to observe the terms of their contract for the lease of property, if the majority of the congregation requests dissolution, if the size of the congregation drops below twenty, or if their meeting site is required for urban redevelopment, although in the latter case alternative accommodations are supposed to be provided.

Local authorities in the town of Zhitomir closed the Cathedral of the Epiphany in 1973 and demolished the building two years later against the will of believers. In 1979 parishioners in the Byelorussian village of Rechitsa were permitted to repair their church, only to find, after they finished the work, a lock on the door and a notice that the building was closed because of "a gross violation of the fire regulations." Sometimes a church building is closed for a short period as a means of exerting pressure on an "overactive" community. This was the experience of a registered Pentecostal church in the Byelorussian town of Molodechno, closed in October 1985. Here authorities objected to the association's work among children and young people. Initially it appeared that because the pastor was held responsible for this violation, the church would remain closed until a new pastor was selected. It was reopened in December, however, under the same but presumably more cautious leadership.

As we have seen, under Khrushchev the generally harsh interpretation of registration requirements led to the closure of as many as half of the religious associations between 1959 and 1964. Thus by the time Brezhnev became first secretary, there were at most only some 20,000 churches remaining. Most Soviet spokesman continue to cite that figure,[13] but it certainly is not correct. In 1975 V. G. Furov, a deputy chairman of the CRA, stated off the record that there were 16,000 registered religious associations.[14] By 1985 the number had dropped to 15,000, a figure confirmed by CRA chairman Kharchev in an interview published in November 1987.

The Life of Registered Associations

Once a community has been registered, its first task is to find a building. Religious associations are permitted to acquire property free of charge or to lease it from the local *soviets*, as well as to use buildings put at their disposal by private individuals. They have no right of ownership, however, and if the association dissolves, its building reverts to the state. At least one draft of the new law under consideration in 1988 returns to churches the right of juridical personality and consequently the right to own property.

To find a building is often not easy. Not all are considered by the authorities suitable for religious use. As mentioned before, proximity to a school can disqualify a site for religious use. Also, despite the Soviet authorities' notorious laxity about enforcement of safety regulations, buildings previously considered adequate for public use may be judged to be fire or safety risks once they are proposed for use as churches. Some registered congregations go for years without a church. Lithuanian Catholics in the parish of Ryliskai lost their building in a fire in 1953. For the following thirty years they met in private homes; since 1983 they have met in a cemetery. Despite their registered status, their lack of a church building has meant that their meetings are persistently disrupted.

A second problem is finding a priest or pastor, for in may

areas these are in short supply, and their appointment requires CRA approval. In 1974 the priest in the village of Istino was transferred, and no replacement seemed forthcoming. Without a priest, the community was in danger of losing its registration. Parishioners appealed to their archbishop, who replied that nothing could be done without the permission of the commissioner for religious affairs. But when they appealed to the commissioner, he said that clerical appointments were the concern of the church, not the state.

Soviet law prohibits a priest or pastor from doing administrative work, and the congregation elects an administrative committee of three—subject to the authorities' approval:

> The registration agencies reserve the right to reject individual members of the executive body of a religious society.

The authorities may choose to remove those whom they suspect of excessive religious zeal and impose administrators with little real interest in the affairs of the church.

In some areas, CRA commissioners have even used their powers of intervention to impose unworthy clerics on congregations or to protect some whose behavior reflects badly on the church. During the early 1970s, parishioners from the Church of Saint Nicholas in the Ukrainian city of Nikolaev complained that one of their priests abused his colleagues and forced his attentions on women in the congregation. The local commissioner said he would close the church if the community refused to renew the priest's contract. In 1975, the believers elected a new *dvadtsatka*, the council of twenty parishioners that controls a church's affairs, only to have eleven of its members rejected by the commissioner as "unreliable." When their archbishop sought to intercede, he was "retired," presumably at the instigation of the CRA. Unworthy clerics do far more damage to the churches than does atheistic propaganda.

Petty interference in the affairs of religious communities remains the norm. A Seventh-Day Adventist pastor, for example, may have to combine his pastoral duties with a regular job, make frequent visits to the CRA commissioner or local authorities to gain permission for a baptismal or funeral service, and sort out problems stemming from meetings in private homes held by members of his congregation. In the latter case, the pastor might be held responsible and fined even if he knew nothing about the gatherings—and this is a registered pastor. The one Catholic priest active in the Moldavian republic during the 1970s had to get permission from five separate persons or organizations before he could take the last sacrament to the dying, by which time it was often too late.

Control Over Church Leadership

Political and administrative control over religion is more systematic and thorough at the churchwide level than at the local level. However, neither Soviet law nor theoretical writings on church-state relations provides any real basis for state intervention in central church affairs. Separation of church and state is generally defined in the following terms:

> The state does not interfere in the internal activities of the religious associations and the church in its turn does not interfere in state affairs.

But not all writers have accepted this formulation with its implicit assumption of equality between church and state. As an expression of the will of the workers, they argue, the state has supreme powers that give it the right to regulate all aspects of social life.

Numerous *samizdat* documents illustrate the state's involvement in the internal workings of the church leadership. An anonymous account of the 1961 Synod of Russian Orthodox bishops noted the presence of three well-dressed men sitting behind the assembled hierarchs, men who "were well known to one another":

> In each locality, in each diocese sat a colleague of these men, the special commissioner for church affairs . . . with the power of decision to forbid services and remove clergy.

Orthodox Church—the Furov Report

Official Soviet sources give little information on the exercise of state control over institutional religious life at the center, and one must rely mainly on *samizdat* critiques. But in recent years two important documents were leaked to the West. The first is a collection of laws and unpublished instructions governing religious life and marked "for official use only."[15] Perhaps even more significant is a report produced in 1974 for the Communist Party Central Committee by CRA deputy chairman Furov, describing in some detail the current state of the Russian Orthodox Church.

Although a spokesman for the government news agency Novosti initially denounced the Furov Report as a forgery, and while it has some minor errors in dates and figures, the document appears to be genuine, and it conforms with what Western experts know from other sources about state interference in church life. It also seems significant that Novosti rather than Tass produced the single denunciation of the report, since Novosti's publications are often for foreign rather that domestic consumption, and also that, untypically, the Furov Report was not mentioned in recent books and articles on "bourgeois falsification" of Soviet religious policy. These two points suggest a desire not to revive its memory.[16]

According to the 1945 Statute of the Russian Orthodox Church, the supreme head of that church is the patriarch, who administers it together with the Holy Synod. It appears that the appointment of patriarch, synod, and all hierarchs is subject to CRA approval, and in the case of the patriarch, also to Politburo approval. Furov states:

> Not one consecration . . . takes place without the careful checking of the candidature by the responsible members of the Council [for Religious Affairs] in close contact with its commissioners and appropriate interested bodies.

The latter presumably includes local party authorities and the KGB. Moreover:

> The Council has reports on each hierarch. We systematically receive characterizations from the commissioners, and a procedure has become established whereby the ruling hierarch visiting the Patriarch with his annual report also visits the Council. We have thorough talks with him.

For hierarchs who act "inappropriately," the fate is either transfer or "retirement." During the 1970s this happened to Archbishop Pavel of Novosibirsk and Archbishop Feodosi of Poltava after they criticized the actions of local CRA officials.

Furov makes it quite clear also that the Orthodox Synod is firmly under the control of the CRA:

> The selection and appointment of its permanent members was and remains in the hands of the Council. All questions raised for discussion in the Synod Patriarch Pimen and Synod members talk over beforehand with the Council leadership and its departments. . . . Exercising personal control over the activities of the Synod the responsible members of the Council systematically carry out educational-explanatory work with members of the Synod, establish confidential contacts with them, shape their patriotic ideas and attitudes while helping them to exert the necessary influence on the whole episcopate.

Other Religious Groups

Similar forms of control appear to operate in other church bodies, though occasionally the evidence is more ambiguous. At the 1979 Baptist Congress, for example, delegates refused to elect to the AUCECB council one of the candidates on a list presumably cleared with the CRA prior to that gathering. Against this one should note that the CRA, in seeking to draw dissenting congregations back into the controllable fold of the AUCECB, may have decided to grant the Baptists an apparently more independent conference than it would have allowed the Orthodox.[17]

In the Georgian Orthodox Church, the mid-1970s were a time of what might be called "control through demoralization." In April 1972 Patriarch David V was elected to head that church amid rumors of corruption implicating both church and state officials, including the wife of the first secretary of the republic. A report produced by a local official revealed that both religious and political authorities were turning a blind eye to—or even encouraging—entry into the church of rather dubious characters. Most notable of these was Metropolitan Gaioz, who had been expelled from the university for homosexuality (an unequivocal sin in Orthodox teachings and a criminal offense in the

USSR), convicted in the courts for "hooliganism," and thrown out of theological seminary for peddling drugs. Since all hierarchical appointments require state approval, the selection of Gaioz as a metropolitan can be seen as a further attempt to undermine the church. After the death of Patriarch David in 1977 and his replacement by Ilya II, however, Metropolitan Gaioz was removed from his position, tried, and sentenced to fifteen years.[18]

Control of Church Institutions

As a function of its "totalist" aspirations, the state also seeks to control admission to theological seminaries and monasteries. One *samizdat* document noted:

> When an applicant for admission arrives at the Zagorsk seminary, the full name and address of the applicant is forwarded to Trushin, the commissioner for the Moscow *oblast*.

The *Chronicle of the Lithuanian Catholic Church* reported:

> In the spring of 1972 . . . the seminary administrators sent a list of seventeen candidates to Tumenas, the CRA commissioner. With his KGB and Lithuanian Central Committee advisors Tumenas crossed five from the list.

Should the applicant pass state scrutiny and be admitted to the seminary, he will face persistent efforts by the CRA or others to recruit him as an informer or in other ways to weaken his commitment to his priestly vocation. In Lithuania, for example, attempts were made from the late 1970s on to steer seminarians away from the influence of so-called extremist priests, those who were active in defending the church against state intervention.

In addition, the CRA possesses a *de facto* right to oversee the appointments of those who head educational and monastic institutions. During the late 1970s a certain Archimandrite Gavriil became head of the Pskov-Perchersk monastery. Soon there were a number of *samizdat* complaints about Gavriil—that he infrequently held services, refused to pray for the opening of churches, turned away beggars, and, most surprisingly, appeared able to give orders to the local militia.

From the Furov Report about the Russian Orthodox Church, this too is known:

> The output of religious literature is effectively under the control of the CRA. . . . The Council annually examines the plan of the publishing section.

It is safe to assume that the CRA performs a similar censorship role with regard to the rather limited publications of the other religious groups.

Both the CRA and the KGB are regularly involved in briefing those church people who travel abroad or meet with foreign delegations. Furov suggests that some of the clerics use their loyalty in international matters or in the propagation of Soviet peace proposals to strengthen the position of their church at home. In speeches given to religious gatherings, however, CRA officials frequently assert that the Soviet state greatly values church activities in the international arena.

The Outlook

Despite official distinctions between state "neutrality" and party "activism," the state has involved itself extensively in both the control of and struggle against religion. This involvement is required by both the ideological commitments and the "totalist" aspirations of the Soviet regime. Nevertheless, institutional religion shows no signs of disappearing. With the option for terror no longer available, the current situation could be described as a stalemate in which the state seeks to strengthen its control over religious life while religious organizations pursue ways to minimize the effects of that control and ensure their survival.

Both "natural" and "strategic" factors play a part in the existence of institutional religion under the rule of a state committed to its overthrow. The natural factors function independently of religious organizations. Religious beliefs occur naturally in every kind of society and must be acknowledged and responded to by those in authority. In recent years a number of

Soviet writers have moved away from stereotyped depictions of believers as elderly, poorly educated village women. Some have spoken of a "new type of believer," one who is young and well qualified, lives in one of the new industrial cities, and, as a hard-working and sober citizen, is everything the "new Soviet person" should be—except an atheist! If it were to become more widely accepted that the believer is an ideal citizen rather than a social pariah, a regime eager for economic and technological advances might find it advisable to accommodate rather than alienate those with religious beliefs. Perhaps liberalization is a necessary concomitant of modernization.

Strategic Factors

The "strategic" factors are those pursued by religious bodies to strengthen their position within a Marxist-Leninist ideology. Over the last twenty years, four broad, interrelated strategic approaches have been adopted: dissent, nationalism, political loyalty, and direct negotiations.

In some cases, *dissenting activity*, usually by those standing outside the "official" community, has resulted in concessions to religious bodies. The most notable example has been the Baptists, where pressure exerted by a strong dissident movement—enjoying considerable support from some of the most dynamic and conservative elements within the denomination—undoubtedly led the state to adopt a more flexible approach toward the registration of religious associations during the 1970s. Such large-scale dissident activity appears to be limited to Protestants, with their traditional willingness to break with church leadership deemed to have moved away from the true faith, and to Islam, where unofficial activity is not incompatible with adherence to officially recognized institutions. This contrasts with the Orthodox and Catholic traditions, where schism is completely unacceptable. (However, unofficial Catholic activity—distinguished from schism—has had an effect similar to that of unofficial Protestant activity in areas such as Lithuania, where the church is closely linked with the national culture.)

A second strategy pursued by some religious groups to

strengthen their positions has centered on the *national-religious link*. During the 1970s, Orthodox spokesmen made much of the role of their church in the development of the Russian state and culture, an approach that perhaps was strengthened by the emergence, after Khrushchev's fall, of nationalistic trends within the Russian political and cultural elite. Although the church has continued to exploit this avenue in the 1980s—for example, in its promotion of the 1988 Millennium of Russian Christianity—it has had to face up to the fact that first Andropov and then Gorbachev have appeared hostile to Russian nationalistic trends.

Religious leaders have also attempted to reinforce the positions of their communities through *political usefulness* to the regime. Since 1927 the Russian Orthodox Church has given public support to the socialist system, and more recently it has been active in propagating Soviet foreign-policy initiatives. For example, Soviet churchmen who promoted Soviet peace policies at ecumenical conferences may have had some influence upon Western Christian peace movements, though they can hardly be said to have initiated them.

Finally, religious organizations sometimes enter into *direct negotiations* with state bodies. For example, the All Union Council of Evangelical Christians–Baptists has undoubtedly been helped by the split within its community. Because the state is eager to prevent congregations from going underground, it is open to AUCECB suggestions for concessions that might mollify dissenters. Similarly, the Islamic establishment might use its foreign-policy activities to argue for more religious literature or mosque openings, developments that might improve the Soviet image in the wider Islamic world.

Will Modernization Foster Liberalization?

Is the legal and administrative position of religious bodies likely to change under a regime committed to the extensive socio-economic modernization of Soviet society? When Gorbachev first came to power, many dismissed his criticism of previous leaders and his calls for change as typical of a new Soviet leader. Three and a half years later it is clear that he means business. In his own words, *perestroika* (restructuring) is entering a new phase, one that will put words into practice and set Soviet society on the road to a fairly fundamental renewal.

During Gorbachev's first two years in power, religious communities experienced little change. As the Millennium celebrations approached, however, signs of a shift in official policy emerged. Beginning in February 1987, a number of religious prisoners were released before completing their sentences, and by the end of that year there were only about half as many prisoners as there had been twelve months earlier. More significantly perhaps, the number of those arrested for religious offenses was reduced to a handful in 1987–88. From mid-1987, religious believers were portrayed more favorably in the press. In June 1988 the authorities gave the Millennium celebrations a high public profile, albeit one that emphasized their Russian character.

Although by fall 1988 little formal change had occurred in the state's legislative and administrative control of religious bodies, there had been some modification of practice. In late 1986, some Soviet newspapers and journals began to publish articles criticizing local authorities who refused to register religious communities that had applied in the appropriate manner. At about the same time the Council for Religious Affairs began to register more churches. Reportedly, more than 300 religious associations have received legal recognition since Gorbachev came to power; the overall downward trend has been not only stopped but slightly reversed. But as yet there are no signs that the tens of thousands of places of worship closed down since 1917, mainly against the will of believers, will be reopened.

In 1988, drafts of a new law to supersede the 1929 Law on Religious Associations were being discussed. One of these became available to Keston College in July 1988, and this, together with the Orthodox Church Statute adopted by the *sobor* (church council) held during the Millennium celebration, indicates the types of legal changes that might be expected. It should be made clear, however, that this particular draft appears to be one of the more liberal ones, and that whatever draft becomes the working one will be subjected to, and probably altered by, political infighting. (Two drafts that appeared later are discussed in the Appendix of this book.)

Among the *possible* changes are:

- the return to the church of juridical personality;
- restoration of the priest's right to be involved in parish administration;
- an end to the right of local authorities to remove people they don't approve of from the parish executive body;
- recognition of the right of religious bodies to carry on charitable activities;
- some broadening of religious education;
- some form of alternative to compulsory military service.

The long-term implications of *perestroika* for believers are at best a matter for speculation. Undoubtedly, the atmosphere has changed somewhat; believers belonging to recognized religious groups no longer are overtly treated as second-class citizens. There have also been some welcome institutional and administrative changes—the opening of a few new churches and monasteries, the *de facto* recognition, however qualified in practice, of religious involvement in charitable activities, and the importing of a limited amount of religious literature. Moreover, the state has given legal recognition to the Hare Krishnas, one of the groups traditionally liable to especially harsh treatment. Yet a much larger group, the Ukrainian Catholics, still cannot function legally.

Despite the change in atmosphere, by fall 1988 the same laws remained in place, enforced by the same institutions and officials that previously operated in a more repressive and restrictive fashion. And changes in laws or enforcers would provide no cast-iron safeguards in a society where policy still prevails over law.

On a more optimistic note, however, we should not forget Gorbachev's stated aim—spelled out in not unambiguous fashion at the Nineteenth Party Conference in June 1988—of moving the USSR toward the status of a law-governed state. Here, when policy and law worked together, there might be real hope of substantial changes in the position of religious bodies and their members.

4

Anti-Religious Propaganda and Education

Marite Sapiets

As an inherent part of Marxist-Leninist ideology, atheism has almost inevitably acquired an official position in the Soviet system. Religion, according to Marx, is the tool of capitalism; invented by human beings to make sense of their unhappy situations on earth, it is "the sigh of an oppressed creature—the opium of the people."[1] Because of the "perverted social order," religion cannot simply be abolished—it will disappear only when the world itself is "put straight."[2] As material conditions on earth improve, especially after socialism is established, Marx believed, people will gradually abandon their religious beliefs.

The Bolshevik party, however, consisted of more militant atheists. Lenin considered every form of religion "vileness of the most dangerous kind." He regarded religion redundant in the presence of triumphant socialism and was impatient with the idea of its gradual disappearance. Together with many other Bolsheviks, he believed that all forms of religion must be actively combatted.

Specifically, the Bolsheviks proposed to eliminate religion by means of universal education and the improvement of general economic conditions, combined with militant anti-religious

---

Marite Sapiets is a member of the research staff of Keston College, specializing in religion in the Baltic states. She is working on a book on Seventh-Day Adventists in the Soviet Union.

propaganda and legislation designed to make religious belief unacceptable intellectually and socially. This actively anti-religious policy was considered necessary to remove the influence of the Russian Orthodox Church, seen as the spiritual support of the tsarist regime and thus a focus of alternative loyalties. While the Bolshevik party proclaimed the separation of church and state in the 1918 Constitution, it could not accept the idea of any institution's remaining independent of the state in practice.

In the seventy years since then, the reasons given by Marxist-Leninists for championing atheism as a state doctrine have hardly changed. Religion has always been presented as the embodiment of superstition and backwardness in a scientific world, while atheism is seen as a weapon of "political progress" against reaction. Religion is said to "distract people from labor and lead believers away from participation in the life of society"; its "petty, egotistical concern with saving one's soul" is opposed to the spirit of collectivism, and its emphasis upon concern with life after death denotes a lack of interest in earthly activity. In addition, religion is often identified with supposedly unhealthful practices, such as the Muslim ritual of circumcision, or socially harmful attitudes, such as the Muslim veiling of women. Religious links with the past, as in the Catholic or Muslim areas of the USSR, are thought to encourage disloyalty to the Soviet system and to support "bourgeois nationalism." The pacifism common to many Protestant sects is also seen as political disloyalty if it involves refusal to serve in the Soviet army. Marxism-Leninism, observed one Western author, is "incompatible with any faith but a faith in its own infallibility."[3]

The aims of the Communist Party regarding religion have also remained much the same since 1917, and to some extent have been achieved: churches and religious institutions have been deprived of political and economic influence. Church buildings, mosques, and synagogues belong to the state and are merely rented to the believers who worship there. Services can be held only in buildings registered with the state authorities. Religion has been completely eliminated from the schools and the educational system, and atheism is taught as an official ideology.

Still, no new generation has emerged without what the state considers an unacceptably high proportion of religious believers. And the traditional authority of the clergy has been eliminated only to some extent; among Muslims in Central Asia and the Catholics in Lithuania, for example, it is often still strong.

Anti-Religion Since the Revolution

After the Revolution, the anti-religious campaign gathered force only gradually as the constitutional "separation of church and state" was turned into its opposite during the 1920s.

From 1917 to 1929

Although the 1918 Constitution permitted not only religious worship but also "religious" as well as "anti-religious" propaganda, it was largely the non-Orthodox denominations that benefited from this clause. Old Believers, Seventh-Day Adventists, and other "sects" were at first tolerated by the Soviet government as part of its campaign against the Orthodox Church, whose leader, Patriarch Tikhon, had labeled the Bolsheviks "outcasts of the human race." Indeed, because of the harassment the Bolsheviks had suffered at the hands of the Orthodox in pre-revolutionary times, they were willing to encourage "sectarianism" insofar as the non-Orthodox were also often anti-Orthodox. Therefore the Soviet authorities allowed the publication of a number of Protestant books, pamphlets, and periodicals; Adventists, for example, had three periodicals. According to a decree of 1919, religious conscientious objectors—mostly members of Protestant churches—were allowed to spend their periods of military service as medical orderlies in hospitals. Bolshevik "experts" on the sects, such as Vladimir Bonch-Bruyevich, regarded "sectarians" as potential socialists who needed only to abandon their religious misconceptions to become full-fledged members of the new society. Baptists and Adventists even established some collective farms.

The Bolsheviks soon discovered, however, that the "sectarians" would not be so easily transformed. They used their newfound privileges to evangelize and increase their numbers.

So by 1923 the Communist Party decided to include the non-Orthodox in its anti-religious campaign, and by the late 1920s it was treating them on an equal footing with the Orthodox.

A breakaway radical movement within the Orthodox Church in the 1920s known as the Renovationist Church was favored by the Bolsheviks, since it openly espoused socialist policies and attracted considerable support among the parish clergy. This alternative movement was used by the Soviet government to bring the Orthodox hierarchy to heel. The imprisoned Patriarch Tikhon, fearing that the Renovationists might acquire significant influence within the Orthodox hierarchy and try to abolish the patriarchate itself, was induced by this fear to make a declaration of loyalty to Soviet power in 1923. As the Soviet government then reduced its active aid to the Renovationists and as the clergy linked with this movement were opposed by the Orthodox hierarchy and most of the laity, the Renovationist Church rapidly declined in influence and survived only until the Second World War.

The 1921 Tenth Party Congress called for an organized "battle against religion," and from then on atheistic propaganda was a normal part of Soviet life. Perhaps because the atheists still had to contend with the vestiges of "religious propaganda," the atheistic campaign during the 1920s retained elements of talent and sincerity that later nearly disappeared. Even then, however, there were some extremely crude posters, such as one that showed the the Virgin Mary gazing at an advertisement for a film about abortion and exclaiming: "Oh, why didn't I know that before?" Debates were arranged between atheists and clergymen. On the eve of religious festivals the Young Communist League (Komsomol) held "anti-religious carnivals" during which young people would march to city centers carrying banners and anti-religious posters or caricatures while singing hymns and burning religious images. Such demonstrations often ended in violent conflict with believers, however, and the Party was forced to restrict these "godless marches."

The authorities made a more effective change in everyday life and attitude by abolishing religious festivals as public holidays and substituting "official" secular holidays, such as the anniversary of the October Revolution and International Labor Day. Secular marriages, funerals, and "name-giving" ceremonies were introduced, while religious ceremonies were deprived of legal significance.

The 1920s "God-builders" movement, led by the writers Maxim Gorky and Anatoly Lunacharsky, was an attempt to replace theistic religion with a form of mystical atheism that centered "divine power" on the perfected human collective. The God-builders concentrated on a glorious future and the powers that humanity, in perfected form, might acquire. The collective would "resurrect 'God'" out of its own midst, developing even the power to heal the paralyzed, as Gorky "prophesied" in his novel *Confession*. Not surprisingly, Lenin despised this movement and its ideas, describing God-building as "no better than God-seeking" and as "copulating with a corpse."

In 1924, the State Publishing House for Anti-Religious Literature was founded in Moscow, with ten branches throughout the USSR, to produce books, pamphlets, and periodicals. In addition, the weekly newspaper *Bezbozhnik*—"Godless"—was founded to coordinate anti-religious work throughout the country. This gave rise to the organization "Friends of the Newspaper 'Godless,' " which in 1925 became the "League of Militant Godless." The League soon became responsible for virtually all anti-religious propaganda throughout the country. It organized atheistic lectures, films, museums, "propaganda trains," and public demonstrations such as the "unmasking of religious frauds," during which religious relics were shown to be wax images or the result of natural preservation. In one such exhibit, mummified rats were placed in shrines next to the preserved bodies of saints.[4]

From 1929 to World War II

With the adoption of the Constitution of 1929, only anti-religious propaganda remained legal. "Religious propaganda" was no longer permitted, and so evangelization outside religious services was illegal. During the decade after the Revolution, "private" religious instruction had at first been allowed (1918), then restricted to groups of three minors at a time (1923). Now the Law on Religious Associations, also adopted in 1929, banned the religious instruction of minors by anyone except their parents; to hold a Sunday school or catechism class was a criminal act.

By 1929, "godless" shock brigades had been established in factories, and completely "godless" factories and collective farms had appeared. In these, workers vowed to fulfill high production quotas while at the same time carrying on antireligious propaganda. Their zeal in propagating militant atheism, however, was often so deficient that they were attacked in the atheistic press for harboring believers among them. Still, the League of Militant Godless reported a membership peak in 1932 of 5.5 million.

The 1929 Law on Religious Associations made registration of religious buildings compulsory and unregistered religious services illegal. This law continues to be the basis of Soviet legislation on religion, though a revision was being undertaken in 1988. The law made it possible for the authorities to close churches and confiscate church buildings merely by refusing registration; only a few hundred Orthodox churches, together with a handful of others, remained open throughout the country. Ironically, while churches of all denominations were being closed, the clergy's "right to vote," abolished after the Revolution, was restored in 1936.

The League of Militant Godless was gradually revealed to be ineffective, corrupt, and dishonest; its membership figures were found to be greatly inflated, with half the "members" not paying dues. Yemelian Yaroslavsky, head of the League, admitted that the organization had exaggerated its successes and stressed that caution was necessary to create an "atheistic mentality" among the population. Sensing the reasonableness of this view, the Central Committee in 1936 called for more subtle and sophisticated efforts to undermine religion. Atheistic propaganda continued but was far less strident, and by 1941 the League of Militant Godless had been disbanded.

The War and Post-War Years

Apart from the revelations of corruption in the 1930s, the central reason for the liquidation of the League was the war with

Germany. During 1941–44, anti-religious propaganda was almost completely abandoned. Attacks on the Orthodox Church in particular were halted. A major reason for this was the German policy of opening churches in the Soviet territories it occupied, which proved so popular that it was imperative for the Soviet government to re-elevate the Orthodox Church to the status of a Russian patriotic symbol, stressing the need for atheists and believers alike to unite against the invader. In some films of this period, such as *The Rainbow,* heroes refer to "our God," cross themselves, and bow to icons.

Nonetheless, the regime remained militantly atheistic. In September 1944, the Central Committee decreed the renewal of anti-religious efforts to combat the "survival of ignorance, superstition, and prejudice," and by 1945 atheistic propaganda had again been intensified. Much of the immediate post-war atheistic propaganda, however, was directed against the Catholic rather than the Orthodox church, which was still benefiting from its wartime role as the embodiment of Russian national culture. Catholics, who in Lithuania, Poland, and Ukraine had resisted the Soviet takeover, were depicted in films of the period—such as *Dawn Over the Niemen*—as Nazi supporters and poisoners of the population. In the newly occupied territories of western Ukraine and the Baltic states, a violent anti-religious campaign was carried out in all sections of society, especially schools, and large numbers of clergymen of all denominations were executed or deported to camps.

The anti-Catholic hostility resulted in some permanent gains for the Russian Orthodox Church in the post-war years. Hundreds of churches confiscated from the Eastern-rite Catholics of Ukraine, whose churches the Soviet government banned because of their links with Ukrainian nationalism, were handed over to the Orthodox. In addition, many churches that had been opened during the war remained open, as did eight seminaries and a number of monasteries.

A few religious journals, such as the Orthodox *Journal of the Moscow Patriarchate* and the Baptist *Brotherly Messenger*, were allowed to begin publication in the post-war period. No

Catholic periodicals were permitted, and none were permitted in succeeding years until 1989.

The Khrushchev Campaign

Apart from a brief four-month atheistic "leap forward" in 1954, the half decade after Stalin's death in 1953 saw a thaw in relations between the atheistic state and the religious denominations. Anti-religious propaganda was superficial and attempts to combat church influence sporadic. Clergymen of all denominations returned from the Stalinist camps and took up their work in churches that had been reopened during the war.

In 1959, however, Khrushchev unleashed a new campaign against religion. Thousands of churches were forcibly closed. By 1966, only 7,500 Orthodox churches remained out of 17,500 and only three Orthodox seminaries out of eight. Control over church affairs was taken out of the hands of the parish clergy and given to a council of twenty parishioners, the *dvadtsatka*, who could be more easily intimidated or replaced by the local state authorities. In addition, the registration of church buildings was often made conditional on the selection of a church committee that would be acceptable to the local *soviet*—"people who would honestly carry out Soviet laws and requests,"[5] as officials in Moscow phrased it.

Article 227 and Article 142 of the 1959 Criminal Code made it illegal to organize, direct, or advocate "activity carried on under the guise of preaching religious beliefs or performing religious ceremonies which are connected with causing harm to citizens' health or with any other infringement of the person or rights of citizens." These articles were used to classify as criminal offenses such acts as circumcision, baptism, or refusal to let a child wear a Pioneer scarf (Pioneers is the Communist organization for young people ten to sixteen; members wear a red scarf). They were also used to prosecute congregations that had been deprived of registration but tried to remain active.

The results of Khrushchev's campaign substantiated the saying attributed to Anatoly Lunacharsky, minister of education, in 1928: "Religion is like a nail—the harder you hit it, the deeper it goes in."[6] That the campaign was in many ways counterproductive is illustrated by the Soviet Baptists. The increase in cases of deprivation of parental rights (the state can take children from their parents and send them to a children's home if the parents are judged to be lacking in responsibility) for bringing up children in a "religious spirit," as well as the attempt to enforce a policy banning children from church, contributed to the split among Baptists that endures to this day.

The development of the unofficial Council of Churches of Evangelical Christians–Baptists from congregations that in the 1960s refused to accept government registration under the conditions imposed has been nothing but an embarrassment to the Soviet state. In fact, the Khrushchev anti-religious campaign could be said to have sparked the beginning of a movement for religious rights that included the dissemination of *samizdat* literature by a large network of unregistered but active churches all over the USSR, as well as the sending of appeals to fellow believers in the West. The large number involved in the unofficial Baptist movement—25–30 per cent of all the Baptists in the USSR—meant that the anti-religious campaign against the official Baptist churches had to be eased to make these churches more attractive to the ordinary believer. More recently, some of the "unofficial" Baptist congregations have registered independently with the state while remaining part of the unofficial Christian-Baptist council.

The Post-Khrushchev Years

After 1966, the state's anti-religious propaganda campaign continued in a less violent form. Facts about religious harassment and discrimination have been made available by unofficial religious-rights groups from all denominations, such as the Christian Committee for the Defense of Believers' Rights (founded in 1976), a similar Catholic Committee (founded in 1978 in Lithuania), and the Baptist Council of Prisoners' Relatives (founded in 1964). Such publicity probably helped somewhat to restrict official harassment of religious believers, but it certainly did not put an end to it.

Neither did adoption by the churches of a "progressive," pro-government stance on both domestic and foreign issues eliminate harassment. The Soviet regime had shown that it expected conformity and open support for its policies from the officially recognized churches, but it appeared to care very little whether such support was internally consistent and sincere. Where it was sincere, as in the pre-war socialist-oriented Renovationist Church, the Soviet authorities were willing to exchange that support for enforced declarations of loyalty by the Orthodox hierarchy. In fact, the existence of an underground "alternative" among Baptists, Adventists, and others led the state to make certain concessions to the "official" churches, but only as long as the alternative churches threatened to take members away and thus lessen the extent to which the state could exercise control. Loyalty to the state was seen by the regime as an all-or-nothing attitude: if it did not include loyalty to the state's atheistic ideology, it was considered not loyalty but rather submission.

Atheism as Official Ideology

Atheism holds a position similar to that of a state religion in the USSR today. Official thinking and discourse on atheism assume that it is an unquestionable truth, the standard right answer. Public debates between religious believers and atheists no longer take place, and no public dissent from the "sacred texts"—the writings of Marx, Engels, and Lenin—is permitted. Pictures of these three secular prophets of Marxism-Leninism hang in prominent places at all public meetings and in state institutions, such as schools. Their words are quoted as "infallible" statements. This can sometimes prove embarrassing, as when present-day conscientious objectors quote Lenin's 1919 decree in support of their own objections to military conscription.

The cult of Lenin, as the creator of the October Revolution and the new Soviet society, began before his death in 1924 and has been greatly encouraged by the Soviet regime ever since. This is especially true in schools: Lenin is presented in textbooks as an ideal ruler and kindly benefactor, and children write poems and stories along these lines. Lenin's embalmed body in the mausoleum on Red Square was intended by the Party to be a permanent reminder of him. (The embalming and the mausoleum were decried by Lenin's wife and certain other Old Bolsheviks as redolent of the public display of saints' relics in the Orthodox Church. Lenin himself, they felt, would have opposed it.) The "Lenin Corners" or "Red Corners" in factories and schools, which often feature Lenin's works as well as atheistic propaganda, could be viewed as secular shrines.

The Institutions of Atheism

Atheistic institutions may be either a part of local government or sponsored by the central Soviet authorities. All official state relations with the clergy and lay leaders of religious bodies are handled by the Council for Religious Affairs (CRA), established in 1965 by the USSR Council of Ministers. Through its officials in each republic, the Council for Religious Affairs passes on state instructions to church leaders. It has closed churches, intimidated members of the clergy, and in other ways furthered the state's atheistic policies. Instructive and fairly entertaining reports of meetings between CRA officials and senior clergy can be read in *samizdat* documents—for example, in the *Chronicle of the Lithuanian Catholic Church*.[7] Such unofficial accounts, which are clearly "leaked" by members of the higher clergy, may by their very existence influence the conduct of future meetings.

Ultimate responsibility for anti-religious propaganda is vested in the Propaganda Department of the Communist Party's Central Committee and its subordinate bodies. These set the goals and supervise the methods of the Party's atheistic program. The work at each administrative level—i.e., in each district, city, region, or republic—is controlled by a party secretary and a staff of experts known as the "Council of Scientific Atheism." Such councils are a major stimulant to atheistic propaganda in almost all cities and districts, as well as in some farms and factories. They enlist members of the Party—especially scientists, schoolteachers, former believers, and pensioners—to create and organize "atheistic public opinion," since otherwise, it is often admitted, the official doctrine of "scientific atheism" will fail to penetrate "to the depths of the collective."

The Knowledge (*Znanie*) Society, founded in 1947, is the spiritual successor of the League of Militant Godless and the most important institution of atheistic propaganda in the USSR. It is organized according to the Communist Party model, with branches in each republic, town, district, and region, and even some individual factories, farms, and villages. Most branches have a section dealing with "scientific atheism" that is responsible for organizing atheistic clubs and activities and delivering anti-religious lectures. The Knowledge Society is less openly militant in its atheism than its predecessor and tries to keep the anti-religious struggle on a relatively intellectual, "scientific" plane. The Knowledge Society has two publications: the monthly journal *Science and Religion (Nauka i religiya),* since 1959 the leading atheistic periodical in the USSR, and the Ukrainian-language monthly *Man and the World* (*Lyudina i svit*). The latter was formerly known as *The Militant Atheist.* The change in title reflects the Society's difficulties in recruiting volunteers and contributors from the Soviet intelligentsia, particularly scientists, who often regard anti-religious propaganda as a vulgar and unnecessary repetition of prepared conclusions. The journals contain no real dialogue with believers; the believer's viewpoint is always presented as inferior and not deserving of respect, and is almost always accompanied by atheistic comment.

Atheistic clubs, often linked with the Knowledge Society, are important sources of propaganda at the local level, as their membership includes the community's most zealous atheists. The clubs are attached to libraries, factories, or farms and are usually involved in planning the local atheistic program.

Museums of atheism exist in former churches or mosques in many Soviet towns, such as the former Kazan Cathedral in Leningrad. The museums have often presented very crude attacks on religion and its history. In recent years, however, many displays have been toned down; they now concentrate on the marvels of science and the origins of religion. The number of visitors to the Leningrad museum has reportedly increased, though a large proportion of these are school children on educational tours.

The center of atheistic academic research is the Institute of Scientific Atheism, founded in 1964. It is responsible for training the more scholarly atheistic propagandists but keeps a certain distance from anti-religious propaganda as such. Post-graduate dissertations on scientific atheism may be written under the aegis of the institute. Its main publication, *Questions of Scientific Atheism (Voprosy nauchnogo atheizma)*, focuses on historical and philosophical problems as well as providing "concerted sociological research," which often gives useful statistical information to observers in the West.

Atheism in Education

The place of atheism in the state educational system is so far undisputed. Academic work in the field is carried out in departments of "scientific atheism," housed in various universities. Fewer than half the departmental graduates, however, later work as professional atheistic lecturers or propagandists. At Voronezh Evening University of Marxism-Leninism in the late 1960s, for example, only 22 per cent of the graduates in scientific atheism went on to become professional propagandists. When this became known, a program of "practical work" was introduced into the course. Students now deliver anti-religious lectures to the public or conduct "agitation tours" on farms as class assignment. While a course in the "fundamentals of scientific atheism" has been compulsory for all university students since 1964, it is usually very superficial. Textbooks are outdated, tendentious, or even unavailable. A well-known Soviet joke has a student who passes his exam in scientific atheism exclaiming, "Thank God!"

Schools are seen as the Party's most powerful weapon in the anti-religious campaign. Theoretically, teachers should be able to counteract any religious influence upon children by scientific education and anti-religious propaganda from an early age. Over the years Soviet researchers have shown, however, that family religious training is often impervious to atheistic logic. A not untypical child, confronted by a teacher with the fact that God had not been seen by any Soviet cosmonaut, replied that only the pure in heart could see God.

Atheism can be woven into many subjects, such as physics, history, and literature. Some pupils have been asked to write essays on "Why Must We Fight Against Religions?"[8] Other assigned topics—such as, after Easter, "How I Spent My Holidays"—are designed to reveal a child's religious views and thus permit "individual work" by an atheistic teacher. Communist youth organizations, the Pioneers and Octobrists, are atheistic in orientation, and refusal to join them is usually a sign of religious affiliation. These organizations are also officially represented as ultra-patriotic, and atheistic teachers often clash with religious parents over the matter of membership. It is not uncommon for teachers to try to persuade pupils to join the Pioneers without their parents' knowledge, or to intimidate children into wearing the Pioneer scarf. Fellow pupils of Valery Bezdushny, an Adventist child, were instructed by their teacher to tie a Pioneer scarf around his neck by force. Meanwhile, the teacher called him an "angel" and asked other children to "find his wings."[9]

"Young atheists clubs" are found in most schools; some even operate their own anti-religious museums. Both these and the Young Communist League (Komsomol) with its 27 million members, most of whom join as teenagers, have been criticized by the press for their failure to produce a generation of militant atheists. Since membership in Komsomol is necessary for most careers, many religious believers, especially members of the Russian Orthodox Church, have joined this officially atheistic organization.

Because religion is seen as backward and unscientific, the continuing presence of religious pupils in the classroom reflects badly on the teacher. Teachers have been known to tell religious pupils that, even if they know their schoolwork subjects as well as the other students, they must still be marked "unsatisfactory" if they persist in their religious views.[10] Adventist pupils who could not attend exams on Saturdays because of religious respect for the Sabbath were not allowed to take them on another day.[11] Russian Orthodox or Catholic children who wear crosses to school risk having them confiscated.

Attempts are often made to find out which schoolchildren

attend church; questionnaires distributed at school ask children such questions as where they were on Sunday morning and whether their parents attended religious services. (These are not very effective, because many children have been instructed by their parents to lie about such matters.) A teacher in Lithuania used to attend church services herself to see which pupils acted as altar boys, so that she could ridicule them in front of their peers.[12] Religion, especially that of "sectarians," is often identified with foreign influence or lack of patriotism; for example, some Adventist children were told by their teacher: "You're spies: your religion came from America, together with the Colorado Beetles."[13]

Religious parents are attacked also, primarily at parents' meetings or in the local newspapers. Such attacks may serve as a threat that their children may be removed from the home, as has happened to some Adventist and Baptist parents. The hostile treatment of religious parents and schoolchildren is used to dissuade others from behaving in a similar manner. As the disputes over the Pioneer scarf have shown, however, often what is required is simply outward conformity; children are reproached for "shaming the collective" not so much because they *have* religious beliefs but because they have not disguised them.

Not all teachers are atheists, but those who hold religious views risk losing their jobs if their views become known. In 1978, Tatyana Shchipkova, a lecturer at Smolensk teachers' training college, was dismissed and her title of lecturer revoked because of her "idealistic and religious viewpoint." Of course, many teachers are simply uninterested in either religion or atheism. "Atheistic education" is therefore often conducted episodically, to coincide with major religious festivals. Those teachers who lack enthusiasm, however, are attacked in the Soviet press, which asks: "Are we not committing an unpardonable error in sometimes keeping the sword of atheism in its scabbard during school lessons?"

The position of atheism as a state ideology makes it almost impossible to conduct a sincere dialogue between atheists and religious believers in public or in any situation that may affect a believer's career. Such discussions take place almost exclusively in private.

Atheism in Daily Life

Some "new traditions"—secular rituals and ceremonies—have been very successful in helping to establish atheism as a part of Soviet daily life. Although ceremonies to replace baptism have not become popular, state-provided rituals to celebrate "coming of age" have largely replaced confirmation services in areas such as Latvia and Estonia, where the majority used to belong to the Lutheran church and most young people were confirmed at sixteen or eighteen. The state ceremony is followed in Estonia by two weeks in a summer holiday camp. Only 8 per cent or fewer of Estonian teenagers are now confirmed in church.

In addition, some non-Christian holidays have been added to the official calendar. In Latvia, for example, the old Ligo festival (Midsummer Day), though banned at one time for its links with "bourgeois nationalism," is once again permitted as an occasion "to worship the spontaneous forces of nature."[14] A Harvest Festival is celebrated throughout the USSR on October 9.

State-sponsored marriages and funerals have changed greatly since the 1950s, when many people with no religious beliefs were holding these events in churches anyway because of the bureaucratic and uninspiring nature of the state ceremonies. "Wedding palaces" have been established where marriage ceremonies can be as elaborate as those celebrated in church, with appropriate songs and other music. The new form of marriage vows may include the use of a stole ornamented with "embroidered quotations about the family" from the *Moral Code of the Builders of Communism*, which the official performing the ceremony wraps around the couple's hands.[15] The many references to the state and "fatherland" during the ceremony substitute a directly political authority for the discarded religious symbols of the past. State funerals have also been reformed to give them more of a ceremonial air: the body is placed in a special room of the local House of Culture, funeral music is played, and farewell speeches are given stressing the deceased's contributions to the national military or economic effort. Often there is a procession to the cemetery. In many parts of the USSR a majority of marriages and funerals are now state-sponsored. In the more religious areas, however, such as Muslim Central Asia or Catholic Lithuania, half or more of these ceremonies are still religious.[16]

Atheism in the Media

The press is today viewed by professional atheists as the principal vehicle for educating the masses. Atheistic articles appear regularly in the newspapers, usually in columns such as "The Atheist's Corner." Newspaper attacks on religious believers are often made in the form of "readers' letters" complaining about particular believers—who may, of course, be disliked by the state authorities for reasons quite different from those stated. A typical example would be this letter to the editor of *Sovetskaya Latvia*:

> Dear Editor,
> I am a believer. I am worried about the behavior of our pastor. He loves to drink and consorts with several women. He threw his former housekeeper out of the house, as she could no longer work because of her age. Our pastor drinks not only with his own funds but with church funds too. Could a surprise audit of the church's funds not be carried out? . . . Help us please.

Many atheistic and anti-religious articles are simply reprinted from one newspaper to another after being published by Tass, the government news agency. The language used is often lurid and insulting, under such headlines as "The Howls of the Obscurantists" and "A Rosary in One Hand, a Truncheon in the Other." Material of this kind has changed little in forty years, but at least some propagandists now admit that it is convincing only to the atheistic faithful.

Besides being offensive and crude, atheistic articles and books often remain on a very primitive level, failing completely to tackle the real doubts or problems of believers. The cosmonaut who failed to "see God" is an example of an official atheistic answer to a question few religious believers have asked. More complex atheistic books on recent religious thinkers, such as

E. M. Babosov's work on Teilhard de Chardin, are often bought by religious believers for the technical information and quotations they contain, as the works from which they quote are nearly unobtainable in the USSR. Recent works that use modern biblical criticism in a religiously debilitating way are often translations from Polish; the standards of atheistic scholarship in Poland are necessarily higher, to combat the influence of the Polish clergy, who are better educated and highly respected.

The high point of anti-religious film-making came in the 1960s; since then there has been a decline. But the basic story line remains the same: the pure hero falls victim to a conspiracy by wicked churchmen or "sectarians" whose leader is almost inevitably a criminal or a former Nazi collaborator. In *I Love You, Life*, the villains are Jehovah's Witnesses, who receive direct instructions from abroad. In *Clouds Over Borskoye*, Pentecostals attempt to crucify a young girl. As one Soviet anti-religious specialist said in condemning such films as ineffective: "This sort of thing is not typical of the activity of most churchmen . . . and is indeed condemned by them."

Ironically, certain recent films use religion in an entirely different manner, as a means to express Russian nationalism and messianism. In *Andrei Rublyov*, the Orthodox Church is portrayed as the bearer of Russian culture. Since the entire story takes place in the Middle Ages, this is ideologically permissible. *The Ascension* gives a symbolic religious aura to the sufferings of the Russian people in the last war, again an eminently "sacred" subject in Soviet ideology.

The Russian Orthodox Church still is seen as a guardian of Russian national culture. This often makes attacks against the church counterproductive, especially among the intelligentsia. It is not uncommon for some members of the intelligentsia, though they have no formal religious beliefs, to attend Orthodox services in order to "support" Russian culture. This attitude is even more common among the Soviet Muslim nationalities or the Catholics of Lithuania, where even an atheist might frequent the mosque or Catholic church as a demonstration of national allegiance.

The least effective atheistic media productions are the programs produced infrequently for radio and television. These usually consist of discussions on atheistic themes, sometimes in response to listeners' letters. The audience is not captive; as in the West, viewers will switch off programs that are dull or unconvincing.

While atheistic public lecturers are better trained than they once were, their talks are still a byword for boredom in Soviet society. A Soviet cartoon shows believers praying for an atheistic lecturer to visit the district, presumably because such lectures are counterproductive.[17] Two of the most effective forms of anti-religious activity, however, are meetings that expose religious "miracles" and those featuring former believers. A talk on "Why I Broke With Religion," particularly by a former clergyman, will attract both believers and unbelievers and stimulate debate. Although a clergyman who becomes an atheist does have a shattering effect on his former fellow believers, the impact is lessened by the fact that his change of viewpoint has made his life much more comfortable. Seen as a defector who has profited from his defection, he generally does not arouse much admiration among either believers or non-believers.

Effectiveness of the Anti-Religion Effort

The true degree of success of atheistic propaganda and education in the USSR is hard to estimate, since it is impossible to determine how many people remain religious believers. The last full survey of religious affiliation was taken in 1937 and was never published—apparently, despite the Stalinist terror of the time, too many people claimed religious faith. According to Soviet estimates cited in 1981, at least 20 to 30 per cent of the population believe in God.[18] A more recent official estimate is 34 per cent. The reliability of these estimates is open to question. For one thing, to report a higher proportion presumably would be ideologically unacceptable, except in certain areas known to have a high concentration of believers (for example, in Lithuania, where 45 to 50 per cent might be the upper limit permissible) or in territories such as Central Asia that are considered backward technically or economically. Another difficulty in assessing

Soviet polls is that respondents might, understandably, choose to conceal their religious faith.

According to Soviet surveys, most religious believers come from religious families, which are usually very closely knit and largely impervious to atheistic propaganda. It is also clear from the surveys that few believers—between 2 and 15 per cent—ever attend anti-religious lectures or atheistic meetings.[19]

Also difficult to judge is the extent to which official propaganda rather than the natural process of secularization common also in the West has furthered atheism. Indeed, by some standards, the West might appear to be more secularized than the USSR. An important part of the secularization of the USSR was the uprooting of large numbers of the rural peasants—once the stronghold of religious belief—from their traditional ways of life. They were sent to work in the new suburban areas of towns and cities, where permission for new churches was rarely given. Also, the pervasive materialism of the twentieth century generally is undoubtedly exacerbated in the Soviet Union by the low living standard of the urban populations.

The most effective time for converting believers to atheism is during childhood, by lessons at school or in individual conversations, as a survey of former believers indicates.[20] Still, state anti-religious policies of discrimination and official hostility against religious believers have probably been more effective than atheistic propaganda in reducing the number of active believers. Almost all primary atheistic propaganda directed at adults is irrelevant to true religious belief, whether it tries to prove its point by "scientific" means, attacks the excesses of the Inquisition, or exposes the failings of individual clergymen. Paradoxically, the state-inspired controls over the production of religious literature create difficulties not only for believers but also for atheistic propagandists who wish to study their opponents' primary sources.

Because of its position as a Communist Party doctrine, atheism has become more of a political dogma than an individual belief. Active atheists remain a minority, often seen as an officious and interfering group by the much larger number of passive atheists and agnostics who make up much of the population of the Soviet Union.

"Restructuring" Anti-Religious Propaganda

Mikhail Gorbachev's policies of *glasnost* (openness) and *perestroika* (restructuring) have led to certain changes in the state's anti-religious policy. Public statements on religion are often less aggressive and hostile than in the past, and the need to review methods of atheistic propaganda is much discussed in official circles.

In the Soviet press, far fewer attacks on religion are published than before, and many of the published ones concern the activities of foreign missions or of pre-war church leaders. Writers on atheism and religion are often prepared to admit that atheistic propaganda, especially in the field of education, has not been succeeding. The number of baptisms and religious marriages has been growing rather than declining;[21] even members of Komsomol are said to be participating in religious rites.[22] Young people are indifferent to atheism, but many show interest in religion. Many newspapers also make it clear that atheistic lecturers are generally regarded as boring, ignorant, and unscientific, which makes it difficult to attract recruits for this work.[23] A "new approach to atheistic education" is therefore required.

An article by Professor E. G. Filimonov in *Kommunist Tadzhikistana*[24] is typical of this new approach, in which it is accepted that religion cannot be got rid of as fast or as easily as Soviet atheists formerly imagined. In Filimonov's view, it is not a betrayal of Marxist principles to abandon certain out-of-date stereotypes: for example, religious believers are not necessarily secret opponents of socialism or fanatics of some kind. Atheist activists should avoid insulting believers and, as he said elsewhere, should abandon the "sledge-hammer" approach,[25] as this merely gives people an excuse for complaints about persecution.

In some ways, then, the press is now showing a more critical attitude toward atheistic propaganda and education and a more tolerant attitude toward religious believers, as having "a place in Soviet society." Since 1987, believers have occasionally been permitted to put forward their views in the press without hostile commentary. However, the "restructuring" called for in this sphere is intended to make atheistic propaganda more effective, not to put religion on an equal basis with atheism. Press articles often include reminders that, according to Marx, religion will decline only as a result of improved social and economic conditions (the aim of *perestroika*), but its decline is still officially regarded as inevitable.

More Openness Toward Religion

The state's more open attitude toward religion is linked with the 1988 celebration of the Millennium of Christianity in Russia by the Russian Orthodox Church. State authorities not only permitted the celebrations but also gave the Orthodox Church various privileges for the occasion, such as the use of the Bolshoi Theater for an anniversary concert. Press articles on the church stressed its contribution to Russian history and culture; it was identified with the Russian national past and patriotic feeling. The religion of the church was praised mainly for its artistic beauty, and writers stressed that the majority of Soviet citizens were atheists. However, publicity was also given to the difficulties certain Orthodox believers had had with the local authorities[26]—for example, in obtaining a church building or getting rid of a priest who was an informer. Suggestions were made that the laws on religion were inadequate for the needs of believers and would be changed. A number of writers made the point that religious associations should have the right to own property and to be represented in court.

At the *sobor* (council) of the Orthodox Church held during the Millennium celebration, church leaders spoke, more freely than usual, of their need for more religious literature. They also suggested that charitable activity by the church and religious instruction for minors might become possible. From the new Church Statute adopted by the *sobor*, it is clear that the parish priest has been restored to his pre-1960s position as head of the parish council, a change to which the Soviet authorities must have given consent. Although many Orthodox lay activists, such as Aleksandr Ogorodnikov, considered this discussion too timid and felt that the Orthodox leaders might have taken advantage of the situation to ask for more concessions from the state, the amount of open discussion that did take place on previously forbidden themes was unprecedented.

New Law on Freedom of Conscience

In mid-1988, both Mikhail Gorbachev and Konstantin Kharchev, head of the Council for Religious Affairs, promised a new law on "freedom of conscience," which would apparently replace the 1929 Law on Religious Associations. In a speech at the Nineteenth Party Conference in July, Gorbachev said that, while the Communist view of religion as "unscientific" had not changed, this was "no reason for a disrespectful attitude" toward believers. Although church-state relations "had not always developed normally," believers and unbelievers were united as "citizens of their Soviet homeland." Believers were citizens "with full rights" and were "participating actively in our economic and public life." The new law would be "based on Leninist principles" as well as "present-day realities."

Kharchev went into more detail. In an interview with the journal *Ogonyok*[27] and a similar talk to party lecturers,[28] he admitted that the church was not only surviving under atheistic rule but in some cases was even growing. He gave a figure of 70 million religious believers in the Soviet Union, which, though probably lower than the actual number, is much higher than previous official estimates—which, he made clear, had been falsified. Kharchev suggested that a new policy of cooperation and toleration must be devised to prevent believers from becoming hostile to the state. He mentioned the large number of requests and complaints he had had from believers asking for the return of confiscated church buildings, and stated that local *soviets* should no longer obstruct the registration of religious congregations without good cause. Churches should be able to have legal representation. He also hinted at the possibility of charitable work by religious bodies and of private religious instruction for children, both illegal since 1929.

One version of the draft law on religion under consideration appeared unofficially in a Moscow *samizdat* journal in July 1988.[29] It reveals changes in a number of areas, but also a degree of ambiguity. Religious organizations are granted the right of juridical personality, making it possible for them to be legally represented in court. Article 17 of the 1929 law, which forbade charitable activity, youth groups, Bible-study groups, and a number of other church activities, has been omitted from this draft. If, as Gorbachev once said, "everything not specifically forbidden by law is to be permitted," this would open up numerous possibilities. The draft seems to give parents the right to "ensure the religious education of their children"; however, this could conflict with the Family Code of the USSR, which requires parents to bring up children "in the spirit of the moral code of the builders of Communism"—so far taken to mean "in the spirit of atheism." The draft law states that believers may not use religion as a means of evading civic responsibilities, but suggests that a court may be able to substitute one civic responsibility for another—presumably a reference to possible alternatives to military service.

In this draft, registration of religious organizations remains in force. However, the number of church members needed for registration is reduced from twenty to eleven, and local *soviets* could refuse registration only if persons involved were guilty of legal violations. It is not clear whether religious activity without registration would be strictly illegal, though this is implied. Restrictions on religious ceremonies in the home are dropped. Local *soviets* would no longer have the right to remove members of church executive and financial organizations.

These changes would respond to much of the criticism made by religious believers over the years. Several points should be kept in mind, however. First, this is only one of several drafts under discussion. (Comments on two other drafts are in the Appendix.) Second, all of the drafts are just that—drafts. Whether the laws restricting religion will actually be changed remains to be seen. Third, any actual changes in the laws will almost certainly depend on Gorbachev's staying power. And fourth, the proposed changes are likely to be seen by the state authorities not as the *beginning* of change but as a final concession.

Gorbachev's reasons for conceding anything to religious believers should not be misinterpreted. He has shown no sign of being a liberal, an idealist, or a secret religious sympathizer. His main interest is in reforming the Soviet economy. Since this will require sacrifices from Soviet citizens, his government will need broad-based support. Even according to official figures, religious believers form 34 per cent of the population.

Neither Gorbachev nor any other Soviet leader has indicated that atheism should no longer be part of the official ideology. On the contrary, it is continually stressed that atheism is the only "scientific" viewpoint and the only one acceptable for members of the Communist Party. Atheistic propaganda is officially regarded not as obsolete but as ineffectual. The state intends to continue (1) promoting atheism and (2) keeping religious believers out of influential positions in society, while simultaneously (3) avoiding serious offense to believers and (4) trying to obtain their support for government policies by means of minor concessions. This multi-faceted aim may well prove self-contradictory.

5

How Religious Bodies Respond to State Control

Philip Walters

THE CHURCHES and other legally existing religious organizations in the USSR are in a unique and anomalous position. They are the only permitted institutions that are not inspired, founded, operated, and controlled by the Communist Party of the Soviet Union. They are also the only ones that bear witness to an idea antithetical to Marxism-Leninism: simply, that God exists. As previous chapters have shown, the state carries on a full-fledged program of atheistic education and anti-religious propaganda, while it places all manner of restrictions on religious activity. Still, religion survives and, at certain times and in certain places, even flourishes.

The churches' survival is due at least in part to their varied membership and an equally varied range of responses to state pressure. At one extreme are certain hierarchs who display undiluted *discretion* (to use the term applied by Trevor Beeson in his 1982 book *Discretion and Valor*). They understand not only the letter but also the spirit of Soviet regulations governing religious life and carefully abide by both: they are prepared to endorse all aspects of the Soviet system, and to allow the range of their religious activities to be defined by the secular authori-

---

Philip Walters is research director of Keston College, whose staff he joined in 1979. He studied modern languages at Cambridge and completed a doctorate in Russian religious philosophy at London and Moscow universities.

ties. At the other extreme are certain believers who have moved beyond dissent, who have given up trying to influence either the religious or the state authorities, and who simply wish to leave the country. These would-be emigrants are likely to have gone through a period of undiluted *valor* before feeling forced to make a final break. Between these two extremes, hierarchs, clergy, and individual believers may occupy a wide range of positions.

Five Categories of Response

The Furov Report (described in chapter three) has given the West insight into the state control and supervision of religious activity. In one section of this lengthy document, bishops are divided into three categories according to their perceived loyalty to the Soviet state and its interests. The report refers specifically to the Russian Orthodox Church, but the categories would presumably apply to any religious group.

1. Undiluted Loyalty

In the first category are Patriarch Pimen, the head of the Russian Orthodox Church, and those other prelates who, the report says, appreciate the essential spirit of Soviet legislation on religion. These are hierarchs who "in their words and deeds," says Furov,

> confirm not only their loyalty but also their patriotism to Soviet society, strictly observing the laws on cults and educating their parish clergy and believers in this spirit, and who have a realistic understanding that our state is not interested in enlarging the role of religion and the church in society, and, understanding this, do not display any particular energy in expanding the influence of Orthodoxy among the population.

Patriarch Pimen tends to avoid any initiative that will annoy the authorities. In contrast to his predecessor, Alexii, for example, Pimen reportedly has undertaken few if any visits to peripheral diocesan centers and churches. While on a cruise down the Volga River, the patriarch apparently made no effort to visit local religious communities but isolated himself on the upper deck of the ship. By contrast, Metropolitan Nikodim of Leningrad on a similar cruise went ashore each time the steamer docked, met local clergy and laity, and celebrated religious services.

The ideal hierarch from the Soviet point of view has a "loyal attitude towards the organs of Soviet power," does nothing to foster the growth of faith within his diocese, and helps to dampen the troublesome zeal of religious activists. Of Metropolitan Palladi, Furov writes:

> As far as religious activity is concerned, the Metropolitan limits himself to periodical services in the cathedral on religious festivals, and he never travels outside the town.

And in a similar vein:

> There have been no significant changes in the activity, attitudes, and conduct of Bishop Iona. . . . He delivers regular sermons, but they are very short and not very expressive. . . . In the seven years he has been head of the diocese he has never visited any of the rural parishes of the region.

A church hierarch is expected to be vocal in support of Soviet policies, particularly in refuting any suggestion that Soviet citizens are not free to practice their religion and in expressing the Soviet desire for world peace. The *Journal of the Moscow Patriarchate* states that "the Russian Orthodox Church has for decades been involved in the global peace movement *in accordance with the foreign policy of the USSR*" (italics added).

What is more, while representing Soviet policies to the world, religious leaders are expected to do so in their capacity as loyal Soviet citizens and not as religious believers. Religious faith is, after all, reactionary by definition. A basic assumption in the Furov Report is that "the clergy of the Orthodox Church, although loyal to the Soviet state, still remains a body with an ideology which is incompatible with our world view."

The specialist in atheism named Gordienko takes this idea further and denies that religious leaders' support for the policies of the state automatically fashions them into positive participants in the building of Soviet society *as religious believers*:

> We must assess the social aspects of the activity [of the Russian Orthodox Church] in a different way from the religious aspects. The

> social activity of the church (for example, its participation in the peace movement, support for the Peace Fund, and so on) is assessed positively by the Soviet people, including non-believers. But we have a different attitude to those activities of the church which are directed towards the preservation and strengthening of religiosity in socialist society—here we see a hindrance to the spiritual development of Soviet citizens who are believers.

In another article we read:

> Loyalty of a religious organization to Soviet society is an absolute condition for it to function in our country . . . [but] in those cases where the church . . . acts in accordance with the spirit of religious ideology, it is following a reactionary political course.

2. Accommodation With Discretion

In Furov's second category are hierarchs who, while sincere in their efforts on behalf of the state, are at the same time determined to strengthen their religious communities. Furov describes them as follows:

> those leading hierarchs who are loyal towards the state and who have a correct attitude towards the laws on cults and observe them, but who in their everyday administrative and ideological activity are seeking to activate the servants of the cult and active church members, and who are making efforts to expand the role of the church in personal, family, and social life.

The history of Metropolitan Nikodim, placed by Furov in this second category, shows how complicated it is to walk this "middle way." Nikodim, born in 1929, is said to have been brilliant at school while already a believer. He went on to study biology, while simultaneously enrolled in the correspondence course of the Leningrad Theological Academy. When his double life was exposed in 1947, he was expelled from the university. He became a monk in the same year and rose rapidly in the church. By 1950, when he was twenty-one, he was a parish priest; in 1960 he became a bishop; in 1961 he was selected for the prestigious position of chairman of the church's Department of External Church Relations and was made archbishop; in 1963 he became metropolitan of Leningrad. He retired from the chairmanship in 1972 because of serious health problems but remained very active in foreign affairs until his death at the Vatican in 1978, during an audience with Pope John Paul I. In 1961 Nikodim led the first Russian Orthodox delegation to the World Council of Churches. From then until his retirement he was the primary source for church statements in favor of all aspects of the Soviet system. So energetic was he in this respect that some observers suspected he was an agent of the KGB. Many of those closest to the situation, however, felt that the reality was far more complex.

Nikodim consistently asserted that Communism as established in Russia was aiming to realize fundamentally Christian principles and that the Soviet regime was established by the will of God. At the same time, however, he always held that Christianity and Communism are irreconcilable on a spiritual level, and he never believed in the possibility of Christian-Marxist dialogue. To say how he reconciled these two views is impossible. While the vast majority of Western church leaders, as well as most Russian Orthodox clergy, are convinced of Nikodim's genuine Christian faith, most people who had dealings with him were unable to fathom what his beliefs actually were. On a practical level, however, Nikodim's aim was clear: to render the church indispensable to the Soviet regime by offering full cooperation, especially in foreign relations, and thereby gradually to win for the church a secure place in the Soviet social organism and make it impossible for anti-religious campaigns such as that of the Khrushchev era to occur again.

Nikodim was also deeply convinced of the need for continuing ecumenical contacts between the Russian Orthodox Church and the Christian community outside the Soviet Union, particularly the Roman Catholic Church. Part of his motivation was doubtless spiritual, but once again practical considerations played a role. While denying the Soviet persecution of believers in world gatherings, Nikodim seems to have realized that exposure of the Russian church on the world scene would in fact consolidate its position at home. When challenged by a Western churchman that his statements on freedom of religion were denied by a mass of documentary evidence, Nikodim said: "Let's come to an agreement. You publish the documents, and we'll deny what they say."

As metropolitan of Leningrad, Nikodim worked ceaselessly to improve the academic level of the seminary and academy, establishing the custom of receiving foreign students and sending Soviet students abroad in exchange, and of inviting foreigners to lecture. In these ways he improved the church's international contacts and helped break down its isolation from new theological ideas; and at the same time he made it much more difficult for the authorities to apply crude pressure on the theological educational establishments, because of the presence of foreigners there.

Nikodim was in general also eager to do all he could to improve the morale of the church at home. In his lectures at the Leningrad Academy, for example, he often stressed the need for the church to gain the status of a legal person, without which it would remain powerless; the implication for his students was that they should continue to struggle for this status. In his diocese he instructed the laity on how to form *dvadtsatki* (a *dvadtsatka* is the community of twenty believers required for registration as a religious association) and how to negotiate with the authorities to get churches opened. On the level of personal contacts, he readily received young people in search of God and gave generous financial help to those in need—ordinary believers as well as theological students and their families.

Not surprisingly, Nikodim's reformist and especially ecumenical activities were deeply resented and opposed by the more conservative and timid bishops, including Patriarch Pimen. Nikodim was very active in ordaining young bishops who were well educated, intelligent, and progressive, and many of these are now in positions of influence in the church. Some of them do not share his belief that one must show unconditional loyalty to the atheistic state, and they may develop new strategies in continuing to pursue his aim of consolidating the strength and self-confidence of the church.

Metropolitan Nikodim, then, is an example of a prelate concerned to expand the influence of the church while expressing solidarity with, and operating fully within, Soviet society. He once articulated his hope that the Christian community would be able

> to persuade the state to recognize the church legally as part of the national social organism and to make its peace with her, recognizing in her a positive moral role and force in the state.

In contrast, Patriarch Pimen, seemingly satisfied with the *status quo*, has never publicly ventured to offer such an aspiration for the place of the church in the Soviet Union:

> In putting into practice its religious life the Russian Orthodox Church is guided by the teaching of the Gospel of our Lord Jesus Christ. . . . But in their activities in society and at work the Orthodox Christians of our country, like all believers in the Soviet Union, follow the principles that were proclaimed sixty years ago when Soviet power was established in Russia.

3. Accommodation With Constraint

The third of Furov's categories is for those prelates who, like Nikodim, are settled in their resolve to strengthen and enlarge the Christian community, yet who, unlike him, are not prepared to offer uncritical defense of all Soviet policies and actions, choosing at times the path of valor rather than that of discretion. Furov describes the category like this:

> That portion of the episcopate who at various times have attempted to get around the laws on cults. Some of these are religious conservatives; others are capable of falsifying the situations in the dioceses and the relations that have developed there with the organs of state power; and a third group have been noted for attempts to bribe the authorities and have slandered them and the functionaries of local administrative organs.

This third category, then, includes those who press for the rights of religious communities and of individual believers more boldly and in a manner more antagonistic to the authorities than those in category two. Furov describes Bishop Pimen of Saratov:

> In his activities one can see his dissatisfaction with the situation of the church in the USSR and his tenacious efforts to make the churches "magnificent" and to expand the staff of the clergy.
>
> For instance, in his conversations with his closest co-workers he

> expressed criticism of the 1961 reform of the Russian Orthodox Church. He thinks that the government imposed the reform and that it contradicts the interests of the church and handicaps the clergy not only in the material but also in the ethical and legal sense by making them dependent on the church elders.
>
> In his personal conversation with the Commissioner he would often voice his dissatisfaction with the situation of the cadres of the Russian Orthodox clergy. In his view this is the most crucial problem for the church at this time.

Similarly Khrisostom, bishop of Kursk and deputy chairman of the patriarchate's Department of Foreign Affairs, is placed in category three for his "religious fervor" and desire to "revitalize the dying parishes." "With that in mind," writes Furov, "he does not shrink from anything, not even from slandering the Commissioner of the Council so as to compromise him." As partial evidence, Bishop Khrisostom is quoted as having said:

> As for the Commissioner's charges against me and my activation of religious life, I do not travel around visiting my churches and I have never suggested that the believers petition to have their churches reopened. They come to me on their own.
>
> Yesterday I learned from the head of the Belgorod cathedral that in September 1975 the Commissioner's secretary had come in the cathedral and forbade baptism of children on weekdays. Baptism was to be permitted only on Sundays. This is impossible because it is against the law. I have not seen the Commissioner and could not discuss this issue with him.

Despite the protests of some, the hierarchs in all three of Furov's categories are committed to operating within the official church structure and in cooperation with the Soviet authorities. This should not be surprising, as the Russian Orthodox Church has traditionally functioned in close association with the secular powers. Neither should it be surprising that some older hierarchs who have personally experienced the near-destruction of the church—such as Patriarch Pimen—may wish to avoid church-state confrontations at almost any cost.

In addition to Furov's three categories of those basically committed to cooperating with the state, there are two other categories of response.

4. Dissent

Certain groups of religious believers question the very notion that an atheistic state should be able to dictate the conditions under which they can function, especially when it restricts what the believers see as purely religious activities. This attitude is expressed most systematically by those who have separated from the official churches and carry on their religious life underground. At times, however, dissenting views are offered from within the registered churches.

Broadly speaking, the modern religious dissent movement was set off by the Khrushchev anti-religious campaign. Certain believers, both lay and clerical, began writing to the leaders of their churches, pleading with them to be bolder in standing up for the rights of the community in the face of intolerable state interference. In November 1965, the Orthodox priests Nikolai Eshliman and Gleb Yakunin wrote a long open letter to Patriarch Alexii that said in part:

> It is clear that the Russian church is seriously and dangerously ill, and that her sickness has come about entirely because the ecclesiastical authorities have shirked from fulfilling their duties.

In June 1966, Christians in the Kirov diocese wrote to the patriarch expressing their support for the Eshliman-Yakunin letter, which had just become known to them "completely and in full." In November 1967 Archbishop Yermogen, formerly of Kaluga, wrote to the patriarch to protest his recent removal, which, he said was uncanonical, brought on by a demand by the chairman of the government's Council for Religious Affairs. Yermogen went on to raise fundamental questions about uncanonical government interference in church appointments. In the same year the Orthodox layman Boris Talantov wrote an account entitled "The Secret Participation of the Moscow Patriarch in the Fight of the Communist Party of the Soviet Union Against the Orthodox Christian Church: A Crisis in Church Leadership."

Aleksandr Solzhenitsyn in 1972 spoke forcefully from among the intelligentsia in his Lenten letter to Patriarch Pimen. This was the noted author's first public acknowledgment that he was a Russian Orthodox believer. While fully recognizing the canonical validity of the patriarchal church, Solzhenitsyn called upon the church leadership to provide a sacrificial example for their flock rather than give in to the dictates of atheism:

> We have lost the radiant ethical atmosphere of Christianity in which for a millennium our morals were grounded; we have forfeited our way of life, our outlook on the world, our folklore, even the very name by which the Russian peasant was known. We are losing the last features and marks of the Christian people—can this really not be the *principal* concern of the Russian Patriarch? . . .
>
> Why are the pastoral letters which are handed down to us by the supreme church authorities so traditionally submissive? Why are all ecclesiastical documents so complacent, as though they were being published among the most Christian of peoples? . . .
>
> Ask the Lord what other purpose but sacrifice there can be in your service to your people, who have almost lost their Christian countenance and even the spirit of the faith.

Of course, Patriarch Pimen was not in a position to respond to Solzhenitsyn's charges. This was brought out in an eloquent reply to Solzhenitsyn in which Father Sergei Zheludkov defends the hierarchs in their extremely difficult position.

> You have made a written accusation that has been publicized throughout the world, against a man who, as everyone knows, has no possible chance of replying to you . . . [and] you did not tell the whole truth, you gave half-truths.
>
> The *full truth* is that the legal church organization cannot be an island of freedom in our strictly unified society, directed from a single center. . . . There exists this strictly centralized system, and within it, surprisingly, is preserved an alien body—the Russian Orthodox Church. It exists in very strictly determined conditions. We are *not permitted* . . . to do many . . . things necessary for the existence of real church life. *We are permitted only one thing*—to conduct divine worship in our churches, whereby it is supposed that this is something from the past preserved only for a disappearing generation.
>
> What can we do in such a situation? Should we say: all or nothing? . . .
>
> Hence today all the evil about which you very rightly wrote, as well as all the evil you did not mention. But there was no other choice. . . . Never, never before have our completely unique conditions of human existence been known.

The debate over discretion vs. valor, accommodation vs. dissent, is endless. Temperament and personality probably play a significant role in determining the path a believer chooses. Father Gleb Yakunin has said that under present conditions any church should ideally consist of two parts: one registered, the other underground. Using the analogy of two vessels containing liquid and connected by a narrow tube, Father Gleb comments that at times of increased pressure on the registered "official" religious communities, the unregistered, underground communities increase to compensate. Thus the two kinds of religious witness are in a mutually supportive balance. The history of the religious communities in the Soviet Union appears to support Father Gleb's analysis.

5. Emigration

The dissent of Lithuanians and Ukrainians arises from a deep concern over the welfare of their nations; many Russian Orthodox believers are similarly concerned for "Mother Russia." Such persons are patriots, even if deeply critical of the regime in power, and are firmly anchored in the traditions and cultures of their lands.

For some groups of believers, however—chiefly among the smaller Protestant denominations—the major objective is to leave the Soviet Union altogether. The Jews are the only ones who have been allowed to fulfill this ambition to any degree: a quarter of a million emigrated in the 1970s. Emigration was subsequently reduced to a trickle, then was increased considerably under Gorbachev.

A substantial minority of Pentecostals—more than 30,000—have sought permission to leave, but only a handful have been allowed to do so. The "Siberian Seven" won their right to emigrate only after spending five years inside the American Embassy in Moscow and exciting world interest in their plight.

A larger group of Pentecostals from Chuguyevka in Siberia—called the "Siberian Seventy"—then began seeking permission to leave, claiming that they could not practice their faith freely under Soviet conditions. After 1981, when they moved to Chuguyevka from Uzbekistan, various members of the congregation were fined, sentenced to cuts in wages, and imprisoned for periods of ten to fifteen days. They refused to accept the restrictions entailed in official registration and held their religious meetings in secret.

The majority of the Chuguyevka Pentecostals are of German descent. In 1983 they renounced their Soviet citizenship and applied for emigration visas to West Germany, their historic homeland. After that they were refused visas several times and undertook long hunger strikes. By September 1984, seven of them had been fired from their jobs and threatened with criminal prosecution for being without passports. Eight families have described how their children were victimized, insulted, and beaten at school without intervention by the teachers. The Pentecostals' pastor, Viktor Walter, was arrested in December 1984, and he and seven other members of the church were sentenced in April 1985 to imprisonment for from three to five years. The rest of the congregation were left with very little money and faced severe shortages of food. They could not receive food parcels from abroad since they could not afford to pay the duty.

The first three families were allowed to emigrate in April 1987. In January 1988 some of the Chuguyevka Pentecostals staged a demonstration outside the Supreme Soviet in Moscow. Since then the pace of permission has accelerated, and most of the families have either left the Soviet Union or received permission to do so. The release of those in prison began in 1988; Viktor Walter was released in July.

Like the Jewish *refuseniks*, the Pentecostals are not interested in working for the reform of the religious community or of Soviet society. The only government restrictions they are protesting are those that hinder freedom of emigration and, on a local level, the free and full practice of their faith until their departure. Their goal, which has gone beyond dissent, is simply to leave the USSR.

Attempts to Extend Religious Freedom

Most Russian Orthodox bishops are eager to encourage the growth of the faith in their dioceses and parishes. They envisage a gradual extension of the area in which the church is free to manage its own affairs. Dissenters, by contrast, believe that action outside the law is necessary if there is to be any significant increase in the freedom of believers to practice their faith. Let us look at some areas in which religious freedom is restricted and at some efforts being made to overcome these restrictions.

Religious Education and Literature

Ever since theological educational institutions were set up in the mid-1940s, the Orthodox Church has made efforts to improve the quality of the students admitted. A stricter selection procedure was introduced, together with more testing, in an effort to eliminate those without a vocation (a divine calling to God's service). The Orthodox Church, like some other churches, also offers correspondence courses for candidates for the ministry who are unable to enroll in theological institutions.

A fundamental problem is that the academic courses may contain nothing about contemporary political or social realities or about problems faced by religious believers in an atheistic society. Moreover, sermons, according to the Furov Report, "must contain no political or social issues or examples." Priests and laypersons have tried in various ways to provide what is lacking here. In the new climate of *glasnost*, religious issues are raised in novels and films much more openly than before. Yet the authorities are still vigilant; writers are wary of expressing unequivocal approval of religious ideas and do not attempt to expound them in any systematic way.

The vast majority of religious believers in the USSR are loyal Soviet citizens who genuinely desire the best for their country, and for some this means that they cannot remain silent about certain political or social problems. They resort to *samizdat*, literature that is clandestinely printed and distributed. Between 1971 and 1974, ten issues of the *samizdat* journal *Veche* appeared, totaling many hundreds of pages. The editor, Orthodox layman Vladimir Osipov, hoped that *Veche* could become a forum for "loyal opposition," an organ in which loyal Soviet citizens who were also religious believers could discuss abuses and shortcomings in Soviet society in a positive spirit. But the authorities closed the journal and arrested Osipov; he was sentenced to eight years' deprivation of liberty.

In the early 1970s Father Dmitri Dudko, a Moscow parish priest, instituted what was considered a revolutionary practice: he invited the members of his congregation to tell him their problems, and publicly tackled the issues they raised in his sermons. Young people particularly flocked to hear him. As his popularity increased, the state brought pressure on the church authorities, and Father Dmitri was moved from parish to parish. Eventually the church could no longer protect him, and in 1980 he was arrested and kept in solitary confinement until he recanted his "anti-Soviet activities" on television. He was then allowed to return to parish activities. During the 1980s he has kept a relatively low profile.

Lay members of the Orthodox Church and new converts have formed discussion groups for the exchange of ideas and for mutual support, trying to create Christian communities in a country that discourages the concept of the "parish" as a living social organism. The Christian Seminar, founded in 1974 by young Orthodox converts in Moscow, was an early example of this kind of group. Its leaders were arrested in the late 1970s and sentenced to many years in labor camps. Since 1985 they have been released, and discussion groups of this kind have again begun to proliferate.

Soviet citizens who are interested in knowing more about religion face a fundamental problem—there is virtually no printed matter available. Between 1956, when the Russian Orthodox Church received permission to publish certain types of religious literature, and 1986, it was able to produce only some 450,000 copies of the Bible and New Testament. Most of these have never entered general circulation in the USSR.

Beginning in 1987 the Baptists and Orthodox were able to import Bibles, hymnbooks, and Bible commentaries in much greater numbers than before, and the Orthodox Church was also given permission to print 100,000 copies of the Bible in Russian. These are very welcome developments. Yet the importing of hundreds of thousands of volumes now under way still will go nowhere near satisfying the thirst for religious literature. It is still impossible to find any religious literature on open sale in the Soviet Union except occasionally in churches, while on the black market it is extremely expensive.

Valeri Barinov is a Baptist rock musician from Leningrad who, unable to secure permission to perform his Christian music in public, sent to the West a recording of his rock opera *Trumpet Call* that was broadcast back to the Soviet Union by the BBC. Barinov received hundreds of letters from people all over the Soviet Union inquiring about the Christian faith. One said:

> I have a question about God. God is Jesus Christ, isn't he? But wasn't he crucified and didn't he die? I've forgotten—he was resurrected later—but who resurrected him, and why was he crucified in the first place? . . . Please write to us without fear: we aren't just asking casual questions out of boredom, we really are interested.

The unregistered Baptists produce Bibles and other religious literature on homemade printing presses. Constructed of parts from bicycles and washing machines, the presses can be dismantled and transported in suitcases. During a raid on a secret press in Central Asia in 1984, authorities confiscated 30,000 printed Bibles and six tons of paper.

It is not only those directly involved in clandestine printing who risk arrest and imprisonment: any priest who tries to supply his flock with religious literature falls under immediate suspicion. Father Aleksandr Pivovarov turned down a theological teaching position to serve a parish in Siberia, where he became known for his faith and exceptional preaching. Although church authorities tried to protect him, the state began to put pressure on him. He was interrogated and his house searched. In 1982 he was implicated in a case being brought against some Moscow Christians for producing unofficial religious literature—Father Aleksandr had been distributing it to his parishioners. Arrested in 1983 and charged with "engaging in an illegal trade" (he supposedly sold the literature for profit), he was sentenced to four years in a labor camp.

Meeting Places

For perhaps three million Baptists in the Soviet Union there are about 5,000 registered churches, roughly one church for 600 people. For some 50 million Orthodox believers there are something over 6,000 churches—roughly one for 8,000 people. Obviously many Soviet believers cannot exercise their only legal religious right—to meet in a registered building for an act of worship.

To open new churches is very difficult. Since 1985 the rate of opening has increased; but a positive reply is by no means certain when a religious association applies for permission to use a building, and since 1975 government authorities no longer have to respond within a given time limit to such an application. In the city of Klaipeda, Lithuania, almost the entire population campaigned without success for years for the return of their Catholic church, confiscated in 1961; a 1979 petition to the authorities was signed by more than 148,000 people! In August 1987 the authorities finally announced that the church would be returned "within two years."

Under *glasnost*, newspaper articles of an unprecedented kind have taken up the cause of named local groups of believers who have experienced difficulties in registering a place of worship. These have had some effect but have done nothing to alter the situation fundamentally.

Some new churches are being opened, then, but the number is never adequate. And there are always reports of the closing of churches, usually against the wishes of local believers. Frustrated at this situation, many groups of believers—particularly in the evangelical denominations—decide not to pursue their legal rights; they meet for worship in non-registered buildings and apartments and even in the open air. Such meetings, if discovered, are regularly broken up and the participants questioned or arrested.

The Defense of Persecuted Believers

Believers have frequently criticized church leaders for failing to protect their flocks against arbitrary and unjust actions. Nevertheless, there is evidence that church hierarchs do make efforts in this area, particularly when the persecuted believer is a priest or church employee. Father Dmitri Dudko was first moved from church to church rather than suspended from his priestly functions. Father Aleksandr Pivovarov was protected by being moved from his parish to become secretary to the bishop of Novosibirsk. Father Gleb Yakunin was suspended as a priest by the patriarch for writing a protest about excessive government interference in the internal life of the church, but he was later given the post of reader in a Moscow church. He may later have declined an offer of reinstatement as a priest but was able to accept such an offer in 1987. Church leaders are less likely to intervene in the cases of lay dissenters and indeed have often specifically disowned such activists as lawbreakers unrepresentative of the mass of believers.

Defense of the lay dissenters falls to a number of activist organizations that have sprung up across the country to defend human rights, promoting their causes both within the country and abroad. After the Soviet government signed the Helsinki Agreements in 1975, citizens set up groups to monitor their government's adherence to those clauses concerned with religious and other human rights.

Father Gleb Yakunin founded the Christian Committee for the Defense of Believers' Rights in 1976. While the members of the committee were all Orthodox, they concerned themselves with the rights of believers of all denominations, even non-Christians. The committee sent to the West more than 3,000 pages of documentation about infringements of believers' rights. They hoped to excite large-scale concern and thereby bring pressure on the Soviet government to uphold the Helsinki Agreements. Very little response was forthcoming, however, and Father Gleb was arrested in 1979 and sentenced to ten years' deprivation of liberty.

A Catholic Committee for the Defense of Believers' Rights was set up in Lithuania in 1978, modeled on the Christian Committee but concerned primarily with Lithuanian Catholics. In Lithuania, the Catholic faith of the vast majority of the population is closely identified with nationalistic aspirations; the desire for national freedom and the desire for religious freedom reinforce each other and cannot be separated. This leads to a widespread commitment to *valor* on the part of Lithuanian Catholics. Like the two other Baltic republics, Latvia and Estonia, Lithuania was annexed by the Soviet Union during the Second World War; deep resentment against Soviet rule from Moscow is common in all three. Only in Lithuania, however, is virtually the entire population united in systematic and ineradicable protest. The religious unanimity of the republic provides a moral and intellectual framework for such protest.

The *Chronicle of the Lithuanian Catholic Church*, a regular *samizdat* bulletin, began appearing in 1972. It records discrimination and persecution suffered by Lithuanian Catholics and deplores the economic and moral decay of the Lithuanian nation under Soviet rule. It has survived all KGB attempts to close it down permanently. Indeed, after a general purge of dissenters in the USSR began in the late 1970s, Lithuania was for several years the only area where organized dissent continued. As of fall 1988 it was still going on, and the authorities seem powerless to stop it. Priests and even bishops are united with their congregations in the protest movement.

Another area of the Soviet Union where religion is identified with national aspirations is Ukraine, but here circumstances are rather different. The Ukrainian Catholic (or Uniate) Church owes allegiance to Rome but observes Orthodox rites and traditions. The Soviet authorities, for once in agreement with the Russian Orthodox Church, have always maintained that Ukrainian Catholics are really Orthodox who came under the jurisdiction of Rome when Ukraine was part of Poland. The Ukrainian Catholic Church was dissolved in 1946 and its members and churches declared reunited with the Russian Orthodox Church. It is now the largest illegal religious body in the USSR; as many as three to four million Ukrainians still identify themselves as Ukrainian Catholics. Secret priests and even bishops continue to minister to their flocks under extremely difficult circumstances.

In response to these conditions, in 1982 the Ukrainian Catholic layman Josyf Terelya founded the Initiative Group for the Defense of the Rights of Believers and the Church. He was subsequently instrumental in founding the *samizdat Chronicle of the Ukrainian Catholic Church*. Similar in many ways to the Lithuanian *Chronicle*, this underground journal addresses itself to the physical and moral survival of the nation as well as of the church. Terelya was arrested for the seventh time in 1985 and sentenced to twelve years' deprivation of liberty but was allowed to emigrate in 1987.

Concluding Observations

The five options described in this chapter cover the range of possible responses by Soviet believers to atheistic rule. Between total acquiescence to the system and total rejection of it, there are various ways of combining discretion with valor.

From the point of view of the Soviet authorities, the ideal religious believer does nothing at all as a consequence of his faith—preferably does not even attend church. Any *modus vivendi* worked out between church and state, therefore, must be seen in the light of the irreducible fact that the Soviet Union in both ideology and practice is determinedly anti-religious.

Since Gorbachev came to power there have been a number of limited practical improvements in the situation of religious believers: prominent prisoners of conscience have been released; more religious literature has been made available; some churches have been opened and some monasteries handed back; injustices have been aired in the press. There has been no real indication, however, that the Gorbachev administration is prepared to put an end to the anti-religious propaganda and education that for seventy years have been an integral part of Soviet Marxism-Leninism. And by the close of 1988 the promised new legislation on religion to replace the very restrictive law of 1929 was still in the discussion stage.

A believer who takes any kind of stand in opposition to authority starts out on a path with an uncertain end. If he protests against aspects of the Soviet system from a religious standpoint, he invites reprisals. Protesting these reprisals, he invites more serious reprisals. A handful of believers follow the path of protest to the end and are imprisoned or placed in labor camps or psychiatric hospitals.

When questioned publicly by foreigners about religious liberty in the USSR and the evidence provided by religious activists,

Soviet church officials almost invariably state that for a normal, law-abiding believer there are no problems; the dissidents, it is claimed, are a vocal but unrepresentative handful of malcontents and misfits who find themselves in difficulty for breaking Soviet law. But there is plenty of evidence to suggest that what the hierarchs say in public does not give a full picture of the complex interdependence of discretion and valor.

Is there any truth, however, in the implication that dissidents have a certain kind of combative and irascible personality or hold a certain set of views in an unreasonably dogmatic manner?

Many dissenters do have such strong personalities or hold such strong beliefs that they would probably find themselves involved in controversy no matter what society they lived in. In others, however, the intransigent adherence to a particular set of beliefs is as much a product of the extreme pressure under which they and their families are living as a consequence of their own personalities. They fear that if they concede any point to the state, they might eventually be compelled to concede everything. And many dissidents are driven by their consciences to stand up for their beliefs without having the kind of bold, combative personality that makes it easier. Father Dmitri Dudko, for example, was contrasted with Solzhenitsyn by someone who knew them both: "Solzhenitsyn simply was afraid of nothing and nobody, but this man is afraid all the time. Yet he carries on."

The legally existing churches and their hierarchies owe a debt to the dissidents. What is possible for religious believers in the registered churches is much greater today than in the 1930s. Indeed, by 1939 the majority of those who practiced their faith were dissidents, for with institutional religion virtually destroyed, most believers were forced into an underground existence. This must have contributed to Stalin's decision to normalize relations between the state and the churches during the war: since the people were going to persist in believing in God, better that they be in legally recognized churches where their activities could be monitored.

The traumatic Khrushchev campaign was the last attempt by the Soviet government to eradicate religion, and it is doubtful that a similar attempt could be made in the future. Religious activists who have chosen the course of valor have been speaking out forcefully for some twenty-five years. Surely there would be worldwide reaction to any new large-scale purge of religion. While church leaders at international gatherings routinely disown dissidents and their activities, the deeper feelings they reveal in private make it clear that the persistent raising of issues of religious freedom is by no means unwelcome to them.

It is clear nonetheless that the government's policy of "divide and rule" has had a debilitating effect on the spiritual life of the churches. It may be that a certain amount of adversity purifies the faith of believers and strengthens their commitment; but an ongoing, systematic attempt to break up the believing community into mutually suspicious factions prevents the church from functioning as the Body of Christ.

In the 1920s the Soviet authorities backed the Renovationist Church faction against the patriarchal Orthodox Church. The Renovationist clergy, who had declared themselves positively in favor of socialism as practiced in the Soviet Union, had few followers among the faithful; yet government backing meant that they were able to control a large proportion of the churches, and the distinction made between a "loyal" and a "disloyal" church led to much confusion, suspicion, and bitterness in the Orthodox Christian community. The same policy has been followed at various times by Marxist governments in Eastern Europe and elsewhere in the world. In a more subtle form, it is the policy that has been followed in the Soviet Union to the present day.

6

Religious Persecution and Discrimination

Michael Rowe

THE CONSCIOUSNESS of every Soviet believer is at least partially formed in the crucible of a frightening past. From the smashing of the power of the Orthodox Church after the Revolution to the assault on religious dissent in the early 1980s, the persecution of religion has been a hallmark of Soviet power, although with great variation in degree and form and in the number of persons directly affected. While today blatant *persecution* is the experience of relatively few, *discrimination* is felt by large numbers of believers.

Religious persecution means deliberate acts on the part of authority intended "to injure or distress"[1] individuals or communities because of their religious beliefs. The persecution may be fully integrated within the established legal system. Religious discrimination is the denial to religious believers of rights that are granted to non-religious people.

Most forms of discrimination are illegal in the Soviet Union, but the persecution of believers through imprisonment under criminal law is done mostly on the basis of established legal procedure, however unjustly applied. Information about criminal charges is often incomplete, however, and sometimes the cir-

Michael Rowe is the senior researcher on the Soviet Union at Keston College, with a special interest in evangelical Christians in the USSR. Since 1979 he has edited Keston's series *Religious Prisoners in the USSR*.

cumstances in a specific case are not altogether clear. The cases that will be mentioned in this chapter are all documented in the archives of Keston College. The documentation, which varies in extent and detail from case to case, includes copies of official documents (bills of indictment and court verdicts), transcripts of trials, notices of fines, appeals by the victims of persecution collected by individuals and groups protesting violations of religious liberty, and Soviet press articles. Since much of this material is available only in the Russian language, individual sources have not been cited.

Criminal Prosecution Through Legal Measures

Soviet authorities consistently maintain that no one in the USSR is imprisoned for being a religious believer; persons are sentenced only for violations of Soviet law. In cases of imprisonment under articles of the Criminal Code relating to religious activity, this assertion is generally true. (The question is, of course: Where does the fault really lie—with the law-breakers or with the law itself?)

Prisoners are either (a) sent away to serve their sentence in compulsory labor or as an exile or (b) held under one of five "regimes" of imprisonment. The five, beginning with the most severe, are: (1) prison, (2) special-regime labor camp, (3) strict-regime labor camp, (4) intensified-regime labor camp, and (5) ordinary-regime labor camp. The regime selected by the court depends on the seriousness of the alleged offense and the number of previous convictions. The type of regime determines the type and quantity of rations the prisoner receives, the number of privileges (letters, food parcels, visits), and the scale of punishment to which he can be subjected. Some prisoners are sentenced to *compulsory labor* on a construction project, usually in one of the remoter regions of the USSR; sometimes prisoners are transferred from labor camp to compulsory labor under amnesty or for good work and behavior in camp. A sentence of *exile*, often given in addition to a labor-camp or prison sentence, is similar to compulsory labor. Exiles are forced to live in a designated, normally remote location for the period of the exile sentence, where they may take whatever work they can find.

Religious Offenses: Articles 142 and 227

Two articles of the Criminal Codes of the Soviet republics—142 and 227 in the Russian Soviet Federated Socialist Republic (RSFSR) criminal code, with corresponding articles in the codes of the other fourteen republics—deal specifically with religious activities that are outlawed under Soviet legislation. Article 142 prohibits "violation of the laws on the separation of church and state and of school and church," while Article 227 is called "infringement of the person and rights of citizens under the guise of performing religious rituals."[2]

Of course, the separation of the church from the state and the school system has long been a dead issue in the Soviet Union. No church wields any political power or enjoys any privileged position, and all religious influence has been eliminated from the schools. What Article 142 refers to in practice (and the March 1966 decree of the RSFSR Supreme Soviet clarifying its application is quite explicit) is any failure by individuals or religious communities to observe the restrictions placed by the state upon religious activity (i.e., essentially limiting it to the conduct of worship within the four walls of a registered church building), and any attempt by congregational leaders to influence their members against accepting the state restrictions.

Specifically, it is an offense with a maximum penalty of three years' imprisonment to organize or lead worship regularly in any place other than a registered church building—for example, in a private home or in the open. Thus anyone who leads an unregistered religious community—which by definition has no registered church building—is committing a crime under Article 142. Cases in recent years include Ulyana Germanyuk, wife of an imprisoned Baptist pastor and evangelist, arrested in July 1985 and sentenced to three years' ordinary-regime labor camp, and Afanasi Melnik, superintendent of unregistered Pentecostal churches in the Vinnitsa region of Ukraine, arrested in November 1984 and sentenced to three years' strict-regime camp.

Article 142 has commonly been applied to Christians involved in activities for children and young people. In Kant, Kirghizia, two Baptists were imprisoned in 1977 for organizing a Sunday school, and in 1978 three others were arrested for continuing their work. In August 1979, Galina Vilchinskaya and Pavel and Vladimir Rytikov were arrested for organizing a summer camp for children from the families of Baptist prisoners. Susanna Herzen from the Orenburg region was put on trial for teaching children in April 1985. Of course, such "criminal" activities are considered quite normal activities in most countries, including several other Communist countries.

Applying Article 227

Article 227 carries a stiffer penalty than Article 142—five years' imprisonment or five years' exile; the equivalent article in the Ukrainian Criminal Code provides for a maximum sentence of five years' imprisonment *and* five years' exile. This article is directed against those who are alleged to be religious "extremists," who do not break the law simply by violating regulations but do "active damage." The primary concern of Article 227 is with the leadership and organization of those religious groups that allegedly cause harm to people's health or infringe upon their rights in some other way, or encourage members not to participate in public life and duties. To entice young people into such a group or to be an active member is also an offense under Article 227.

Religious practices that are prohibited as damaging to physical or mental health include fasting, praying for the sick (if medical treatment is neglected), and speaking in tongues. Other "infringements of citizens' rights" are often closely bound up with incitement not to fulfill public duties—for example, encouraging others not to vote (voting is a duty as well as a right). Some religious young people decline to undertake their public duty of armed military service. By encouraging members to separate themselves from the world and to renounce worldly pursuits, religious groups impede believers from fulfilling the aims of Soviet society and of the Communist Party. Refusal to join trade unions, or to attend public meetings and rallies, or to allow children and young people to participate in or belong to Communist youth organizations, has a similar effect. Discouraging the use of secular media, especially television, allegedly infringes upon citizens' right of free access to the press.

Since its enactment in 1959, Article 227 has regularly been applied to Pentecostal leaders. One of the first to be charged was Nikolai Goretoi, whose indictment included, "The children are forbidden to join the Pioneers and Komsomol [Communist youth organizations], to go to the cinema or the theater, to undertake community assignments, or to read [secular] literature." Several children from Christian families confirmed this. The only evidence of damage to health was from a judicial-psychiatric commission that reported three children it had examined were mentally and physically underdeveloped and emotionally unstable. This the commission attributed to their upbringing and their attendance at Pentecostal services. Goretoi was sentenced to five years in labor camp and five years' exile, although after Khrushchev's fall from power the sentence was reduced. In 1979 he was arrested again on charges under Article 227 and also for the political offense of anti-Soviet agitation and propaganda, whereupon he was sentenced to the maximum penalty under the latter charge—seven years' strict-regime camp and five years' exile.

More recent indictments of others have been more detailed, but the evidence of damage to health and infringement of rights appears equally contrived. For example, the indictment of two Moscow Pentecostals in December 1983 stated:

> On the pretext of preaching Pentecostal doctrine, Kostyuk, together with Tsimmerman, systematically circulated among members of the group ideas of an anti-social nature: he preached the separation of believers from the "world" and from an active stance as builders of Communism; he conducted propaganda against Soviet law, calling for non-observance of the legislation on religious cults, and incited religious fanaticism, as a result of which the group of Pentecostal sectarians was not registered with the local *soviet* [council] of people's deputies. They systematically encouraged the uncontrolled production of ideologically harmful literature. . . . They preached against marriage with non-believing citizens, thus infringing citizens' rights. In addition, their activity was . . . causing harm to the health of members of the group. They deliberately aroused religious preju-

> dices connected with belief that the "Holy Spirit" can enter a person resulting in the ability to speak "in other tongues"; they incited them to systematic performance of ecstatic religious rituals with the aim of arousing religious ecstasy which led to personality changes of members of the group [four are named] and caused harm to the health of members of the group [two are named] in the form of pathological personality change.

Article 227, first directed against Pentecostals, has often been applied also to Baptists (usually in conjunction with charges under Article 142), Jehovah's Witnesses, and, more recently, Hare Krishna adherents and practitioners of yoga. The penalty under Article 227 today, however, is far less severe than the sentences faced by Pentecostals before 1959. Afanasi Melnik, for example, was sentenced in 1957 to twenty-five years in labor camp on charges of anti-Soviet activity, the details of which correspond very closely to the charges in the indictments against Goretoi and Kostyuk, though without any reference to harm to health.

Academician Igor Shafarevich, a Soviet Christian and human-rights activist, has pointed out that if actual damage to health can be proved, then those guilty can be charged under articles of the Criminal Code dealing with crimes against the person. The same applies to infringement of rights. Shafarevich quotes Soviet legal specialist V. V. Klochkov:

> For example, the sacrament of communion, as practiced by the Orthodox Church and by Christian sects, brings with it the possibility of transmission of infectious diseases, baptism the danger of catching cold, circumcision of causing complications, etc.

Shafarevich comments:

> One can conclude that in cases where these actions lead to illness the author considers it appropriate to bring charges under Article 227. The question arises: Is there a basis for judicial sanctions if a child's illness is caused, for example, by being bathed in the draught from an open window by some other person, a parent, grandmother, or kindergarten nurse? If the answer if yes, then there is no reason to single out the connection with religious rituals. If not, then there is discrimination against religious acts.

Political Offenses: Articles 190–1 and 70

Two overtly political articles of the Soviet criminal codes limit freedom of expression in general, as opposed to religious expression specifically. In the RSFSR code, these are Articles 190–1, "dissemination of deliberately false fabrications slandering the Soviet state and social system," and 70, "anti-Soviet agitation and propaganda." These articles have been widely applied to those who draw attention to Soviet abuses of human rights, and to Lithuanians, Georgians, Armenians, Ukrainians, and others—many of them Christians—who campaign for the independence of their nations. While concern for human rights is a natural Christian response, it is obviously not one that is exclusively Christian or even religious.

National consciousness and religious faith are also very closely connected, and often intertwined. Under Soviet conditions, the national churches of the minority peoples are the only institutions independent of direct Soviet influence. They play important roles in preserving these nations in the face of a Sovietized culture and the extensive Russification of public life. Although Christians imprisoned for human-rights activities and campaigns for national freedom can legitimately be regarded as religious prisoners of conscience, our concern in this chapter is with repressive measures directed against religious activity *per se*. Therefore many "political" offenders sentenced under Articles 70 and 190–1 will not be considered.

The case against Pyotr Kuzmenko, however, could certainly be classified as purely religious persecution. Kuzmenko, a leader of an independently registered Baptist church in Kiev, was charged under the Ukrainian equivalent of Article 190–1 ("dissemination of deliberately false fabrications slandering the Soviet state") for praying for Christian prisoners during services. Vasyl Kobryn, chairman of the Action Group for the Defense of Believers and the Church, was also sentenced under this article for compiling information on the persecution of the Ukrainian Catholic Church. Article 190–1 carries a maximum penalty of three years' imprisonment or five years' exile.

Article 70, dealing with "anti-Soviet agitation and propaganda,'' is a far more serious charge, with a maximum of seven years' camp and five years' exile for a first offense, rising to ten years' camp and five years' exile for those with a previous conviction under the article. Yet despite the wide difference in maximum penalties between the two articles, the distinction between them often seems to be largely subjective; in some cases investigators reportedly substitute one charge for the other.

Pentecostals campaigning for the right to emigrate in the search for religious freedom have been sentenced under both articles. Nikolai Goretoi, mentioned previously in connection with Article 227, was arrested on charges under Article 70 in December 1979; the deacon of his congregation, Nikolai Bobarykin, was also sentenced under this article, though to one year less. Earlier, Fyodor Sidenko, another member of the same congregation active in the emigration campaign, had been arrested and charged under Article 190–1, although he was sent to a special psychiatric hospital at the recommendation of a psychiatric commission. A number of other Christians prominent in the defense of religious rights have received sentences under Article 70, notably Fr. Gleb Yakunin, leader of the Christian Committee for the Defense of Believers' Rights, Frs. Alfonsas Svarinskas and Sigitas Tamkevicius of the (Lithuanian) Catholic Committee for the Defense of Believers' Rights, and Josyf Terelya, founder of the (Ukrainian Catholic) Action Group for the Defense of Believers and the Church.

Protesting violations of religious freedom can be seen as a political act, and so it is not altogether surprising that Soviet authorities bring charges relating to political expression. Nevertheless, in innumerable case histories analyzed, prosecutors have never tried to establish that any statements forming the basis of charges under Article 190–1 were false—let alone ''deliberately false fabrications.'' Nor has any proof been required that religious activists have, in the words of Article 70, engaged in ''agitation and propaganda conducted with the aim of undermining or weakening Soviet power.'' The cases for the prosecution have always seemed to rest on the fact that reports circulated by the defendants discredit the Soviet regime.

In some instances, however, even this logic seems difficult to apply. Aleksandr Ogorodnikov and Vladimir Poresh were both sentenced under Article 70 in connection with the activity of the Christian Seminar, a religio-philosophical study group. Orthodox writers Zoya Krakhmalnikova and Felix Svetov were sentenced under Articles 70 and 190–1 respectively, Krakhmalnikova for editing and compiling a periodical *samizdat* anthology of religious devotional material, Svetov for writing about the search for religious values.

While it is common Soviet legal practice to formulate charges under several articles of the Criminal Code simultaneously, Articles 190–1 and 70 are never combined, as the distinction appears to be one of degree. Articles 142 ("violation of the laws on separation of church and state and of school and church") and 227 ("infringement of the person and rights of citizens under the guise of performing religious rituals"), however, are often combined, as they cover different aspects of religious activity. Many Baptists have been charged with 142, 227, and 190–1, and religious or political articles are combined with others that cover apparently non-political and non-religious offenses as described below.

Refusing Military Duties: Articles 80 and 249

Another pair of offenses concerns a matter of conscience: "evasion of regular call to active military service" (Article 80, RSFSR Criminal Code) and "evasion of military duties by maiming or any other method" (RSFSR Article 249). If a conscientious objector refuses altogether to obey the call-up, this is an offense under Article 80 with prosecution virtually automatic, as there is no provision under present Soviet law for exemption from military service on grounds of conscience, religious or otherwise. The key phrase in Article 249 is "refusal to perform military duties," which can include a refusal to bear arms and also to swear the military oath of allegiance. Swearing the oath is not a military duty as such, but certain duties (for example, guard duty) can be performed only by recruits who have sworn the oath at the end of their basic training. Therefore to refuse the oath is regarded as the equivalent of refusing such duties. In recent years, the number of reported prosecutions under Article 249 has dropped. There is no indication that this is because there are fewer conscientious objectors. Instead, military commanders seem now to prefer to deploy objectors on such noncombatant duties as driving vehicles, or to transfer them to construction battalions.

Conviction for refusal to bear arms or to swear the military oath involves a minimum sentence of three years' imprisonment, with a maximum of seven years. In wartime or in combat situations (e.g., during the Soviet occupation of Afghanistan), refusal carries the possibility of the death penalty.

An "advantage" to being sentenced to imprisonment under Article 249 is that, since the offense is a military one, those who have been imprisoned for it have been discharged from military service at the end of their sentences. In the case of Article 80, on the other hand, refusing call-up is a civil offense. Thus, while the penalty under Article 80—one to three years' imprisonment—is less than that under Article 249, the objector runs the risk of being called up for military service again when he completes his sentence. This happened to Filip Akhtyorov, who was called up in May 1980 and sentenced to 2½ years' ordinary-regime camp for refusing military service. Released in the summer of 1982 after two years' imprisonment, he was called up again in November 1982, rearrested, and sentenced to an additional three years of camp.

Disrupting Public Order: Article 190–3

In addition to these "crimes" that clearly relate to the expression of religious faith, a whole range of criminal offenses with no apparent connection to religious or political activity have regularly formed the basis for charges against religious believers. The most common is expressed in Article 190–3 of the RSFSR Criminal Code: "Organization of, or active participation in, group actions which disrupt public order." The circumstances to which this charge has been applied vary considerably, from situations in which large crowds have indeed interrupted the flow of traffic to peaceful assemblies that apparently have not obstructed vehicle or pedestrian movement in any way.

In more than one instance, Christians are reported to have gathered in the street only after the authorities prevented them from entering the building in which they were planning to meet. This occurred in Rostov-on-Don in 1978, for example, when the unregistered Baptist congregation came together for worship in a private home that was cordoned off by the militia. As a result, the pastor, Peter Peters, was arrested and sentenced to 2½ years' strict-regime camp. In Krasnodar in 1978, Josyf Bondarenko organized a youth rally at the registered Baptist church. According to local Christians, the authorities withdrew permission for the rally at the last moment and made sure that the designated meeting place remained closed, but it was too late to stop the young people who were arriving for the meeting from Krasnodar and surrounding towns and villages. Bondarenko, the rally organizer, was arrested and sentenced to three years' strict-regime camp. Also in 1978, Pyotr Kravchuk, chairman of the church council of the registered Baptist church in Bryansk-Bezhitsa, was sentenced to two years' camp under Article 190–3. He was held responsible for a procession from the church to the place where an open-air baptism was to be held. The authorities claimed that while they had granted permission for the baptism, the church council had not sought permission for the procession.

Open-air meetings have provided the most frequent cause for prosecution under Article 190–3. Roman Moiseyev and Kharlampi Kirov were arrested in 1983 for organizing a youth rally in the woods near Strasheny in Moldavia; Moiseyev received a two-year sentence and Kirov three years under the Moldavian equivalent of this article. Ivan Danilyuk, pastor of a small unregistered Baptist church in Chernovtsy, western Ukraine, was arrested in 1979 three days after he conducted a baptismal service in a local river. The church reported that when the militia tried to prevent the service from taking place, considerable public attention was attracted. Danilyuk was sentenced to 2½ years' ordinary-regime camp under the Ukrainian equivalents of Articles 190–3 and 142.

Services do not have to be held outdoors to call forth charges of disrupting public order. Vasili Shilyuk, leader of an unregistered Pentecostal church in Rovno, in western Ukraine, was arrested in 1982 following a search of his home, conducted on a warrant to search for one kilogram of stolen meat. While no meat was found, Shilyuk was charged under the Ukrainian equivalents of Articles 190–3 and 190–1. Although all the services he was charged with leading took place in the homes of members of the church, the alleged disturbance was centered on the fact that singing could be heard on the street outside the house. Shilyuk received a sentence of three years.

Resisting a Militiaman: Article 191–1

Another charge that has often been related to the conduct of worship services is "resisting a militiaman or people's guard" (Article 191–1, RSFSR Criminal Code). If resistance is accompanied by violence or the threat of violence, it is punishable by a sentence of one to five years. This article has several times been used as justification for reportedly excessive force used by the militia in dispersing the worship services of unregistered churches: the militiamen allege that they meet with violent resistance. Andrei Yudintsev and Vladimir Timchuk faced this charge after a harvest festival service of the unregistered Baptist church in Khartsyzk, Ukraine, was dispersed in the autumn of 1982. Both were sentenced to 3½ years in labor camp.

A more recent case of "resistance" involved members of the unregistered Baptist church in Leningrad, who were meeting for a service in the woods on a Friday evening in October 1985. Soon after the service began, the militia arrived and ordered it to stop. When church leaders requested permission to conclude the service before dispersing, plainclothes policemen tried to arrest them, whereupon the believers abandoned their service. At the railway station, some of these same policemen allegedly attacked one of the young men from the church in an apparent attempt to provoke a fight, but without success. Nevertheless, one month later four church members, including the leader of the church, Vladimir Filippov, and his son Andrei—who was not even present at the service—were arrested and charged with instigating the "fight" at the station. They received sentences of from 2½ to four years of labor camp or forced labor.

Cases arising from other situations have also been prosecuted under this article. For instance, Andrei Zhuravel reportedly was arrested when he intervened as officials began to beat his father during an interview about the family's desire to emigrate for religious reasons; and seven members of an unregistered Pentecostal church in Chuguyevka, in the far east of Siberia, were arrested because of a demonstration at the district prosecutor's office following the arrest of their pastor, Viktor Walter.

Hooliganism: Article 205

A related but less specific offense than resisting the militia is "hooliganism" (Article 205, RSFSR Criminal Code). Vitali Varavin, a member of the unregistered Baptist church in Leningrad, was arrested on this charge for his alleged courtroom behavior at the trial of three leaders of the church in 1982. In the same month, near Chernovtsy, four believers were arrested and charged with hooliganism after the authorities discovered a meeting of the Baptist church to welcome back their pastor, Ivan Danilyuk, from his term of imprisonment. The meeting was being held in a private home when the leaders were requested by the militia to accompany them to the village *soviet*. They reportedly went in an orderly fashion, joined by the entire congregation, singing hymns as they walked. Yet as a result Danilyuk and three others were arrested for hooliganism. Danilyuk was sentenced to five years' strict-regime labor camp, two others were sentenced to three years' ordinary-regime camp, and one received a suspended sentence.

Prohibited Trade: Article 162

Because very little officially produced religious literature is available, Christians of some denominations engage in the unofficial production of pamphlets, journals, and even entire books. Seventh-Day Adventists, for example, have published a number of the works of the church's prophet Ellen G. White in this manner. In Lithuania, in 1985, a group of Catholics was caught printing religious pictures for sale in Catholic churches. In 1982, some Orthodox Christians in Moscow were arrested for reproducing the Bible, prayerbooks, and other Christian literature.

The most active have been the Baptists, who claim to have produced some one million items of literature on a network of portable clandestine presses. Thus far, authorities have discovered five of these presses while in operation, another in a house with books ready for binding—just after the printing team had left—and a seventh being transported by car.

Usually the printers have faced a combination of charges, including Articles 142, 227, and 190–1, but the basic charge has been Article 162 of the RSFSR Criminal Code, "engaging in a prohibited trade," with a maximum sentence of four years' imprisonment. The fact that believers claim no aspect of the enterprise generates any profit does not appear to be of any significance.

Parasitism: Article 209

While official churches and other religious bodies may employ full-time clergy, office staff, and caretakers, people involved in full-time religious work outside these categories are not officially recognized as being employed. Those who are unofficially supported by churches or religious groups run the risk of being charged with "parasitism" (Article 209 of the RSFSR Criminal Code) on the principle that if one is not gainfully employed, one must be living off others in a socially unproductive manner. This was the fate of Aleksandr Ogorodnikov, leader of the Christian Seminar (before he was charged with "anti-Soviet agitation and propaganda"), and of several Baptist pastors from the unregistered churches.

In 1984, the maximum sentence under Article 209 was raised from one to two years for a first offense and from two to three years for a second offense. One Baptist leader, Grigori Kostyuchenko, has served three consecutive sentences under this article.

Persecution Through Fabricated Legal Charges

All the above charges arise directly out of the defendants' religious activities, and the vast majority of religious prisoners of conscience have been imprisoned under one or more of the articles we have looked at. In some instances, however, there is very strong evidence that charges having nothing to do with religious activity have been fabricated in attempts to discredit believers both in their own communities and in Western eyes. Some of the cases of alleged hooliganism and violent resistance to the militia may fall partly into this category. Other such charges include drugs and weapons offenses, theft, embezzlement, rape, and attempted murder.

"Attempted Murder"

One of the most notorious of these cases was the 1961 trial of the Pentecostal preacher Ivan Fedotov near Moscow. During Khrushchev's 1959–64 anti-religious campaign, Fedotov was indicted on charges of attempted murder, an obvious propaganda exercise to support claims that Pentecostals kill people as sacrifices to God. Fedotov was arrested in an apparently staged incident—there was even a film crew on hand—in which the mother of a young girl pleaded with Fedotov not to force her to sacrifice her daughter. It was also alleged that a young woman who had been attending Fedotov's services and who committed suicide had been encouraged by Fedotov to do so in propitiation for her sins. A "documentary" film was made about Fedotov's group. Another film circulating at the same time showed a group of Pentecostals attempting to crucify a young girl, who was rescued at the last moment by brave Komsomol members. On such "evidence," Fedotov was sentenced to ten years' imprisonment. His lawyer was so outraged by the prosecution's case that he delivered a spirited defense, and after the fall of Khrushchev he even tried to have the case reopened on the grounds that it had been a propaganda exercise with no basis in fact.

Defense law in the Soviet Union is extremely ambiguous. In theory, the Soviet legal system prevents the innocent from being brought to trial. Thus, if the investigation has gathered enough evidence to prosecute, the defense lawyer is regarded as working against the cause of justice if he or she tries to prove the client's innocence. Indeed, who are lawyers to contest the judgments of responsible officials of the Soviet state? Even judges are most unwilling to reach a not-guilty verdict, preferring instead to refer a case back for further investigation if the evidence is unconvincing. Usually the best that a lawyer can do on behalf of the defendant is to plead extenuating circumstances—such as youth, change of heart, or cooperation with the investigating authorities. If a defense lawyer insists on the client's innocence, he or she is going far beyond the responsibilities of a Soviet attorney and staking his or her professional reputation and career on the issue.

Another well-documented case involved Seventh-Day Adventist Pyotr Raksha, accused in 1978 of trying to murder a militiaman and sentenced to six years' imprisonment. The Tashkent city court found him guilty despite claims that he was far away from the scene of the alleged incident on the night in question. Although the prosecution had produced documentation to refute Raksha's alibi that he had flown from Tashkent to Ukraine, the family, with the help of the defense lawyer, was able to secure original documentation from the Soviet airline Aeroflot proving that Raksha did in fact board flights from Tashkent to Kiev and back—this despite his absence from the passenger lists, from which, according to strong circumstantial evidence uncovered by his family, his name had been deleted at the instigation of the prosecution. In addition, sworn statements from independent witnesses testified that he had been present at a family funeral near Kiev, which had been the purpose of his trip. On appeal, the Uzbek supreme court acquitted Raksha, but the prosection promptly pressed fresh charges under the Uzbek equivalents of Articles 227 (infringement of citizens' rights through religious rituals) and 190–1 (slandering the state through fabrications). Since these charges can be brought against almost any active believer found to be in possession of information about persecution, the new case against him was "sound," and he was subsequently sentenced to three years' ordinary-regime camp.

"Embezzlement"

In two remarkably similar instances, the cases for prosecution on charges of embezzlement also came under critical scrutiny from the courts. In December 1977, Mikhail Yurkiv, a Pentecostal leader from Transcarpathian Ukraine, was arrested for embezzlement in connection with private contracts to supply timber to collective farms; essentially, he was accused of making excessive profits on the operation. In September 1978, Ivan Kirilyuk and three fellow Baptists were arrested in Kiev and charged with the same offense after delivering timber under contract from the forests of Karelia to collective farms in Moldavia.

Yurkiv was originally charged with embezzling 168,000 rubles; the regional court, in finding him guilty, reduced this sum to 68,000 rubles; the Ukrainian supreme court further reduced it to 44,000 rubles, and cut the sentence from thirteen to ten years. For the defense, however, each of the collective farm chairmen for whom Yurkiv had supplied timber testified that he had done the job well and with no irregularities. If he had earned large sums for himself and for those with whom he had contracted to accomplish the work, then it was evidently through efficiency and diligent effort.

In the parallel case, Ivan Kirilyuk and his friends were initially arrested on suspicion of involvement with clandestine printing operations. When no evidence could be found, the charge was changed to embezzlement. The four were then apparently approached with an offer to drop the charges if they would collaborate with the KGB; they refused, whereupon the case came to court three times. Two judges, after extensive hearings, sent the case back for further investigation, as the evidence presented was inadequate. The third judge passed sentences of up to twelve years, even though each of the collective farm officials involved spoke in defense of the accused. The defense lawyers who had declared the four innocent were publicly criticized by the third judge for "terrorizing the court." Subsequently, it was reported that two of the lawyers were expelled from the college of advocates for unprofessional behavior.

There have been a number of instances of alleged planting of drugs, and one in which a gun was "discovered" during a house search. The description of the circumstances by the accused and the character references of friends give strong grounds for doubting the veracity of the charges.

Upgrading Minor Offenses

In a few cases the authorities seem to have pressed charges because those allegedly involved in minor offenses were Christians. Student Sergei Yermolayev was arrested after he had shouted out in high spirits, "Down with Communism!"—admittedly an unwise thing to do in Soviet society. He was sentenced to a few days' imprisonment. When someone in the judicial system realized that Yermolayev was a member of the Christian Seminar, he was charged with hooliganism and transferred to investigation prison, subsequently being sentenced to four years in a labor camp.

Another Seminar member, Tatyana Shchipkova, slapped a plainclothes policeman in the face when he allegedly twisted her arm and tried to tear a notebook out of her hand during a raid on a meeting of the Seminar. Subsequently, she was charged with hooliganism under part one of Article 209, which relates to minor incidents. As the prosecution failed to bring the case to court within the required six-month time limit for minor offenses, the charge was changed to the more serious part two of Article 209, in order, one may speculate, not to lose the opportunity to imprison a member of the Seminar. Under this charge, Shchipkova was sentenced to three years' ordinary-regime camp.

The case of Sergei Timokhin and Valeri Barinov, sentenced respectively to two years' and 2½ years' labor camp for allegedly attempting to cross the Soviet frontier illegally, can be viewed in the same light. The two men admitted they had planned to cross the frontier to Finland but claimed they had given up their plan and were returning home when arrested. Since neither had even entered the "restricted zone," which stretches for one hundred miles inside the frontier, it would seem rather difficult to substantiate the claim that either had actually attempted to leave the country. Some of those close to the situation believe that the charges were pressed primarily because the authorities were eager to arrest Timokhin and Barinov for leading a gospel rock group. Indeed, much of the trial concentrated on their religious activities, which were said to have led to their "criminal act."[3]

Detention in Psychiatric Hospitals

In some situations, religious dissent or "fervor" is said to result from a psychological dysfunction requiring "treatment," and one form of imprisonment is detention and treatment in psychiatric hospitals. Religious believers held in such hospitals are usually sent as a result of a court decision on the basis of a psychiatric examination requested by the prosecution during a criminal case. Detention is for an indefinite period of time, which may be either shorter or longer than the period of imprisonment prescribed for the alleged offense. Most prisoners so confined are in Special Psychiatric Hospitals, institutions that until 1988 were within the prison system. Many of the prisoners in these hospitals are violently deranged, and conditions are said to be often very grim.

In addition, some believers have been referred directly to ordinary psychiatric hospitals by the militia. Although such persons usually remain hospitalized only for short periods of time, they may sometimes become long-term patients. Anatoli Ponomaryov, for example, was taken to a psychiatric hospital in Leningrad for the fifth time in December 1978 and was released only in 1986. There are many reports of the use of unnecessary and damaging drug therapies on believers detained in psychiatric hospitals. A great deal of evidence detailing the abuse of psychiatry in the USSR was collected in the 1970s,[4] leading in part to the withdrawal of the Soviet Union from the World Psychiatric Association.

"Malicious Disobedience"

In the early 1980s an increasing number of religious prisoners were rearrested in prison or labor camps, charged with new offenses, and sentenced to supplementary terms of imprisonment. Most commonly, the new charges were under Article 190–1 in connection with complaints about the conditions of imprisonment; a prisoner might be charged anew simply for explaining to fellow prisoners why he was arrested.

In 1983 a new crime was added to the RSFSR Criminal Code: Article 188–3, "malicious disobedience," "proven" by repeated punishments for violation of camp or prison regulations, which prisoners allege are often arbitrarily interpreted by camp personnel. The advantage of this offense, from the prosecution's standpoint, is that the testimony of camp and prison officials is sufficient to secure a conviction; it is virtually impossible for there to be any defense witnesses. A number of Christian prisoners have been given supplementary sentences under this article. In one instance, money (which prisoners are not allowed in camp) was apparently planted in the shoe of Baptist pastor Mikhail Khorev while he was taking a bath; the money was discovered during a "random" search immediately thereafter. In another case, Vladimir Poresh broke prison regulations simply by coming to the aid of another prisoner. (After serving part of his additional sentence, Poresh was released on a legal technicality.)

Trends Under Gorbachev

Under the leadership of Mikhail Gorbachev the Soviet authorities have attempted to reduce the overall prison and labor-camp population, especially of those imprisoned on political or religious grounds. During 1987–88 the number of religious prisoners known to Keston College decreased by more than 50 per cent. The reduction was made through (1) a pardon extended to political prisoners in the spring of 1987 followed by (2) an amnesty, to mark the seventieth anniversary of the 1917 revolution. Under the amnesty some prisoners (mostly women and pensioners) were released outright, while others had their remaining sentence cut by as much as half. Many were transferred from labor camp to compulsory labor.

During this period very few new religious prisoners entered the system; most of those reported are conscientious objectors to military service. The Criminal Codes are under review; it has been suggested that some offenses, such as those covered in Articles 142 and 190–1, could be abolished, and others, such as those in Articles 227 and 70, more narrowly defined. There has also been a suggestion that conscientious objection on religious grounds could be recognized and a form of alternative service introduced. If these changes do indeed occur, the number of religious prisoners could remain low.

Persecution Through Administrative Sanctions

The legislation on religious "cults" is enforced not only by criminal law (Article 142 of the RSFSR Criminal Code) but also by administrative law, as defined by the March 18, 1966, ruling of the RSFSR Supreme Soviet Presidium, and analogous rulings by the presidiums of the other republics.

1. *Fines*. Under the RSFSR ruling, refusing to register a congregation, or organizing services or processions in violation of the rules laid down by the legislation, or conducting children's meetings or other activities not directly connected with worship as strictly defined, may be punished by a fine of up to fifty rubles imposed by the administrative commission of the local *soviet*. For the average worker, this is about a week's wage.

The distinction between criminal and administrative responsibility for violations of the legislation on religion is a fine one; there is often overlap. Refusal to register is an administrative offense, while *incitement* of others to refuse registration is a criminal offense under Article 142. Leading one service is an administrative offense, but repeatedly leading services is a criminal offense.

2. *Administrative Arrest*. In this second form of administrative sanction commonly applied to religious believers, a sentence of up to fifteen days is imposed by the judge of a local court, without any legal representation and without the two "people's assessors" who substitute for a jury in criminal cases. This sanction is employed for only two offenses: petty hooliganism, and disobedience to the militia. Anyone who refuses to disperse when the militia interrupts a church service is liable to arrest for an act of disobedience, though it is often only the leaders who try to continue the services who are sentenced.

The use of either of these administrative sanctions, fines or administrative arrest, can put considerable economic pressure on individual families and on a congregation as a whole. The two weeks' term in prison means not only the loss of wages but also, often, the loss of any bonus for productivity. A consistent campaign of raids against services by the authorities can quickly cost congregational members large sums in fines as well as substantial loss of income.

During the first half of 1974, Ivan Fedotov, then pastor of an unregistered Pentecostal church in Maloyaroslavets, was fined a total of 450 rubles, while other members of the church together paid fines totaling more than 2,000 rubles. On a single day in 1981, twelve of Fedotov's church members were fined 50 rubles each. Fedotov was then arrested for the fourth time in April 1981. One of the most thoroughly documented cases is that of the Pentecostal church in Chuguyevka, located in the far east of Siberia. Between June 1981 and February 1983, members paid 1,315 rubles in fines, had 483 rubles deducted from wages, and were detained for 130 days with an estimated loss of earnings of 1,180 rubles; the total loss amounted to nearly 3,000 rubles.

3. *Surveillance*. Another form of pressure applied without full judicial procedure is administrative surveillance of released prisoners, which is imposed either on the recommendation of the labor-camp administration or by the local militia. The measure usually places an evening and night curfew on the ex-prisoner and limits freedom of movement to the home city; even certain districts of the city may be placed out of bounds. The ex-prisoner must report regularly to the militia and ask permission before traveling beyond the established limits. Repeated violations of the restrictions can lead to imprisonment for up to two years.

Until a few years ago, administrative surveillance was usually applied to prisoners convicted of "crimes against the state" (including "anti-Soviet agitation and propaganda"). Recently, however, several Baptists have been placed under surveillance, apparently in an attempt to hinder their ministries. Galina Vilchinskaya, who traveled widely after completing her first camp sentence, was—upon release from her second sentence—placed under one year's surveillance and restricted to her home in Brest; she was, however, permitted to marry in Novokuznetsk and reside there with her husband, although the surveillance was extended there for an additional six months. Pavel Rytikov, an itinerant evangelist, was placed under surveillance upon completion of a two-year sentence in April 1985. After several official warnings, however, Rytikov decided to continue his ministry in hiding. He was arrested in January 1986 while traveling by train in Siberia and was sentenced to 1½ years for violating his surveillance.

4. *Confiscation.* An additional administrative measure is the confiscation of personal property, included as a supplementary penalty under some articles of the Criminal Code. Of particular relevance to believers is the exercise of this sanction under Article 227 ("infringement of the person and rights of citizens under the guise of performing religious rituals"). If a prisoner sentenced to confiscation of property owns his family's home, it can be expropriated by the authorities, although alternative accommodation must be offered. This occurred in the case of Vladimir Protsenko, in whose home the unregistered Baptist church in Leningrad had met for several years. If the family home is held in joint ownership or belongs to another member of the family, however, the furniture and other belongings may be confiscated, as happened with the possessions of unregistered Baptist leader Georgi Vins in 1975 when he was sentenced under the article corresponding to 227 in the Ukrainian code.

Property used in the execution of a crime may be subject to confiscation under any article of the criminal codes. Two brothers, Aleksandr and Nikolai Chekh, were arrested in March 1979 while transporting 1,330 copies of a clandestine Baptist publication in their car, whereupon they were given eleven-month suspended sentences for "dissemination of deliberately false fabrications slandering the Soviet state and social system" (Article 187–1, Ukrainian Criminal Code). Their car was confiscated. In other instances, the confiscation of property may take place if officials rule that the property is itself illegal or that it is being used illegally. Christian literature is regularly confiscated during searches of believers' homes, and believers complain that it is rarely returned, even if it has been published officially in the USSR and the contents can in no way be construed as anti-Soviet.

Illegal and Extra-Legal Measures

All the forms of persecution discussed so far have some kind of legal basis, even though the laws may be unjust and the application of them biased or dishonest. In addition to these, a wide range of illegal or extra-legal measures are used against religious believers. These fall into two broad categories: intimidation and victimization, and discrimination.

Intimidation and Victimization

Religious believers along with human-rights activists allege various forms of intimidation. The most obvious examples are interviews with branches of Soviet officialdom, ranging from local administrators to officers of the KGB. Such an interview may take the form of an official warning that the person has been doing something that is considered to violate Soviet law and faces prosecution if he does not stop. Other types of informal and off-the-record interviews are also intended to prevent activities considered unacceptable. Sometimes believers are secretly asked to become KGB informers or collaborators: many Orthodox and Catholic seminary students in particular face this kind of pressure.

Surveillance or "tailing" by the KGB is often used to intimidate rather than to gather information. Vladimir Poresh said that on a visit to Moscow three years before his arrest he was tailed by a KGB agent for an evening and the following morning.[5] Then several more KGB officers joined the first and quite openly followed Poresh wherever he went. Poresh reported that when he spoke to the men they responded with threats, and the next morning they roughed him up. They left him after he had purchased a train ticket for home.

Of course, covert surveillance for gathering information also takes place. The family of unregistered Baptist leader Gennadi Kryuchkov, who has been working in hiding since 1970, discovered a bugging device hidden in their electricity meter. The family of another leader in hiding reported that the militia always showed up when family members greeted by name a visitor with the same first name as the missing father.

Various ruses have been used for planting a bugging device. Daniil Frolov, an Adventist from Alma-Ata, was summoned to the offices of the militia in March 1980. After being taken to one room, where he was asked to hang up his hat and coat, he was called into another room and threatened with confiscation of his car if he did not stop using it to transport illegal literature. After a while he was given another appointment three days later and allowed to leave. Then he began to notice that wherever he went he was tailed, and that each tail had a radio receiver. After a search, he and his wife found a microphone and transmitter buried deep in his fur hat.

Threats of arrest or reprisals, while they may not be carried out and may seem unlikely, are another means of intimidation. Before the 1980 Olympic Games, for example, Moscow Baptists from the unregistered church reportedly were told that they would be sent away from Moscow for the duration of the games. Since a clampdown on dissident activity had already begun, this threat probably did not seem empty, though it was never carried out. Even exaggerated threats may leave believers with a disturbing fear that the authorities might take any opportunity to begin criminal proceedings or implement a more outright persecution. Pentecostals seeking to emigrate report that KGB officers have said they would shoot the entire church community as traitors if it were in their power; others have reportedly threatened to send the believers to the Arctic as targets for nuclear missile testing.

While threats such as these seem far-fetched, many believers will indeed know of assaults on fellow Christians and attacks on property that have gone uninvestigated and unpunished. Attacks on property range from stones thrown through windows to arson, and even registered churches may find little sympathy from the militia when they are victims of vandalism. The family of Aleksandr Balak, a Pentecostal seeking to emigrate, claim to have been attacked by neighbors while in their own backyard. One of the children was badly beaten up returning home from school. Indeed, Christian children have many times been attacked at school by fellow pupils, especially after atheistic lecturers have denounced the activities of local churches. Prisoners' children can be particularly vulnerable: in March 1978 the eldest son of Baptist prisoner Viktor Dubovik was beaten unconscious and taken to the hospital after a lecture at school in which his family was mentioned.

Some assaults have very serious consequences. Baptist soldier Nikolai Kravchenko was hospitalized with a broken jaw after a reportedly unprovoked attack by a corporal; with his jaw permanently damaged, he was eventually pronounced unfit for further military service. Other soldiers have been murdered, and in at least one case this appears to have been done with the clear connivance of an officer. Often, however, it is impossible to establish the full circumstances surrounding such a crime, and there are indications of a cover-up—as with the death of Ivan Moiseyev, whose experiences in the army in the period before his death are extensively documented. Civilians too have died in unexplained circumstances, some with at least circumstantial evidence of official involvement. The seventeen-year-old Baptist Nikolai Loiko was shot in the back by a militiaman at a youth rally in May 1974. Although he recovered completely, he missed probable death by inches.

Discrimination

Only a very small minority of believers are subjected to victimization. Various forms of discrimination, however, affect the vast majority of actively religious people, causing many to feel they are second-class citizens. While discrimination is often hard to prove, some striking examples are available that believers claim are symptomatic of a pervasive problem, especially in education and employment.

Religious believers are often expelled from institutions of higher education and even more frequently denied admission; a school report indicating that a pupil is a believer is usually sufficient to block entry to further education. Mathematicians Valeri Senderov and Boris Kanevsky compared the results of the Moscow University Mathematics Faculty entrance examinations with the actual admissions and found clear evidence of discrimination against Jews (whether they were religious or not seemed immaterial). One young Baptist, Anatoli Germanyuk, was prevented from taking his secondary-school graduation exams because he received a failing mark for conduct after he was detained by the militia at a service of an unregistered church. His written reference from school also referred to this incident and drew attention to his "clear religious views and convictions." According to others, his academic standing was quite good. But, unable to take his graduation exam, Germanyuk had no hope of further education, and his educational reference was likely to make it difficult to find meaningful work.

Students who do not disguise their religious convictions often have problems passing "scientific atheism," a compulsory subject in most university programs. Lyuba Oleinik, a Baptist medical student, was failed when she admitted at her oral examination that she was a believer, even though she claims to have had a good theoretical knowledge of atheism. Following protests she was readmitted to her course; others have not been so fortunate in protesting their expulsions.

Naturally, discrimination in education affects work opportunities. Aside from this, believers often have difficulty finding work commensurate with their qualifications. Many senior positions are *de facto* reserved for Communist Party members, though Gorbachev has pressed to have appointments made on the basis of ability alone. In addition, believers report that it is nearly inconceivable for Christians—if their beliefs are known—to be allowed to teach in schools, colleges, or universities; teachers who become believers are likely to be dismissed.

Tatyana Shchipkova, who taught Latin for seventeen years at Smolensk Pedagogical Institute, became a Christian and took part in the Christian Seminar led by Aleksandr Ogorodnikov and Vladimir Poresh, one of her ex-students. When the authorities learned of her participation in the Seminar, her home was searched, she was dismissed from her teaching post, and she later was stripped of her master's degree. Another academic who became a Christian, Vyacheslav Zaitsev, wrote two doctoral dissertations but was not allowed to present either of them, reportedly because of his pronounced religious views. When he was finally baptized as an Orthodox Christian, he was removed from the Institute of Literature of the Byelorussian Academy of Sciences.

Dismissal from work appears to be the experience of Christians in quite ordinary employment as well. Vladimir Markov, a Christian for thirty years, had by 1982 lost his job twenty-seven times and was again facing the threat of dismissal. No doubt his experience is exceptional; still, many others have lost their jobs upon becoming Christians, or once their Christian sympathies are discovered. A secondary-school graduate, Galina Mashnitskaya, who had taken a two-year vocational course as secretary/typist, was fired seven times in four months—on various pretexts—as soon as her employers discovered she was a Baptist. When her mother asked the public prosecutor's office about the legality of this, she reports being told unofficially that a Christian could not be employed as a typist and that her daughter should seek some other kind of employment. Eventually, however, she managed to keep a job as a typist.

Within such a centralized society as the Soviet Union, there are innumerable bureaucratic opportunities to make life difficult for known believers, both individually and as congregations. Registered churches may encounter difficulties when they wish to acquire or adapt buildings for use as places of worship. A newly registered Baptist church in the Bezhitsa suburb of Bryansk faced a series of obstacles before finding a house that the local authorities would allow the congregation to buy. Then, when the church members had nearly finished a total remodeling of the building, the authorities informed them that their purchase contract was illegal. The building was confiscated and demolished.

Two independently registered Baptist churches had such problems with the authorities that they renounced their registered status. When one of them, in the Peresyp district of Odessa, asked to hold an extra service on May 2, 1979, a public holiday, the city's Council for Religious Affairs was unwilling to grant permission, finally allowing it for a maximum length of two hours. On the appointed day, as the two hours were coming to an end, according to the believers' account of events, an official interrupted the service to announce through a portable voice amplifier that only a few minutes remained. As soon as the allotted time was up, he allegedly called in the militia to disperse the congregation. In the second case, in Dedovsk, near Moscow, local authorities often harassed the congregation for continuing to meet in private homes while negotiating the purchase of a church building.

A Catholic pilgrimage in Lithuania is likely to face a whole battery of obstacles, including the suspension of public transportation and road-blocks to prevent people from joining local pilgrims. Many Orthodox pilgrimages are also said to have been suppressed by these tactics. The main service of the Orthodox year, the Easter-night liturgy, is commonly blockaded at numerous churches and cathedrals, with the apparent intention of preventing access by young people.

While high-profile forms of persecution—imprisonment and detention in psychiatric hospitals—have been reduced considerably under Gorbachev, many other repressive measures are still being applied. Unregistered churches report no decline in the dispersal of worship services, fines, and administrative arrests. Some buildings used for worship have been demolished or confiscated. Discrimination, whose extent is always difficult to measure, may have been reduced but does not seem to have been totally eliminated.

Persecution and the Soviet System

With the vast amount of evidence now available in the West, few outside observers would claim that there is no religious persecution in the USSR. Soviet authorities themselves, while denying that anyone is imprisoned for religious *convictions*, admit that some believers are imprisoned for religious *activities* that violate Soviet laws regulating religious communities. The authorities describe this, of course, as the prosecution of lawbreakers rather than the persecution of believers.

Two Views: An Aberration, An Extreme

In response, some Western commentators believe that to focus on persecution is to give a distorted view of the religious picture in the Soviet Union. Such observers usually perceive persecution in one of two ways—as an aberration, or as an extreme on a spectrum. The aberration view is that persecution results from both misunderstandings by local officials and the unreasonable attitudes of some believers. The view of persecution as an extreme in a widely varying situation points to the size as well as the ethnic and religious diversity of the USSR and the likelihood that local officials will implement policy in differing ways. According to either view, however, only an untypical minority is adversely affected. Overall there is more freedom within the country than most people think, and believers should secure and build on that freedom in the hope that persecution will recede.

Undoubtedly, there is evidence to support these views. Even official statements from the Soviet government sometimes refer to difficulties that can arise, claiming that these can usually be settled amicably. A feature in the government newspaper *Izvestia* illustrates this approach. In the article, the assistant church warden of the Orthodox cathedral in Pskov said that when she worked in a factory, someone raised the subject of her religious beliefs. The circumstances are not explained further in the article, but clearly the point at issue was whether a religious person could be entrusted with some responsibility or possibly even employed at all. In this instance, according to the article, the constitutional freedom of conscience was explained to the person who had raised the question, and there were no adverse consequences. Two Baptists also spoke to *Izvestia* correspondents about local difficulties (again, their precise nature was not revealed) but said that local representatives of the Council for Religious Affairs (CRA) had been able to resolve the problems. The chairman of the CRA, Konstantin Kharchev, in commenting on the article, said the problems that arise generally happen because local officials or clergy do not understand the provisions of Soviet law; some believers, however, persist in willfully breaking the law, he said, and they must expect to face the consequences.

Indeed, there are instances of intervention by staff members of the CRA or other government agencies to modify local decisions regarding religious believers individually and in community. In some cases, discrimination in employment against believers was exposed and the believers reinstated. *Samizdat* sources confirm cases in which central or local CRA representatives have, for example, overruled the opposition of local government officials to the registration of new evangelical churches. Here one might conclude that central policy favored the registration of independent congregations as a means of bringing them under some kind of control, and this course was imposed on local authorities.

Changes in policy have also on occasion brought relief to religious prisoners. After Khrushchev fell from power (as after Stalin's death eleven years earlier), cases against many Baptists were reviewed, and many prisoners were either declared innocent or given reduced sentences. Some Pentecostals who had been sentenced to camp followed by exile found upon their release that they were not required to serve the period of exile. In 1976, at a time when independent Baptists were being encouraged to register their congregations, many Baptist prisoners were released before the end of their sentences, with the remaining period suspended. (One prisoner who was subsequently rearrested, however, had one year of this suspended sentence added to his new sentence.)

The treatment of individual believers and religious communities is by no means uniform throughout the country. In Turkmenistan, with more than two million Muslims, there are only four mosques. In the Sverdlovsk region of western Siberia in 1976, there were reported to be no registered Baptist churches at all, though there were unregistered congregations willing to accept registration within the officially recognized union. In parts of Siberia, even Orthodox churches are hundreds of miles apart, and so most believers cannot attend church regularly. Other regions have a much more abundant supply of churches. Some Ukrainian cities have as many as six Baptist churches operating legally. Moscow has some fifty churches, mostly Orthodox; the Danilovsky Monastery in the city was returned to the Russian Orthodox Church, and a small monastic community has been revived there. In Estonia, where some church communities are very lively, few believers are arrested for religious activity, while in other republics even small congregations have reportedly been subject to substantial onslaughts. Some churches conduct youth activities and even Sunday schools without penalty from the authorities, while church leaders from other areas have been arrested on charges related to their work with youth and children.

Certainly the Baptist and Orthodox churches have found their situations improved since the fall of Khrushchev, who did great damage to both. At least since the mid-seventies, the Baptists have opened some fifty new churches each year; since 1969 they also have had a Bible correspondence course to train pastors and preachers, though only a small proportion of their thousands of ordained and lay leaders have benefited. While a certain number of Bibles, New Testaments, and hymnals can be produced regularly, the churches would easily be able to distribute far larger quantities. The Orthodox Church has also made significant gains in theological training: although the five seminaries closed under Khrushchev have not been reopened, the number of students at the three existing seminaries has doubled, and a correspondence course has been established to train priests who have not had any theological education.

Yet between 1979 and 1986, persecution for some intensified. The number of known religious prisoners doubled. Vast sums were collected in fines, and Christians worked hundreds of thousands of hours of free labor in ten- to fifteen-day administrative sentences. Religious people were identified publicly as being particularly receptive to external anti-Communist propaganda, the implication being that any believer is potentially subversive and under foreign influence.

The contrasts are endless and confusing: on the one hand, evidence of some strident persecution; on the other, the appearance of normal church life in certain areas. Probably the average congregation and the average believer live between these extremes, surviving without a great number of problems.

A Third View: A Pyramid

The view that religious persecution and discrimination are aberrations and the view that they are at one extreme on a spectrum of responses are fundamentally optimistic: progress in religious tolerance will result in an end to aberrations and a reduction of extremes as society settles on a middle course.

The monolithic structure of the USSR and the totalitarian aspirations of its rulers, however, suggest another possibility: that the entire range of treatment of religion and religious believers represents a cohesive policy. In this view, the situation is seen not as a spectrum, with apparently unconnected occurrences at each end, but as a pyramid. The peak of the pyramid is small: relatively few people experience the most severe forms of persecution, such as imprisonment and serious assaults. At a lower level, more people are affected by lesser forms of persecution, such as administrative detention, fines, and harassment. Further down the pyramid are the countless believers who have experienced direct discrimination at school, in higher education and in employment. Finally, at the base of the pyramid are millions of believers who may not have been victims of specific incidents of persecution or discrimination, but who nevertheless are conscious of being second-class citizens. The pyramid view seems to integrate the experiences of the persecuted minority with those of the majority who appear to lead normal lives. The differences in experience, then, are of degree rather than of kind.

The pyramid view suggests two possible insights into Soviet policy. First, that the extremes of treatment are aspects of a single "carrot and stick" policy. Soviet legislation on religion has a dual purpose: to control religion and to limit its influence. Registration, under which a religious congregation agrees to work within the limitations laid down by the legislation, is a key aspect of this policy. For evangelical congregations, which in recent years have borne the brunt of persecution, the "carrot" means that conditions for registration have been substantially improved over the last twenty years, while the "stick" involves the active persecution of those who persist in their refusal to register. Allowing a prominent Westerner such as Billy Graham to preach in major Baptist churches is a carrot; the "damage" such a person can cause by his presence and preaching is outweighed, in the state's view, by the credibility that he lends to the registered churches as the state struggles to bring evangelical Christianity under control. In other churches, too, the crushing of dissent has often been accompanied by measures to alleviate some of the difficulties under which the churches have labored.

A second possible insight into Soviet policy stemming from the pyramid view is that in the present relatively stable conditions of Soviet society, the more extreme forms of persecution need to be used in only a relatively few cases in order to exemplify for the rest of the religious community the dangers of "irresponsible behavior." A more severe persecution is applied as "necessary."

The persecution of religious believers in the USSR can be interpreted in several ways, depending upon one's understanding of the broader context of Soviet society and Soviet policy. One thing is clear: persecution exists, in many different forms, in varying degrees, affecting religious groups to differing extents. No denomination or congregation, registered or not, is totally exempt from persecution and discrimination.

7

Buddhism

Hans Bräker

THE FOURTEENTH Dalai Lama visited the Soviet Union in September 1982 at the invitation of the leader of Buddhism in the USSR, the Bandido Chambo Lama. After two days in Moscow he visited the Involginskij Datsan (monastery), the center of the Buddhist religious community. From there he went to the Mongolian People's Republic and then set out on an extended journey through Spain, France, Italy, and West Germany before returning to the northern Indian Himalayan village of Dharamsala, where he has lived since his spectacular escape from Tibet in 1959.

The Dalai Lama's stay in the Soviet Union was particularly notable in several respects. In contrast to his first visit, in 1979, this time he was officially received not only by Patriarch Pimen, head of the Russian Orthodox Church, but also in the government's Council for Religious Affairs, which regulates religious life in the Soviet Union. The visit was officially reported by Tass, the government news agency:

> To honor the esteemed guest, Pimen, the Patriarch of Moscow and All Russia, gave a banquet at which speeches were exchanged. In his welcoming speech Patriarch Pimen said that he "valued the personal contribution of the Dalai Lama toward educating people in the spirit of love and peace. . . ." In the afternoon the Dalai Lama

---

Hans Bräker, formerly deputy director of the Federal Institute for East European and International Studies, Cologne, West Germany, is professor of international politics at the University of Trier. He has written widely on Islam and Buddhism.

met with the Council for Religious Affairs. On Tuesday the guest and his entourage will go sightseeing in the capital before flying on to Ulan-Ude in the evening.

Although a spokesman for the Dalai Lama had said before the trip that the aims were strictly religious and cultural, observers in the Soviet capital ascribed some political significance to the visit of the spiritual and political leader of the Tibetan people. They believed the Dalai Lama was attempting to strengthen his bargaining position with the Chinese government, which for several years had been offering many concessions to induce him to return to Tibet from exile.

At Soviet peace and disarmament congresses in which religious leaders participate, the persecution of Buddhists in China and the devastation of Tibet during the Cultural Revolution have been openly and repeatedly criticized. The magazine *Buddhists for Peace*, printed in Mongolia and distributed in the Soviet Union, stated that "Tibet was the first victim of China's hegemony. China's goal of annihilating Buddhism and the Buddhist cultural tradition in Tibet resulted in the genocide of approximately one million Tibetan Buddhists."[1] Such comments are usually linked to the demand for the "liberation of Tibet" and the return of the 80,000–100,000 Tibetans who followed the Dalai Lama into exile in India.

A Radio Beijing commentary on the Dalai Lama's visit said: "Observers wonder what the Soviet Union has in mind when its authorities for religious affairs invite the Dalai Lama to pay it a visit and its government welcomes him as an official guest" (September 15, 1982).

The visit drew attention to ethnic Buddhist minorities in the Soviet Union, whose problems have been little noticed in the West. Islam, another "foreign religion" in the Soviet Union, enjoys much wider recognition as a result of events in the Middle East and Asia.

How Many?

The exact number of practicing Buddhists in the Soviet Union is unknown since Soviet statistics contain no information about religious affiliation. Three ethnic minorities have traditionally professed Buddhism: (1) The Buryat Mongols, largest of the three groups, in the Buryat ASSR (Autonomous Soviet Socialist Republic), above northeast Mongolia. (2) The Tuvinians in the Tuvinian ASSR, above northwest Mongolia. The region was made a Russian protectorate in 1914, became the Tuvinian People's Republic—popularly called Tannu-Tuva—in 1921, and was annexed by the Soviet Union in 1944. (3) The Kalmyks, in the Kalmyk ASSR, along the Volga, northwest of the Caspian Sea. In 1943 the Kalmyks, together with the Crimean Tatars and Volga Germans, were deported to Siberia as "unreliable" because of their alleged collaboration with the German *Wehrmacht*. Not until 1957 were those who survived allowed to return to their homeland. (There are also some Buddhists in Ordynsk Buryat National Okrug and in Aginskij Buryat National Okrug [the administrative divisions called okrugs are sparsely settled ethnic minority areas].) As of January 1981 these three ASSRs had a combined population of 1.5 million. The ethnic Buddhists in this population number about 666,000—353,000 Buryats, 166,000 Tuvinians, and 147,000 Kalmyks.

These figures, however, reveal little about the actual significance of Buddhism in the Soviet Union. Even if all these 666,000 ethnic Buddhists were practicing believers, which is very unlikely, they would constitute a very small minority of the total USSR population (226.5 million in 1981) and the universal community of Buddhism, estimated at 400–500 million exclusive of the Buddhists in China.

Development of Russian Buddhism

The Buddhist community in the Soviet Union can be historically classified with the Tibetan branch of Buddhism, Mahayana Lamaism, which gained a foothold in Mongolia in the sixteenth and seventeenth centuries and then toward the end of the seventeenth century was spread by monks to the Buryats, Kalmyks, and Tuvinians. Buddhism was originally an ethical atheistic system that developed into a kind of theistic religion in its Mahayana Lamaistic expression. All schools of Buddhism demand renunciation of here-and-now-oriented, "worldly" life and action. Buddhism is a religion of withdrawal from the world, of social and political passivity.

Because of this, Buddhism, unlike Islam, has never been viewed by the Soviet leadership as a political challenge. Yet Buddhism has always been a difficult problem for the Soviet state and party leadership.

In 1728 Lamaism was recognized as a "permitted" religion in the Russian Empire. At its head has stood, since 1764, an elected leader, the Bandido Chambo Lama. Like the Dalai Lama in Tibet, the Bandido Chambo Lama is responsible for not only the political administration but also the spiritual guidance of the Buddhist religious community. Prior to the 1917 Revolution, the Bandido Chambo Lama was confirmed in this position by the imperial governor. His subordinate lamas (monks) had substantial privileges and stood under the protection of civil law.

Lamaistic Modernism: Doržiev

The encounter with Christianity and other Western thought systems made possible by Russia's 1905 Edict of Toleration resulted in the development of a movement in Buddhism generally called Lamaistic modernism. Comparable change did not occur in Lamaistic Buddhism in Tibet until the confrontation with Chinese Communism in 1949.

Lamaistic modernism in Russia was closely linked to Lama Agvan Doržiev, leader of the Buryat clergy, born in 1853. Educated in Tibet, Doržiev became a friend and advisor of the thirteenth Dalai Lama in Lhasa, the Tibetan capital. In 1901 he was granted an audience with the tsar, whose inclination for the mysticism of the Orient was known. Doržiev suggested to the tsar that Russia should declare itself the liberator of Asia and defender of Buddhism, then mount a campaign southward over the Himalayas to "liberate the oppressed peoples."[2]

After the October Revolution, Doržiev tried to develop Lamaistic modernism further by teaching the compatibility of Buddhism with Communism. The point of departure for this could only have been, of course, the atheism of Buddhist doctrine. Leading Russian Orientalists joined in the effort to develop a modern version of Buddhism acceptable for the Soviet Union. For them, as for Lamaism itself, it was a matter of survival.

The new Soviet leadership took advantage of Buddhist modernism and vigorously attempted to associate Soviet authority with the messianic expectations of the Lamaistic world. The first edition of the *Great Soviet Encyclopedia*, in a volume published in 1927, characterized Buddhism as a kind of declaration of the rights of mankind, and of the rights of the citizens in the East. This interpretation derived not from any sympathy with Buddhism but from hard-headed political pragmatism. In the interest of internal consolidation of power, the new Bolshevik leadership had to avoid all conflict with non-Marxist spiritual or religious forces.

The 1918 Decree

But this pragmatic policy did not correspond to actual ideological and political objectives of the Soviet leaders. In January 1918, soon after the October Revolution, they passed the Decree on the Separation of Church From State and of School From Church, its aim being, for all practical purposes, destruction of the institutional framework of religion in the Soviet Union. For Buddhism, the monastery is of central importance. The religious practice of the Buddhist laity as well as the lamas is centered in the monastery. When this institution was suppressed, Buddhism was deprived of its main foundation.

The 1918 decree was very cautiously applied until the end of the 1920s, and for a time the Soviet leaders had to accept a marked revival of Buddhist religious life. The number of lamas increased substantially. The monastic educational system blossomed. Even the Young Communist movement of Central Asia recruited its cadres from monastery schools. According to the *Great Soviet Encyclopedia* (first edition), in 1916 there were 34 monasteries with 15,000 lamas in Buryat Mongolia; by 1923 some new monasteries had been founded (the number is not known), and the number of lamas had risen to about 16,000. In 1928 there were still 73 monastic schools alongside 119 government schools.[3] In the region of the Kalmyks there were 70 monasteries and 1,600 lamas in 1916; by 1923 the number of lamas had increased to 2,840. In Tannu-Tuva, Lamaism was able to develop relatively undisturbed until 1929. At that time there were 22 monasteries and approximately 2,000 lamas in a population of 60,000.

At the height of this development, in the winter of 1926–27, a congress of Soviet Buddhists took place in Buryat Mongolia under the direction of Doržiev. It gained a quasi-international status through the participation of numerous Buddhists from other central and east Asian countries and was therefore instrumental in disseminating the thesis of the compatibility of Buddhism and Communism. The message of allegiance that the congress sent to the Dalai Lama in Lhasa, however, must have provocatively demonstrated to the party and state leadership the dangerous internationalist orientation of Buddhism in the Soviet Union.[4]

1929–44: Attack on Buddhism

The consolidation of Soviet power and Stalin's seizure of leadership led to a radical change in Soviet religious policy. The Law on Religious Associations of April 1929 led to the nearly complete annihilation of Buddhist practices in the Soviet Union by the second half of the 1930s.

To begin with, anti-Buddhist articles appeared in the party press. The ideas that Marxism-Leninism and Buddhism were compatible and that, because of its atheism, Buddhism had a special position among the religions of the Soviet Union were labeled dangerous heresies. In the second edition of the *Great Soviet Encyclopedia*, Buddhism is seen as nothing more than an instrument created by the feudal masters to exploit the working masses.

In 1929 a branch of the League of Militant Godless was organized in Buryat Mongolia. Its mission was to eradicate religious consciousness through ideological influence, i.e., atheistic propaganda. This policy was totally ineffectual, however, because many Buddhists, considering themselves atheists, joined the League. Party and state confronted them with the argument that Buddhist atheism was not related to the militant atheism that is based on the Marxist-materialist understanding of the laws of nature and society.

As ideological tactics against Buddhism proved ineffective, administrative steps were taken. High taxes were imposed upon the monasteries supported by the populace. In 1929 numerous monasteries were forcibly closed, and many lamas were arrested and sent into exile. According to the *Great Soviet Encyclopedia*, in Buryat Mongolia alone the number of lamas decreased from 6,900 in 1929 to 900 in 1936. The reason given was that the stabilization of Soviet power and the advancing economic and cultural development had led to a "mass desertion of religion by the people." Agvan Doržiev was arrested in Leningrad in 1937. He was sent to prison in Ulan-Ude and died in prison in 1938, possibly as a result of torture.[5]

The Japanese expansion (1937–39) into China, as far as the border of Outer Mongolia, served as a pretext for increased persecution. Using the unfounded allegation that the lamas were agents of Japanese imperialism, the Soviet government closed the few remaining monasteries.[6] In 1936 Foreign Minister Molotov could report at a reception in Moscow for a "delegation of workers" from the Buryat ASSR that "the Buryat Mongolians had forever put an end to the many-thousand-headed class of lamas, which had like leeches sucked the blood from the body of the people of Buryat Mongolia."

Liberalization of Soviet Religious Policy

In 1944, right before the close of World War II, two Buddhist monasteries were reopened, Involginskij Datsan, near Ulan-Ude, capital of the Buryat ASSR, and Aginskij Datsan in Chita, capital of the Aginskij Buryat National Okrug. In the mid-1960s there was also a report of a small Buddhist temple in the Astrakan Oblast (region). A Buddhist monastic temple built in Petersburg shortly before World War I was closed in 1937 and is still closed, even to foreign tourists, despite the efforts of Soviet Orientalists and art experts as well as Buddhists.

The two open monasteries have been maintained since their reopening by state funds. The Involginskij Datsan was designated the residence of the Bandido Chambo Lama and, later, the seat of the Buddhist central spiritual authority, the Buddhist Central Council of the USSR, founded in 1950. A special library here displays the remnants of the holy books that had been scattered over the Soviet Union.

Estimates of the number of lamas in the Soviet Union in recent decades differ greatly and are therefore not reliable. Soviet sources put them at 20–40 in 1959, or "only a couple of dozen" in 1960. In 1961 official Buddhist sources in the Soviet Union numbered them at "over 300." Since 1969, Sambal Gamboev, born in 1897, has been the Bandido Chambo Lama. In an interview with the *London Times* (October 6, 1970), he declared that virtually every village in Buryat ASSR had its own lama. More recent figures are unavailable.

The Burmese president of the World Fellowship of Buddhists in the 1960s, U Chan Htoon, declared on a visit to the Buryat ASSR that he had found many deeply devout, mostly elderly, Buddhists. He had also met with some educated lama monks. They were isolated from their fellow believers, however, since they were kept busy in Soviet museums and similar institutions doing research on old manuscripts. U Chan Htoon felt that in the regions he had visited, Buddhism was more of a museum showpiece than a living religion.[7] Professor Malalasekera, however, who founded the World Fellowship of Buddhists in Colombo in 1950 and was the ambassador of Ceylon to Moscow in the 1960s, was more optimistic. He reported that during numerous lectures in the Soviet Union, members of Moscow's intelligentsia had seemed fascinated by Buddhist teaching and doctrine.[8]

The Institute for Ethnography of the Academy of Sciences of the USSR surveyed religious life in the Buryat ASSR in the 1960s, and the results confirmed the observations of both U Chan Htoon and Professor Malalasekera. These surveys revealed that on religious holidays the monasteries and temples were packed with worshipers. Among them were middle-aged Buryats employed either on collective farms or in manufacturing who were only scantily informed about their religion. The number of lamas was extremely small; ceremonies were carried out mainly by older believers who were still well versed in the

Buddhist canon. Among these were often former novices who had fled the monasteries during the persecution of the 1930s and former lamas who had laid aside their office under the pressure of religious persecution.

Even among the young, according to the survey, there was still some interest in religion. Not a few young people shared their parents' reverence for the lamas and retained the monks' services for consecrating marriages, christening newborns, evoking guardian spirits for a newly founded family, and praying after the death of relatives. The survey found it deplorable that in spite of the transformation of the people, Lamaism retained a considerable following.

Motives for Toleration

Why does the Soviet Union again tolerate Buddhism?

The article on Buddhism in the third edition of the *Great Soviet Encyclopedia* was written by a professional expert on India. Its academic precision sets it apart from the articles in the first two editions. Apart from the few obligatory remarks, it dispenses with ideological vocabulary and with Marxist-Leninist arguments against religion, and could be published in a Western scholarly journal. The Moscow leadership is evidently convinced that, thanks to the religious policy of the 1930s, Buddhism in the Soviet Union is reduced to a few insignificant relics. Moscow does not anticipate any revitalization of the Buddhist ethnic minority's self-identity as a result of its more tolerant policy.

At the end of World War II, the Soviet state and party leadership had a great interest in documenting, especially vis-à-vis Asia, the credibility of the "freedom of the principle of practice of religion" as stated in its Constitution and party platform—within the bounds, of course, of existing legislation. The Soviet regime unmistakably wanted to provide itself with a foreign-policy tool when it reestablished the Buddhist Central Council of the USSR. At meetings of the World Fellowship of Buddhists, or the so-called Peace Conferences of Asian Buddhists, for example, Buddhist Central Council delegates have primarily functioned not as representatives of Buddhism in the USSR but as spokesmen for Soviet foreign policy.[9]

The most probable determinant of the policy change toward Buddhism was Moscow's need to react to the Mao leadership's attitude toward the Buddhist minorities in China. Since 1952 the attitude had been increasingly liberalized. In many respects this "new" Chinese policy resembled the Soviet policy of the 1920s. But the Chinese leaders went far beyond the Soviet policy and skillfully tried to reinterpret the teachings and history of Buddhism in the light of dialectical and historical materialism.[10]

The Chinese Reinterpretation

The basic tenet of Buddhism is the renunciation of the world, with the goal of reaching enlightenment or *nirvana*, that is, deliverance from the perpetual cycle of birth-death-rebirth through individual meditation. This tenet was totally incompatible with Communist objectives. Therefore the Chinese Communists reinterpreted it. If the goal of meditation is the purification of thought, word, and deed, then enlightenment cannot be found in the far distance but only in the here and now, in action, in the problems and cares of society today. It is therefore detrimental for a Buddhist to become isolated from the responsibilities of life. The framework of Communist objectives is the only acceptable sphere of religious practice.

According to the Buddha's precepts, monks and nuns are to live a collective life. There is no private property inasmuch as there exists no autonomous, isolated self. To be concerned about one's own life above that of the community is to cling to an illusion of independent existence. If this illusory "self" is not relinquished, then something exists to be born and to die. Thus the "Heavenly Paradise of the West," into which all Chinese Buddhists hope to be reborn, was reinterpreted. The goals and actions of the Chinese Communist Party serve to advance the "Paradise of the West" here on earth. Carrying out the Party's Five Year Plan would be comparable to realizing the Paradise of the West on earth.

With this interpretation, Chinese Buddhists are required, along with all other Chinese citizens, to make their contributions to the Chinese economic plan. Productive work is the fulfillment of the vow of a *bodhisattva* (one who postpones enlightenment for the sake of helping others to realize it), because *bodhisattva*-like behavior ultimately consists in being good to all living creatures, in helping in their redemption. And so the new Chinese interpretation comes full circle. It is argued, with a certain logic, that no *bodhisattva* could attain the highest enlightenment without helping living beings. From this comes the dialectical conclusion that enlightenment in isolation from the working masses is impossible.

This reinterpretation of Buddhism had, above all, the goal of supporting the Chinese policy toward south, southeast, and east Asia. It was also aimed at influencing the Buddhist minority in Siberian areas bordering China.

The Situation in Recent Years

Critical discussions of Lamaistic "practices" appear time and time again in Soviet publications. These are evidence that beneath the surface of the institutional Buddhism that serves the interests of the Moscow leadership, there still remains an active practice of Lamaism.

For instance, *Fundamentals of Scientific Atheism,* published in 1961 in Moscow—obligatory reading in the Communist Party of the Soviet Union—declares:

> At present the majority of Buddhist clergy in the Soviet Union and other socialist countries are loyal to the state. . . . The change in political outlook, however, changes nothing of the unscientific and reactionary character of the Buddhist world view itself. The religious ideas of Buddhism . . . prevent believers from becoming fully conscious and active builders of Communist society.

The *Book of Buddhism* by A. N. Kocetov, published in 1965 but still considered the standard work of atheistic interpretation of Buddhism in the Soviet Union, states:

> The lamas, and those acting as such, constantly violate the laws on religious cults. They even conduct religious rites in the homes of believers. Some still practice traditional Buddhist medicine. The lamas have even revived barbaric customs such as marriage of minors or buying of wives.

A third example is from the *Handbook of Atheism*, published in Moscow in 1971:

> As a result of the victory of the Great October Revolution, of the building of socialism and of the creation of a new culture, the influence of Lamaism on the Buryats, the Kalmyks, and the Tuvinians has constantly diminished. During the thirties, the majority of the monasteries in the Baykal region and all local Buddhist centers in Kalmyk ASSR were closed and the buildings handed over to the workers. Some of the lamas who were banished from the monasteries turned to productive work. Others, however, continued to practice their religious activities illegally. . . . The long-ago superseded customs of Lamaism are far from being completely eradicated. Buddhism perpetuates an unjust social order in the world and promotes a bourgeois attitude toward society.

In a spectacular trial that took place in Ulan-Ude in 1972, B. D. Dandaron, a Buryat expert on Buddhism at the Siberian Academy of Science, was sentenced to five years in a labor camp. Four of his co-workers and students were committed to a mental hospital. Dandaron died two years after the start of his sentence. The charges against him were based on Article 142 of the Criminal Code of the Russian Socialist Federal Soviet Republic, which concerns violations of the 1918 Decree on the Separation of Church From State and of School From Church, and on Article 227 of the code, which deals with "infringement of the person and rights of citizens under the guise of performing religious rituals."[11]

On the Dalai Lama's first short visit in the Soviet Union, in June 1979, he made a short stopover in the Involginskij Datsan. The official Soviet news agency reported then (June 14) that he was welcomed by the Bandido Chambo Lama and thousands of believers.

Clearly, Buddhism has survived the "modernization" of its doctrine, the decimation of its community, the near annihilation of its institutional base, and the state's political use of its central body. Lamaism is still actively practiced in the Soviet Union, though its extent is difficult to know.

8

Islam

Marie Broxup

THE SOVIET UNION has the fifth largest Muslim population in the world today, following Indonesia, Pakistan, India, and Bangladesh, far ahead of Egypt, Turkey, and Iran. In 1979, when the last census was taken, the Muslims numbered nearly 44 million. Islam was brought to what is now the Soviet Union as early as the seventh century, almost two centuries before the arrival of Christianity, and Soviet Islam belongs to the very heart of the Muslim tradition. For over a thousand years Soviet Central Asia and the Caucasus (the mountainous region between the Black Sea and the Caspian Sea) played a central role in the development of Muslim culture. Deeply rooted in popular lore and penetrating all aspects of private and public life, such an old religious tradition as Islam could not be destroyed by half a century of anti-religious propaganda. It still permeates the psychology, character, and behavior of Soviet Muslims, creating a person significantly different from the average Soviet citizen.

The conquest of Kazan by the army of Ivan the Terrible in 1552 marked the first Russian advance into Muslim lands. (Kazan, on the Volga, now capital of the Tatar Autonomous Soviet Socialist Republic, was then the capital of a powerful Tatar khanate.) While these territories were gradually forgotten by the rest of the Muslim world, Russian Muslims never ceased to

---

Marie Broxup is director of the Society for Central Asian Studies, London, and the editor of *Central Asian Survey*. She is co-author with Alexandre Bennigsen of *The Islamic Threat to the Soviet State* (1983).

consider themselves part of the *umma*, the community of believers. This they proved by a continuous cultural, political, and military resistance to the Russian "infidels." Centuries later, their weight of population and strategic location gave Soviet Muslims an opportunity unique among Soviet nationalities to challenge Russian rule and influence Soviet domestic and foreign policies.

Arab Conquest and Mongol Invasion, 650–1550

Islam began to expand in the middle of the seventh century, a century after its founding by the prophet Muhammad. Arabs, Iranians, Caucasians, Oriental Turks, and Ottomans all helped to implant Islam in an immense territory stretching from the Caucasus in the west to China in the east, and from the city of Kazan in the north to Afghanistan and Iran in the south. It was spread into what are now the Soviet Central Asian and Caucasian republics by military conquest, by the diplomacy of the Caliphate of Baghdad and the Ottoman Empire, and by Muslim merchants traveling the "Fur Road," north to south along the Volga, and the "Silk Road," west to east from the Black Sea to China. The main thrust was the missionary activity of the Sufi brotherhoods, religious orders about which more will be said later.

By the middle of the tenth century, Islam was established unassailably in Central Asia. The area became one of the most brilliant cultural centers of the Islamic world and remained so until the sixteenth century. The Arab penetration of the Caucasus was less thorough—Georgia and Armenia, for instance, remained Christian bastions—but Islam was solidly entrenched in some areas, such as Azerbaijan, on the southwest edge of the Caspian Sea. It extended east as far as Sinkiang in northwestern China.

In the thirteenth century the Muslim world suffered a major disaster. The first Mongol invaders appeared in Central Asia during autumn 1219, and in less than two years they had conquered Turkestan, Afghanistan, and the Caucasus, sacked all the great cities, and slaughtered their populations. Although the

Mongol emperor Genghis Khan was tolerant in religious matters, his reputation for destruction and butchery was such that he became symbolic of the deadliest danger ever to threaten Islam. The decline of the cities during the Mongol domination was accompanied by a decline of the old Arab-Persian Muslim religious establishment, which was firmly rooted in urban society. Thus, for almost a century, Islam in Central Asia ceased to be the religion of the ruling classes but survived as the religion of the rural masses, its entrenchment enhanced by the activity of the Sufi brotherhoods.

Recovering from the shock of the Mongol invasion, Islam flourished again under the Pax Mongolica from the middle of the thirteenth century. At the beginning of the fourteenth century, certain Mongol rulers converted to Islam and were responsible for its spread into the southern steppes of Russia (north of the Black Sea and Caspian Sea) and western Siberia. This new phase of Islamic expansion lasted until the middle of the sixteenth century.

The Russian Conquest, 1552–1917

In the mid-sixteenth century the Muslims fell prey to another invader. The expansion of the Russian Empire into Muslim lands started in 1552 with the conquest of the Tatar capital of Kazan and ended in 1900 with the occupation of the Pamir, a mountainous region north of Afghanistan. (It was resumed by the Russians in their Soviet guise in December 1979 with the invasion of Afghanistan.) Nowhere has the past more strongly influenced the present than in Central Asia and the Caucasus. The passionate interest that still surrounds Imam Shamil, the leader of Caucasian resistance to the Russians in the nineteenth century, proves that a heroic past has not been forgotten.

Ivan the Terrible, whose reign marked the beginning of the conquest, was tolerant in matters of religion and eagerly accepted Muslims as loyal subjects. The first Orthodox bishop of Kazan was ordered by the tsar to avoid brutality in dealing with Muslims; conversion to Christianity should be conducted "with love and sympathy and never by force." This religious tolerance, imposed by the tsar personally, was a unique phenomenon in the history of Russia.

After Ivan's death in 1584, a long era of religious intolerance began that lasted until Catherine II, who took the throne in 1762. Native Muslims were given the choice of conversion or expulsion from the major cities. Their richest lands were confiscated and distributed among the Russian nobility, the monasteries, and, later on, the peasants. They were treated no longer as equals but as second-class citizens, denied the rights reserved to Christians, and subjected to an intense missionary activity launched by the archbishop of Kazan. Thus under Tsar Feodor (Ivan's successor) Russia acquired a "nationality problem" that was to be handed to the Imperial Russia of the Romanovs and later to the Soviet Union.

The Russian conquest of Kazan was followed by a continuing expansion south until 1604. The Ottomans and the Crimean Tatars realized the danger and reacted vigorously. They made use of diplomacy, military alliances, and the Sufi brotherhoods to strengthen Islam in the north and central Caucasus. In 1604 Tsar Boris Godunov's army was routed, and the Russian front line was pushed back as far as Astrakhan on the northwest edge of the Caspian Sea. From that time forward, the north Caucasus became a Muslim stronghold, a center of Islamic resistance to the Russian advance in the nineteenth century. Today it is still a bastion of Islam in its most conservative form.

The Seventeenth and Eighteenth Centuries

The Russians remained on the defensive along their southern borders throughout the seventeenth and eighteenth centuries but continued their advance eastward from the Urals and the northern shore of the Caspian Sea to the Tian Shan mountains.

From the time of Tsar Mikhail, the first Romanov, whose reign began in 1613, to that of Catherine II, beginning in 1762, Islam continued to be treated as an alien body, and various measures were taken to liquidate it. Mosques were destroyed or closed, other religious property confiscated. Intense missionary activity was launched, while Muslim counter-proselytism was punishable by death. Muslims were expelled from villages containing converts to Orthodoxy. Local Muslim political structures and ruling classes were eliminated.

Russian expansion in the south resumed during the reign of Catherine II (Catherine the Great). Crimea, the peninsula in the northern Black Sea, was occupied in 1771. The conquest of the north Caucasus started in 1783 but met with fierce resistance from the Mountaineers, led by the Sufi Naqshbandi brotherhood. Indeed, it took all the might of the Russian Empire nearly a century to conquer this relatively small territory.

Catherine was personally interested in Islam and believed it better able to "civilize the wild Asian populations" than Orthodox Christianity. Like Ivan the Terrible, she had an imperial approach and understood that a multinational empire could survive only if all its subjects, whatever their creeds or cultural backgrounds, were treated as equals. In Crimea the Tatars were given the same civilian status as Russians, along with freedom to exercise their religion. The Muslim religious leadership retained its wealth, and Christian proselytism was forbidden. The Tatar nobility was accepted into the hierarchy of Russian society without having to convert to Orthodoxy.

In the Volga region, anti-Muslim campaigns were halted, and Muslims were allowed to build mosques. In 1773 Catherine established a Central Muslim Spiritual Board in Orenburg, chaired by a mufti. (The term *mufti* originally designated a Muslim legal expert but came to be applied in Russia to these religious leaders who were appointed by the state to administer Muslim affairs.) This astute policy gained the Russian government the loyal collaboration of the Tatar merchant class. For almost a century Tatar trading colonies were used as scouts in Siberia, China, and Central Asia (areas still closed to the "infidels"), while in return Russian authorities helped the Tatars build mosques and Koranic schools in the Kazakh steppes. The extraordinary economic prosperity of the Tatar merchant class that resulted from this partnership made possible the "Tatar renaissance" (*jadid* movement) of the nineteenth century. When the conquest of Central Asia was complete, however, this cooperation came to an end, as there was no longer the need for diplomatic and commercial assistance from Tatar middlemen.

Then the Tatar and Russian bourgeoisies, once allied, became competitors. The Russian government brought increased pressure to bear on these religious and economic rivals, and equality between Muslim subjects and their Russian masters was, therefore, to be short- lived. Even during Catherine's lifetime the best land along the Crimean shoreline was requisitioned for her numerous favorites.

The Nineteenth Century

Alexander I, whose reign began in 1801, was an admirer of ancient Greece and decided to make Crimea a home for exiled Greeks. Crimea became the "government of Taurida," and all the major cities were renamed. Pushed into the arid central areas, the Crimean Tatars felt compelled to flee, and between 1783 and 1913 more than a million Tatars left for the Ottoman Empire.

In the Volga region the Russians tried to solve the "nationality problem" by attempting to convert the Muslim population to Christianity. Nikolas Il'minsky of the Kazan Religious Academy devised a policy aimed at creating a Tatar intelligentsia converted to Orthodoxy but speaking and writing Tatar. This new intelligentsia alone was entrusted with missionary work among the Tatars. The policy achieved spectacular results: between 1865 and 1900, more than 100,000 Tatars converted to Christianity. Il'minsky's methods were seen, however, as a threat to the survival of the Volga Tatars and gained Russia the lasting resentment of Tatar Muslim elites and masses alike.

In the Caucasus the Russians applied a different policy. The status of nobility was granted to the feudal lords of some nationalities (Kabardians, Ossetians, and some Cherkess) but was denied to the Daghestanis, who provided the backbone of Imam Shamil's fierce resistance movement. The surrender of Shamil in 1859 marked the end of the Caucasian wars, though Russia was obliged to maintain control by military means rather than by a civilian administration. Russians were encouraged to colonize in the Caucasian lowlands, with the result that during the 1860s over a million Cherkess were obliged to leave the Caucasus for the Ottoman Empire. The mountains of Daghestan, however, remained inviolate: no assimilation policy was introduced, and the Orthodox Church was forbidden to proselytize.

In the Kazakh steppes, Russian missionary activity and rural settlements were discouraged until the reign of Alexander II, which began in 1855. The nomadic Kazakhs preserved their customary laws, and the Tribal Councils of Elders even exercised an embryonic self-government. Russian authorities in the steppes, attracted by the more romantic aspects of nomadic society, encouraged a revival of Kazakh traditional culture, and beginning in 1841 Russian-Kazakh schools were opened.

But this relatively happy state of affairs was short-lived. The immense steppe territory with its sparse population was too much of a temptation to the land-hungry Russian peasantry, and in 1891 the first wave of Russian and Ukrainian settlers reached the steppes. By 1914 more than a million Slavs had settled in the richest areas. The nomads were ruthlessly driven to the poorest regions, and their standard of living plunged drastically. In 1916 the nomad tribes attacked the settlers, only to be slaughtered by a joint force of Russian military and armed peasants. The survivors fled to China.

Muslim Transcaucasia (present-day Azerbaijan), on the southwest edge of the Caspian Sea, was ruled by Persia and its Qajar dynasty. Russian intervention in 1928 relieved the population of the bloody misrule of the Qajars, and therefore resistance was light. The Russians successfully applied a policy of indirect rule through delegation of power.

Turkestan, the large area extending east from the Caspian to China, was the last land to be conquered. Here the Russians applied an altogether different method of rule, rather like South African apartheid. Turkestan, once one of the most brilliant cultural centers of the Muslim world, was set to remain in a state of medieval backwardness and economic stagnation as the country was cut off from any outside influence, Turkish, Russian, or Tatar. The indigenous peoples were not given the status of "citizens," nor were they drafted into military service. Russians and other Europeans settled only in the cities, forming "white colonies" in quarters specially built for them. While proselytism was strictly forbidden to the Orthodox Church, the local administration tried to preserve the most archaic form of Islamic culture: the Tatar modernist *jadid* teachers and schools were banned.

Assimilation and Expansion

Clearly, Russian rule of Muslim lands previous to 1917 had no uniform policy. Methods varied from attempted genocide by slaughter to genocide by expulsion to cooptation of Muslim elites, non-interference, and assimilation.

It has often been said that the Russian people historically have not had a sense of racial superiority, and among Russian peasants there was no sense of superiority toward the native Muslims, whose standard of living was probably not very different from their own. At the top of the social scale as well, the Muslim nobles who had been admitted into the hierarchy of the Russian aristocracy were treated as equals and could reach the highest positions within the establishment. But apart from these circumstances, the Russians were convinced of their cultural superiority, and so there was never any question of a cultural symbiosis. Muslims could hope to gain equal status with Russians only through a cultural assimilation (this is still true today), preferably through conversion to Orthodox Christianity. Voluntary conversion was extremely rare, and so the Russians tried to assimilate the masses of alien Muslims through forced conversion. "Russification" was thus seen as a deadly threat by the Muslim nations; it completely alienated the Muslim elites from the Russians.

Strangely, the expansion of Islam was not slowed down by the Russian conquest; on the contrary, Islam made progress from the eighteenth century onward, owing to the liberal religious policy of Catherine II. Volga Tatar merchants were active in carrying Islam to the half-pagan populations of western Siberia and the Kazakh steppes. The arrival in the Caucasus of the Sufi Naqshbandi order also resulted in further Islamic expansion.

Total religious freedom proclaimed in Russia in 1905 enabled Islam to renew its efforts at expansion, which were halted only in 1928, when the Soviets inaugurated their anti-religious campaign among the Muslim people. During this period the majority of Tatars who were converted to Orthodoxy in the eighteenth century were persuaded to return to Islam, and new converts were made also.

The Soviet Period, I: 1917–45

The Bolshevik Revolution was seen by the Muslims not so much as the beginning of a new socialist era but as the end of Russian imperialist domination. Lenin's "April Thesis" adopted by the Bolsheviks in April 1917 promised the right of secession and political self-determination to all, and did much to rally the support of Muslim nationalists and liberals for the Bolshevik cause—or at least to ensure their neutrality during the civil war. But two major Muslim rebellions soon broke out that were to threaten the very existence of the new Soviet state.

The Basmachi War

When Bolsheviks took power in Tashkent, the main city in the Turkestan region (and now the capital of the Uzbek SSR), in October 1917, they received, rather to their surprise, the support of the entire local Russian population, including former civil servants, officers, merchants, and even the resident Orthodox clergy. This unholy alliance was prompted by common fear of the native population, forced into an apartheid-like condition, and was manifested in a new colonialism that excluded Muslims from any position of power.

Convinced that they could not cooperate with the new regime, Muslim leaders called a congress in Kokand in November 1917 that proclaimed the independence of Turkestan. The local Soviet government, the Tashkent *soviet*, reacted by attacking Kokand on February 5, 1918. The city was razed and its entire population of some 50,000 slaughtered. The sacking of Kokand, as well as an unsuccessful offensive against the Emir of Bukhara by the Tashkent *soviet* in March 1918, sparked the "Basmachi War" (*basmachi* means "bandit" in Uzbek). The resistance lasted from 1918 until 1928 (and in some areas until 1936), in parts of what are now the Uzbek, Kirghiz, Tajik, and Turkmen republics.

The Basmachi War was a spontaneous response to a variety of different threats: it was a *national* war against an old enemy reappearing in a new, Soviet guise; it was a *class* war of poor rural elements, including some nomads, against rich colonizers; and it was a *religious* war against the hated "infidels." Most of all, however, it was an attempt by Muslim conservatives to preserve their traditional way of life. The campaign against the Basmachis, employing more than 150,000 Red Army troops under the command of the best generals, proved to be one of the most difficult the Soviet Army ever had to face.

The North Caucasian War

Sufi brotherhoods of the north Caucasus viewed the October Revolution and ensuing Civil War as an opportunity to shake off Russian rule and expel the "infidels." The uprising that began in the spring of 1920 was in the same territory that Imam Shamil had defended in the nineteenth century. It was led by a Naqshbandi Sufi sheikh, Imam Najmuddin of Gotso, and was inspired by Sheikh Uzun Haji. The war in the north Caucasus was even more ferocious than that in Central Asia; no quarter was given and no prisoners were taken. The rebels fought to the last. Najmuddin was captured and executed in 1925. The tomb of Uzun Haji is now one of the most venerated places of pilgrimage in the north Caucasus.

The repercussions of this war were, if anything, more lasting than those of the Basmachi War. After their defeat, all the religious elements in the north Caucasus were subjected to a bloody persecution, and Sufis were fighting again in a major revolt in 1928. Similar revolts followed in 1934 and in 1940–42.

Another Muslim people, the Kazakhs, also suffered heavily under the new Soviet regime when, in the forced sedentarization program of the early 1920s, the Soviets killed the nomads' livestock. The result was the death by starvation of more than one million Kazakhs.

The State Attack on Islam

The first efforts to destroy Muslim institutions were several years later than similar measures against Christians, primarily because the Soviets could not risk alienating the entire Muslim population during their fight against the Basmachis. But in 1924, Koranic courts were abolished; around 1928 all primary and secondary religious schools were closed (before 1917 there had been some 15,000); finally, around 1930 all remaining *wagf* (religious endowment) properties, which provided the financial independence of the Muslim establishment, were requisitioned.

The direct attack against the Islamic religion itself was launched in 1928 and continued until the beginning of World War II. During this time the number of mosques declined from some 26,000 to about 1,000 in 1941. This onslaught was accompanied by violent anti-religious propaganda—organized by the League of Militant Godless—and the targeting of Muslim clergy and believers, variously accused of parasitism, counter-revolutionary sabotage, and, later, spying for Germany, Britain, and Japan.

Post-War Persecution

As World War II was nearing its end in 1944, five Muslim nationalities were accused of collaborating with the Germans, even though some of these nationalities had remained out of reach of the German armies. As a result, the Crimean Tatars, Karachays, Balkars (north Caucasian Turks), Chechens, and Ingush were deported under appallingly inhuman conditions to the most forbidding areas of Siberia, Kazakhstan, and Kirghizia. (The Germans living along the Volga and the Buddhist Kalmyks were treated the same way.) All together more than one million Muslims were deported. It is estimated that more than 20 to 30 per cent died in transit; an unknown number were exterminated in death camps.

Another Muslim nation, the Meshketians, was deported to Kazakhstan and Uzbekistan, although there was no suggestion of collaboration with the Germans. The number of Meshketians deported has been estimated at between 100,000 and 200,000; at least 50,000 died en route of cold and hunger.

On November 30, 1945, the Crimean Republic (proclaimed after the 1917 Revolution) was liquidated by decree and the area absorbed into the Russian Soviet Federated Socialist Republic

(RSFSR); it was subsequently given to the Ukrainian SSR. The Crimean Tatars, who for five centuries had played a major part in the history of eastern Europe, simply ceased to exist as a nation. Thus the Soviets proved more successful—because they were more ruthless—than their tsarist forebears at solving the Crimean question. In the case of the other four north Caucasian Muslim nationalities, however, the attempted genocide proved unsuccessful. After Stalin's death, the Chechens, Ingush, Karachays, and Balkars were cleared of treason, and their national territories were restored to them.

According to Soviet sources, it was Islam in its most conservative form that provided the deported Muslims with their only basis of identity, helping them resist extinction and assimilation. This singular achievement was a result of the activity of two Sufi brotherhoods, the Naqshbandiya and the Qadiriya. What is more, the revival of Islam among the Kazakhs and Kirghiz—whose faith used to be fairly superficial—is attributed by Soviet sources to the presence of deported Chechen Sufis in their midst.

The Soviet Period, II: Since 1945

According to the 1979 census, the Muslim population of the USSR was nearly 44 million. In the Soviet Union, however, the word "Muslim" has historical, cultural, and social as well as religious meanings and does not necessarily imply spiritual dedication. The term "non-believing Muslim" is often heard. Practically all Soviet Muslims, including those who are high-ranking members of the Communist Party and Politburo, observe certain basic Muslim rites and customs and lead a more or less Muslim way of life. To call the native inhabitants of Central Asia and the Caucasus "Muslim" is therefore not inaccurate.

During World War II an agreement was reached between the Soviet government and the Muslim establishment as the result of an initiative taken by Abdurrahman Rasulaev, one of the few Muslim clerics to have survived the fearful persecution of the 1930s. Rasulaev approached Stalin with a view to "normalizing" relations with Islam and obtaining legal recognition. In exchange for a promise of Muslim support for the Soviet war effort, anti-religious propaganda was toned down, and several Muslim Spiritual Boards were created to administer the few remaining Muslim institutions. This system was modeled on the reforms of Catherine II and has no parallel among Muslims in any other country.

The period of relative tolerance that ensued lasted only until Stalin's death, whereupon Khrushchev's "return to Lenin" policy brought on a new and violent anti-religious campaign that began in 1954 and lasted for a decade. More than two-thirds of the mosques were closed: there were approximately 1,500 in 1958, fewer than 500 in 1965. After Khrushchev's fall, relations between the Soviet government and Soviet Islam entered a new phase of relative détente—or, rather, subtle bargaining—that continues today.

Official Islam

The Muslim community has no central organization apart from a coordinating center, established in 1962, that oversees the international relations of the four muftis with the rest of the Muslim world. Administrative affairs are divided geographically among four Spiritual Boards. The Sunni are the main, orthodox branch of Islam. About 85 per cent of all Muslims are Sunni, and the rest are Shia (the branch of Islam followed in Iran). Three of the Spiritual Boards are Sunni, the fourth mixed Sunni-Shiite: (1) The Spiritual Board of Central Asia and Kazakhstan (Sunni, Hanafi Rite) has its seat at Tashkent in the Uzbek SSR; (2) the Spiritual Board of the Muslims of European Russia and Siberia (Sunni, Hanafi rite), at Ufa, Bashkir ASSR; (3) the Spiritual Board of the North Caucasus and Daghestan (Sunni, Shafei rite), at Makhach Qala, Daghestan ASSR; and (4) the Spiritual Board of the Transcausian Muslims (Shiite, Ja'fari rite, and Sunni, Hanafi rite), at Baku, Azerbaijan SSR.

These four Spiritual Boards are the only recognized Muslim institutions in the Soviet Union. All religious life, public or private, is supposed to be conducted under their auspices; religious activity outside the Boards is strictly forbidden by law. It is difficult to ascertain the number of "working" mosques controlled by the Spiritual Boards today; board executives are cautious when asked direct questions, and the data published by Soviet sources are incomplete and unreliable. A figure of 350–400 mosques serviced by 1,500–2,000 clerics seems plausible. The majority of the mosques are in the cities, since there are not enough "registered" clerics to operate those in rural locations. Some new mosques have been opened since 1978.

The Spiritual Board of Central Asia and Kazakhstan controls the only two Islamic educational institutions left in the USSR, the *madrassah* (secondary school) of Mir-i-Arab in Bukhara and the *madrassah* Imam Ismail al-Bukhari in Tashkent. The Spiritual Board executives, official clerics, and *ulama* (theological scholars) produced by these two madrassahs have high professional standards. Their intellectual ability is excellent and sometimes outstanding, the equal of that of Muslims anywhere else. Most of the clerics, including the four muftis appointed by the state to oversee Muslim affairs, are relatively young. Graduates of Mir-i-Arab become *imam-khatib*—prayer leaders or heads of mosques—or go on to study at madrassah Imam Ismail al-Bukhari. The syllabus of this madrassah is said to resemble that of well-known Islamic universities in the Middle East. After four years of studies, the best students are sent for six years to foreign Muslim universities, such as al-Azhar in Cairo or the University of Damascus.

In addition to operating the only two madrassahs, the Spiritual Board of Central Asia and Kazakhstan is also the only one to produce a number of publications. Among these is *Muslims of the Soviet East*, a quarterly review published in Arabic, Persian, Uzbek (in Arabic script), English, and French. This well-produced and nicely illustrated journal is aimed at a foreign Muslim readership; within the USSR it is accessible only to those few scholars who can read Arabic. The board also publishes a calendar in Uzbek, a few editions of the Koran, and collections of *hadith* (narratives of the sayings and customs of Muhammad).

State Use of Official Islam

After the fall of Khrushchev, the Soviet government gradually raised the iron curtain that had isolated the Muslim territories for decades. Muslim leaders began functioning as "roving ambassadors" to the Muslim world at large, presenting Central Asia and the Caucasus as showpieces of Communist achievements and testifying to the freedom and prosperity of Muslims. Of course, the purpose was to help promote Soviet foreign policy.

The help provided by Muslim officials in establishing contacts with conservative, pro-Western Muslim states such as Saudi Arabia, Morocco, Jordan, Tunisia, and Sudan has proved invaluable to the Soviet government. Soviet muftis frequently lead Muslim delegations to Muslim countries; usually the members of these delegations speak perfect Arabic and have a thorough knowledge of Islam. They are, therefore, the best possible ambassadors that the Soviet Union could send to the Muslim world. In addition, the muftis organize international Islamic conferences and host numerous foreign Muslim delegations in their own regions.

Another important contribution is the propaganda value of broadcasts by the muftis and other representatives of the Soviet Islamic establishment. These broadcasts in Arabic, Persian, Pashto, Urdu, and Turkish vary little from the standard Soviet fare: they praise the Soviet government, glorify the freedom and happiness of Muslims in the USSR, and denounce various "enemies" such as American "imperialists," Chinese "hegemonists," and Israeli "colonialists." The impact, however, is much greater on foreign Muslim audiences because the broadcasts originate from the highest religious authorities.

At first sight it seems paradoxical that Soviet Islam should further the aims of the atheistic state that has persecuted it for so long, but Islam has had to adapt itself to the realities of life under the Soviet regime. To Soviet Muslims there is little difference between the present "infidel" masters in Moscow and the former tsarist ones—they are still Russians. If anything, the atheists may appear less dangerous than the proselytizing Christians of the past, since Marxism-Leninism is not considered a rival ideology so much as a political and economic system.

The Soviet government for its part has had to make important concessions to the religious establishment, such as toning down anti-religious propaganda, allowing new mosques to open, and permitting publication of the Koran and *hadith*. These concessions strengthen Islam in the USSR. The position of the muftis, therefore, appears to be somewhat stronger than that of Patriarch Pimen of the Russian Orthodox Church.

Intellectually, Soviet *ulama*—theological scholars—are the heirs of the prestigious nineteenth-century *jadid* reform. Like the liberal, modernist scholars who were their predecessors, they reject *taqlid*—blind obedience to scholastic authority—and advocate *ijtihad*, the right to interpret the meaning of the Koran. They are thus in a better position to reconcile Islam with science and "progress" and to guarantee its survival in a socialist environment. They have contributed to preserving the purity of Islam while at the same time saving it from the two main dangers that threaten religion in the USSR: ignorance and relapse into superstition.

Whatever concessions Muslim leaders have been able to secure from the Soviet state, however, it is difficult to imagine that official Islam, with its limited means—a mere 350–400 mosques, two schools with fewer than 100 students, and a single religious journal that can be read by only a minority of believers—is able to satisfy even the most basic spiritual needs of the Muslim.

"Parallel" Islam

The submissiveness of the official Muslim leaders has not been accompanied by any disaffection of the masses towards Islam. For several reasons, Islam has fared better than any other religion in the USSR.

First, Islam is a religion without a clergy. Muftis, though they oversee the religious life of the faithful within their jurisdiction, are not the equivalents of Christian bishops. When a mufti makes an official statement, he is not necessarily speaking for Islam, or for the *umma*, the community of believers. Consequently, a mufti's cooperation with the Soviet state does not undermine the community, as it often does in the case of an overly accommodating Christian leader. Second, anyone with enough knowledge of Arabic to read the Koran can perform the basic Muslim rites. Again, an official clergy is not necessary.

Third, although the destruction or closing of mosques is regrettable, such buildings are not essential to the performance of religious rites. Finally, the strength of Soviet Islam is due in part to the existence of the Sufi brotherhoods.

As early as the twelfth century, the fundamentalist Sufi orders provided the only effective Muslim response to the "infidels" (at that time, the Qara Khitays and the Mongols). The same orders fought the Russians in the eighteenth and nineteenth centuries and the Soviets in the 1920s. In fact, from 1917 to the present day, the only serious, organized resistance encountered by the Soviets in Muslim territories has come from Sufi brotherhoods, referred to in Soviet sources as "Parallel," "Non-official," or "Sectarian" Islam.

The Sufi Structure

Sufi brotherhoods are closed but not wholly secret societies, well-structured, hierarchical organizations bound by a strict discipline and total dedication to a religious ideal. The adept (*murid*) is accepted into a brotherhood after a period of initiation and remains all his life under the spiritual guidance of a master (*murshid*). His life is regulated by a complicated ritual of prayer—the *zikr* (remembrance of God), either vocal (and sometimes accompanied by musical instruments) or silent, depending on the order.

As Sufi orders are outlawed and therefore operate outside the control both of Soviet authorities and of official Islam, they are most active in those territories where official Islam is weakest. Sufi brotherhoods in Central Asia are more active in the Turkmen republic, where only four small mosques remain open, and the Kirghiz republic, with probably fewer than fifteen working mosques, than in the Uzbek republic, where some 150 mosques are functional. In the north Caucasus, traditionally a bastion of Sufism, the brotherhoods dominate the private and collective life of the Muslim population, and almost all the religious leaders belong to a Sufi brotherhood. Soviet sources agree that the north Caucasus is one of the most "fanatical" Muslim territories of the Soviet Union.

Sufi adepts perform the necessary religious rites—circumcision, marriage, and burial—and run numerous schools and clandestine mosques. Their activities are usually centered around "holy places," often the tombs of Muslim saints. Pilgrimages to these sites serve as substitutes for the pilgrimage to Mecca, since no more than thirty officially selected pilgrims are allowed to journey to Mecca each year. The brotherhoods also provide a forum for believers to gather and learn Arabic prayers and elementary theology, as well as to listen to propaganda against the official atheism of the state.

Soviet sources report that in some areas of the north Caucasus, the Sufi brotherhoods are so influential and public opinion so "conservative" that non-believers are obliged to hide their atheistic ideas from relatives and friends, while teachers do not dare teach atheism in schools—an ironic situation after seventy years of official state atheism. Sufi brotherhoods are fighting not only Communism but also the presence of the Russians, who, in their view, are responsible for the evil of Communism. Not surprisingly, the Sufis are accused by the Soviets of promoting xenophobia and of acting as the guardians of national traditions.

According to recent Soviet reports, Sufi brotherhoods are not small units but mass organizations with hundreds of thousands of followers. The figures are almost certainly higher today than before the 1917 Revolution. The adepts are not exclusively from the poor, rural masses but also include growing numbers of industrial workers and intellectuals. Unlike Orthodox Christians, who may be obliged to leave the church if they strongly disagree with the policy of the Moscow patriarch, the Muslim believer simply joins a militant Sufi brotherhood if he feels that the official Islamic leaders have become too submissive to the godless regime. Sufi brotherhoods, even the more extremist, are perfectly orthodox, and, despite constant pressure from Soviet authorities, the muftis have refused to condemn Sufi Islam save on one or two minor points.

There are five main Sufi orders in Soviet Islam. (1) The most influential, because of its historical importance, is Naqshbandiya, founded in Bukhara by Sheikh Muhammad Bahautdin Naqshband (1317–89). Branches of this order operate in the Middle East and elsewhere. It is an intellectual order but popular among city craftsmen. (2) The largest Sufi order in the USSR is probably the Qadiriya, founded in Baghdad by Abd-al-Qader al-Djilani (died in 1166). There are branches throughout the Muslim world. The other main orders are (3) Kubrawiya, (4) Yasawiya, and (5) Kalendariya.

Anti-Religious Propaganda

The themes of Soviet anti-religious propaganda were elaborated between 1925 and 1928 and have changed little since that time, though the emphasis has varied. Anti-religious propaganda is considered the moral duty of all Soviet citizens. As chapter four has shown, the Soviet anti-religious propaganda machine is a massive, costly bureaucracy employing tens of thousands of specialists.

From the standpoint of ideology, Islam is one of the most frequently attacked, though attacks against the Spiritual Boards are, of course, forbidden. Arguments used against Islam have four main themes: (1) Islam is a foreign religion, brought by Arab conquerors and Ottoman sultans. (2) Islam is an anti-social religion, the most reactionary and conservative of all. It humiliates women, submits youth to an abusive authority from their elders, and encourages such barbaric practices as circumcision and Ramadan fasting. (3) Islamic morals are opposed to Communist morals. Islam annihilates any spirit of initiative and inculcates submission, fanaticism, and xenophobia. (4) Islamic art and literature are ossified, unable to evolve or progress.

How effective is the anti-Islam campaign? An official Soviet survey conducted in the Chechen-Ingush ASSR in 1978 revealed that only 20 per cent of the Chechens and 22 per cent of the Ingushes felt favorable toward atheists; the other 80 per cent were either indifferent or frankly hostile. Admittedly, the survey was made in a bastion of Islam at its most conservative. Give or take a few points, however, its findings can be considered fairly representative of the feelings of the entire Muslim population of the USSR.

Levels of Religious Belief

Most Muslims in the USSR, Sunnis as well as Shias, observe the practice of *taqiya*: a Muslim has the right to renounce his faith publicly if the pressures against it become too strong, so long as in his heart he remains faithful to God. Moreover, Islam is a religion that encompasses every aspect of life, not just the spiritual; it is almost impossible, even for a proclaimed "non-believer," to cease to be a Muslim. A Muslim who does not follow the teaching of the Koran, fast during Ramadan, or pray five times a day does not thereby become an "infidel." To give up Islam, to become an "infidel," a Muslim must declare publicly in front of his peers assembled in the mosque that he rejects God. This is never done, as such a person would be immediately ostracized and effectively condemned to become a "Russian."

Soviet specialists generally divide Muslims into six categories of belief:

1. *Believers by Conviction*: "fanatics" who proselytize. They are intolerant of atheists, strictly observe the teachings of the Koran, usually know Arabic, and often refuse to take part in Soviet society. Members of Sufi brotherhoods are in this category.

2. *Believers by Tradition*: those who follow the teachings of the Koran and practice traditional customs but who do not attempt to impose their ideas on others.

3. *Hesitants*: those who believe in God and follow the moral principles of Islam but who do not maintain a conscious religious outlook. They do not pray five times a day or fast throughout Ramadan, usually do not know Arabic, and are more interested in the national than the spiritual aspects of Islam.

4. *Non-Believers-1*: those whose religious experience is limited primarily to observing certain religious rites, such as circumcision, religious marriage, and religious burial, paying *sadaqa* (a contribution toward the upkeep of the mosque), and celebrating Kurban Bayram (the feast of the sacrifice).

5. *Non-Believers-2:* those who observe certain religious rites under family pressure. They generally hide their religious indifference and claim to be Muslims.

6. *Atheists*: those who do not openly observe religious rites and festivals. Almost without exception, however, they still conform to the three basic religious rites of circumcision, marriage, and burial in a Muslim cemetery.

Unfortunately, there are no surveys of levels of belief that cover all the Soviet Muslim territories. In the past decade and a half, however, several have been conducted in parts of Central Asia and the north Caucasus. The Central Asia survey revealed that only 23 per cent of the men and 20 per cent of the women claim to be atheists. Similar surveys in the Daghestan ASSR and the Chechen-Ingush ASSR show that nearly 50 per cent claim to be "believers of conviction." Of the avowed atheists, nearly half were from the 18–30 age group. The proportion of believers is slightly higher among women than men.

The authorities' reason for conducting these surveys was to try to find out why religious belief has remained high among the Muslim population. The data were collected in a reasonably scientific way, and the findings can be considered fairly objective. For many people, such surveys seem rather like police questioning, and some are likely to avoid giving true responses for fear of persecution. In light of this, the high proportion of avowed believers is quite remarkable. The number of true believers is very likely higher than the surveys disclosed.

On the basis of the available data, it is fair to surmise that roughly 80 per cent of Soviet Muslims are believers. By contrast, in some "Christian" areas only 20 per cent are believers. Furthermore, there are frequent cases of former militant atheists who, once retired, return to the fold and resume religious practices. This may signify not a genuine change of heart but a desire not to be deprived of social contact with the local community.

Religious Rites and Customs

Five religious rites are considered to be the pillars of Islamic faith:

1. *Zakat*, alms given to the mosque to be distributed among the poor. This is strictly forbidden by Soviet law (officially, there are no poor under Communism), and *zakat* has been replaced by *sadaqa*, the voluntary contribution for the upkeep of the mosques. It seems, however, that the Sufi brotherhoods of the north Caucasus continue to collect *zakat* from their adepts.

2. *Haj*, the pilgrimage to Mecca. Since only a handful of believers are allowed to make this, *haj* is replaced by a pilgrimage to any of numerous local holy places, usually tombs of saints. These are run by the Sufi brotherhoods and thus escape control.

3. *Sawn*, fasting during Ramadan. This practice cannot be officially forbidden but attracts violent disapproval in anti-religious propaganda. Still, it appears to be observed by 40 to 60 per cent of the rural population in Muslim areas. Soviet writers point out that many non-believers—even some atheists—- fast as a matter of national custom or simply good manners.

4. *Namaz*, praying five times a day. (Friday noonday prayers are to be at the mosque.) This too is impossible to forbid, but it is regularly denounced as a ridiculous, archaic, and anti-social habit that slows down production. It seems to be practiced regularly by 20 to 40 per cent of the rural population.

5. *Shahada*, the profession of faith ("There is no God but Allah, and Muhammad is his prophet"). This is said privately, and therefore the extent of the practice cannot be estimated.

Soviet specialists consider that of the five pillars of the faith, alms for the poor and the pilgrimage to Mecca have lost their significance for Soviet Muslims, whereas prayers, fasting, and the profession of faith remain. Friday prayers at the mosques still attract believers, but because of the small number of open mosques and competition from the clandestine houses of prayer run by Sufi brotherhoods, attendance cannot be used to judge the level of belief among Muslims. In the north Caucasus, village mosques are filled with several hundred of the faithful on Friday, whereas in Central Asia, Friday prayers attract only about 1 per cent of believers.

The four great Muslim festivals of Id al-Fitr (or Uraza Bayram, marking the end of Ramadan), Id al-Kebir (or Kurban Bayram, the feast of the sacrifice), Mawlud (the birthday of the Prophet), and Ashura (a Shiite commemoration of the death of Iman Hussain) are celebrated by the majority of the population in Muslim areas—believers, non-believers, and official atheists. Soviet observers agree, however, that this is because the festivals have acquired a national rather than a purely religious significance.

The three main family rites are observed by the vast majority of Muslims: circumcision, religious marriage, and religious burial. Although denounced by officialdom as "barbaric" and "unhygienic," circumcision is practiced by almost the entire Muslim population of the USSR, including high-ranking members of the Communist Party and the Politburo. Religious marriage, too, is practiced by the majority of Muslims, despite government efforts to promote the Soviet "Red marriage." A religious marriage is probably seen by Muslims as a protection against ethnic assimilation by the Russians. In the Chechen-Ingush ASSR, a survey showed that 92.7 per cent of Chechen and Ingush marriages were religious. Even more pervasive is religious burial (in purely Muslim cemeteries), which is observed by the entire population. In areas where tribal or clanic structures have survived, cemeteries are not only Muslim but also tribal or clanic.

Demographic Changes

Soviet ideologists describe their society as dynamic, engaged in building socialism, and striving toward Communism amid constant change and evolution. In this process the various Soviet nationalities, including Muslims, will, it is said, draw closer together. The final stage will be the merging of all nationalities into one "Soviet" nationality with one "Soviet" culture. A new human being, the Soviet man, will emerge, with a "Soviet," "international," "proletarian," supranational consciousness. National differences will disappear; national cultures will survive only as folklore. In this context, of course, "Soviet" simply means "Russian": the other nationalities are expected to speak Russian, to adopt a Russian way of life, to learn Russian literature and history.

The demographic development of the Soviet population will be an important factor in Muslim-Russian relationships over the next twenty years. According to the censuses of 1926 and 1939, the growth of the Muslim population was then slower than that of the Slav, and slower than the average for the USSR as a whole. Since the war, however, Soviet Central Asia has been undergoing a "revenge of the cradle." The best defense Muslims have against their alien overlords is their demographic dynamism, which has canceled out all Russian attempts at assimilation. Between 1959 and 1970, the Muslim growth rate at 3.25 per cent was almost three times the Russian figure and nearly 2.5 times the national rate. Between the 1970 and the 1979 census, Muslims had the highest growth rate in the USSR. This situation is expected to continue.

Several continuing and interrelated trends revealed by the three post-war Soviet censuses will have a considerable effect on the evolution of the Muslim regions: the increasing concentration of the Muslims within their national territories (with the consequent reduction in Muslim minorities elsewhere), the slowing of Russian and other "European" emigration into Muslim regions, and, in some areas, the beginning of Russian emigration from Central Asia and the Caucasus back into the European areas of the USSR.

Refusal to Migrate

The 1979 census shows that over 99 per cent of ethnic Central Asians (with the exception of the Kazakhs) still live in Central Asia despite government incentives and pressures to move to labor-short northern Russia and Siberia. The Central Asians simply refuse to cooperate. In fact, over the last ten to twenty years there has been a gradual shift of Muslims back to their homelands.

There are several reasons for the Muslims' refusal to migrate. Most of the Muslims are of Turco-Mongol origin, and Turco-Mongols are not migratory. Their notions of "land," "people," "nation," "state," and "army" are confused—the same words describe them all. Even in the case of nomads, migration has always been considered a sin against the "nation," since it means that people—perhaps even an entire tribe—are lost to the community and condemned to assimilation by an alien environment. The only possible exception is when a whole "nation" moves to new lands—but then only as conquerors, not as emigrants.

To the traditional reluctance of Central Asians to go beyond the boundaries of their "land" can be added the notion of Dar ul-Islam, the "Abode of Islam," which in the USSR has come to mean the "Muslim homeland." Despite an officially anti-religious regime, Soviet Muslims still consider Central Asia and the Caucasus part of Dar ul-Islam, while the RSFSR and Siberia are part of Dar ul-Harb ("Abode of War"). For Muslims, the *umma* (community of believers) must not be forsaken, and thus permanent exile cannot be voluntarily accepted.

Another reason for the Central Asians' strong reluctance to migrate is their deep attachment to their "imperial" land, cradle of the Irano-Turkic civilization and of all the great Muslim dynasties. Samarkand, Bukhara, Khiva, and Tashkent, with their 2,000-year histories, are symbols of past glories and enhance every Central Asian's feeling of belonging.

As a result of the "nativization" of Muslim borderlands and the growing xenophobia of local populations, Russians and other Europeans have begun to move out of Muslim areas. It is probable that the four capital cities of Baku, Tashkent, Ashkhabad, and Dushanbe have now regained a Muslim majority. The prospect, therefore, of assimilating the native Muslims into Russian culture seems remote. The psychological gap between Russians and Muslims is widening.

Demographic changes have given a new impetus to the process of *mirasism*—rediscovery and rehabilitation of the national patrimony. The rediscovery of their brilliant Irano-Turkic culture and past, common to most of the Muslim world, has enhanced the Soviet Muslims' feelings of solidarity with and interest in their Muslim brothers abroad. This search for the past is not limited to the golden age of Turkestani literature, which shone uninterrupted from the ninth to the eighteenth century, but includes more recent events such as Imam Shamil's Holy War and numerous other nineteenth-century rebellions and wars against the Russians—almost always in the name of Islam. The great writers and philosophers of the Irano-Turkic literature of Turkestan were, if not Sufis themselves, thoroughly impregnated with the ideas of Sufism. When their writings are rediscovered, some Muslim spirituality inevitably filters through to the readers.

Effects of Iran and Afghanistan

Accurate information is always slow in reaching the West from the Soviet Muslim areas, but enough is now available from various sources—Soviet publications, *samizdat*, reports from Afghan students in the USSR and from *mujahidin* and Muslim travelers—to justify the assertion that the Iranian revolution and the Soviet failure in Afghanistan have resulted in an upsurge of Muslim assertiveness. To Soviet Muslims, the Islamic revolution in Iran has one meaning: If it is possible for the Iranians to overthrow a seemingly strong regime backed by foreign imperialism and the largest army in the Middle East, as well as to emasculate the oldest and strongest Communist party in the East (the Tudeh), then there may be hope that one day Soviet Muslims can rid themselves of the Russians and the Communists. Soviet officials' concern about recent developments in the Muslim republics can be gleaned from the local press. Several new themes emerged in Soviet writings following the invasion of Afghanistan:

1. *New "enemies."* Previously, the main adversaries were U.S. imperialism, Zionism, Western capitalism, and the like. Now there are increasing references to "enemies" from the Muslim world, such as Ikhwan al-Muslimin (Muslim Brothers) and the Afghan resistance parties, Hizb-i Islami and Jamiat-i Islami.

2. *The "obnoxious" and illegal activity of the Sufi brotherhoods*. Such references occur with increasing frequency, and in recent years there have been specific references to Muslim "extremists" in the USSR. ("Extremist" in Soviet terminology refers specifically to people who use religion to further political aims. It was used in the past only to qualify foreign Muslim "fundamentalist" groups such as the Ikhwan al-Muslimin and Jamaat-i Islami of Pakistan.) Growing Soviet concern over Sufi brotherhoods can also be detected in the authorities' numerous appeals for a "counter-propaganda" to stem the flow of Islamic contamination from abroad, and for a strengthening of the KGB border-guard units to protect the Muslim republics from foreign infiltrators.

3. *Religion and nationalism*. The more serious Soviet specialists in Islam, such as Saidbaev, now admit openly that the Central Asian and Caucasian ideas of nationalism and religion are so closely interrelated as to be sometimes indistinguishable, that an upsurge in nationalist feelings will probably assume a religious character, and that any Islamic revival will automatically sponsor anti-Russian xenophobia.

Two trials, one in Dushanbe (Tadzhikistan) in 1982 and one in Tashkent (Uzbekistan) in 1984, revealed to the West for the first time the existence of a wide-scale Muslim *samizdat* in Central Asia. The Tajiks standing trial in Dushanbe were accused of being linked to Afghan partisans and of distributing mujahidin literature and anti-Soviet propaganda. The trial in Tashkent dealt with the distribution of purely religious literature, pieces from the writings of Sufi poets and writers and pamphlets about Islam. Afghan *mujahidin* are well aware of the long-term political advantage of gaining Soviet Muslim sympathies and have been encouraging existing pan-Islamic trends by providing religious and political literature printed in Russian for Soviet Central Asia.

The report to the Twenty-first Congress of the Communist Party of Uzbekistan by the party first secretary highlighted the dilemma:

> One of the serious problems facing the republican party . . . is that some party organizations connive at and sometimes openly flirt with religion and pander to backward traditions and customs. Party committees do not notice, or else refuse to notice, that souvenirs and goods bearing religious symbols and the dictums of theologians are produced in state enterprises. Religious rites, with their extravagance, have captivated many people. These are by no means isolated cases of Communists, Komsomol members, and leading personnel taking part in the performance of religious rites. . . . It must be constantly remembered that religion clears the way for nationalism and chauvinism [*Pravda vostoka*, January 31, 1986].

Russian dissidents and intelligentsia also are concerned about developments in the southern Muslim republics. As evidenced by Russian *samizdat*, a letter written by a Russian opposition activist states: "In general the atmosphere in the eastern republics created apprehension among thinking people in Moscow. According to observers, on the streets and towns in the region close to the Iranian border graffiti have started to appear saying, 'We are filling our irrigation ditches with Russian blood.' There are especially strong anti-Russian attitudes among young people'' (*Possev*, March 1985). The longer the military and political situation in Afghanistan remains unresolved, the greater the danger of solidarity between Soviet Muslims and their Afghan co-religionists, with consequent anti-Russian sympathies.

Concluding Observations

Soviet sources now frequently refer to a Muslim ''revival'' in the USSR rather than to mere survival. A number of factors are contributing to this. There is the growing intermingling of the notions of ''nation'' and ''religion.'' In addition, Soviet Muslim elites are increasingly interested in the ''people''—more precisely, the poor people. The poor are seen both as better Muslims and as a symbol of the national character in its purest form. This ''populism''—another expression of nationalism—can also be viewed as a sign of Islamic revival. Also, the blending of faith and morality persists in spite of the efforts of official *agitprop* to implant a new Communist moral code. The term *imansiz* (non-believer) is still synonymous with an immoral scoundrel.

Finally, the rediscovery of the spiritual, aesthetic, and cultural wealth of Islam has sharpened the contrast with the intellectual and spiritual misery of an alien, Marxist-Leninist doctrine. The imam-khatib of the mosque of Urgench said to a French journalist in September 1980:

> Atheists attack religion in general but not the believers. Their propaganda cannot have any impact on our Muslims. As for our customs, they are those of our ancestors. We believe as our ancestors have believed. . . . Compared to the previous generation of young people, the level of religious belief is rather higher today.

Both tsarist and Soviet leaders have underestimated the power of Islam; both have failed to appreciate its tenacious hold upon its people. Islam has survived more than four centuries of oppression and persecution at the hands of the Russians, and its leaders are therefore justified in viewing the future with optimism. Indeed, Muslims are the only group in the USSR today who feel confident that time is working on their side.

9

Judaism

Jerry Goodman

ANNIHILATION, assimilation, or emigration: these, according to an advisor to the tsar in the latter part of the nineteenth century, were the three options open to Jews in Russia. Anti-Semitism did not begin with the Revolution; it has been part of the Russian landscape for centuries.

The 1.8 to 2 million Jews in the Soviet Union today bear more than their share of anti-religious harassment and persecution. The one option among the three that does not involve cultural or physical genocide, emigration, was open to fewer than 1,000 each year until Gorbachev began easing restrictions in 1987. The plight of Soviet Jews must remain a pressing concern for all who believe in human freedom and the preservation of cultural values.

UNDER THE TSARS (TO 1917)

"It is not convenient to allow Jews to come with their goods into Russia," said Tsar Ivan in 1550, "since many evils result from them. For they import poisonous herbs [i.e., medicines] and lead astray Russians from Christianity." The modern-day Soviet assault against Judaism has its origins in a deep-rooted

Jerry Goodman is the founding executive director of the National Conference on Soviet Jewry. He formerly was a specialist in European affairs for the American Jewish Committee. The author gratefully acknowledges the assistance of William Korey, director of international policy research for B'nai B'rith International, in the preparation of this chapter.

anti-Semitism characteristic of Russia under the tsars. As early as 722 B.C.E. (before the Common or Christian Era), legend has it, Jews settled in Georgia and Armenia in the first diaspora, following the destruction of the ten northern tribes of Israel.

The first evidence of Jewish settlements, however, is found on the northern shores of the Black Sea, tracing to the early centuries of the Common Era. Following the expulsion of Jews from Constantinople in 740 (a disputed date; possibly 865 or later), they settled in the area of Khazar, a kingdom incorporating the Russian plain. The local ruler converted to Judaism, and Hebrew script was used for official documents of state; but, unlike the situation in Christian realms, the conversion of the ruler did not mandate the conversion of the people. They remained religiously pluralistic—pagan, Christian, Muslim, and Jewish—and relatively pacifistic for their age. The Jewish population grew as a result of persecutions in the Byzantine Empire from the seventh to the tenth century, and the region was benignly described by a contemporary as one where "sheep, honey, and Jews exist in large quantities."

By 970, Khazar kingdom had been destroyed by invaders. Shortly thereafter a Jewish community was established in Kiev, by this time the political and economic center of the area. When the local prince, Vladimir, converted to Christianity in 988, much of the population was baptized also. This marked the start of a religious intolerance that would prove to be characteristic of Russia. In 1563, Ivan IV (the Terrible) ordered that all Jews in his area of conquest who refused baptism were to be drowned. In 1648–49, between 100,000 and 500,000 Jewish men, women, and children were massacred in the Ukraine (then under Polish rule), and some 300 Jewish communities were devastated.

Sources of Discrimination

The noted historian Salo Baron traces Jewish discrimination in Russian history to two main sources: a pervasive anti-Semitism imported, in part, from the Byzantine Empire along with Eastern Orthodoxy, and a more general xenophobia on the part of the Russian people. Where Jewish assistance was required to service the needs of the nobility in commerce or medicine, local restrictions were often relaxed. Otherwise, Jews were prohibited from inhabiting Muscovite Russia (the state centered around Moscow that gradually gained ascendancy over the other Russian principalities), with some exceptions, and faced varying degrees of persecution aimed at assimilation or even elimination. The religiously fanatic Tsarina Elizabeth Petrovna (1741–62) expressed this Judeophobia most plainly:

> All Jews, male and female, of whatever occupation and standing shall, at the promulgation of this Our ukase, be immediately deported, together with all their property, from Our whole Empire. . . . They shall henceforth not be admitted to Our Empire under any pretext and for any purpose, unless they be willing to adopt Christianity of the Greek persuasion.

Unwilling to relax this policy even for reasons of industry and commerce, the tsarina wrote: "From the enemies of Christ I desire neither gain nor profit."

Across the border, life was quite different for the Jewish community in the Polish-Lithuanian state. The Jews were largely of recent German origin, speaking a dialect from which Yiddish would derive. The community was integrated with society but also maintained its cultural distinctiveness. To be sure, its separateness was in part enforced by the state; Jews were restricted to their ghettos and were compelled to wear special attire. Still, the *kahal*—community—thrived. It was not subject to regular civil administration. Jews elected their own officials, who governed them after the Mosaic Law in matters of religion and economics, and operated schools and *yeshivot*. A census conducted in the late eighteenth century revealed that while Jews constituted one-eighth of the population, only fourteen Jewish families were engaged in agriculture. Approximately half were involved in the liquor industry and small businesses, and many were artisans; Jews controlled 75 per cent of the export trade. They were welcomed by the nobility for their business acumen, but this engendered the hostility of the peasants.

Catherine: A Transitory Toleration

With the reign of the Tsarina Catherine the Great (1762–96) and the adoption of numerous reforms, an easing of restrictions on the Jews might have been expected. Catherine certainly was more intellectually inclined to such a position than her immediate predecessors, and in 1776 she proclaimed "the free exercise of religion and the inviolability of property for one and all." Yet, while she was intent on building a society on the principles of the Western Enlightenment, she saw the Jews as a threat to progress because of their cultural adhesiveness. This potential problem to the empire was of special significance in light of the three partitions of Poland during Catherine's reign—1772, 1793, and 1795—when parts of Poland were annexed by Prussia, Austria, and Russia. As a result of these annexations, more and more Jews found themselves living under tsarist rule. Professor Salo Baron writes:

> The partition of the once-powerful Polish-Lithuanian Commonwealth proceeded so swiftly and encountered so little armed resistance that few Jews had a chance to leave their residences before they suddenly found themselves facing a new sovereign [*The Jews Under Tsars and Soviets* (Macmillan, 1976), p. 348, n. 1].

With the partitioning of Poland and the addition of other regions conquered during Catherine's reign, large numbers of Catholics, Lutherans, and Muslims were added to the religio-ethnic mix. An immediate and thoroughgoing Russification of all these disparate elements seemed a practical impossibility. Still, according to Baron, Catherine was wary of progressing too rapidly on the Jewish question, mindful of her position as defender of the Orthodox faith as well as responsive to the fervent belief of the masses and the strength of the clergy. Catherine's relative ideological openness on the Jewish question did create a more tolerant atmosphere for the Jewish communities in the earlier period of her reign than they had previously experienced in Russia. The first partitioning of Poland added only some 27,000 Jews to Russian rule. But as more Jews came under Russian dominion, their interests began to collide with those of the Russian people. Anti-Semitism and concern over Jewish competition in business grew, and conditions were ripe for strengthening anti-Jewish policies. Following an attempted expansion of Jews into Smolensk and Moscow, Catherine in

1791 created the Pale of Settlement—territories annexed from Poland in the first partition—to contain the Jewish population and prohibit the spread of the "Jewish problem" into the interior of the country. Jews were restricted to this area, required to register as members of the burgher or merchant classes, and forced to pay taxes at twice the normal rate.

Nicholas I: Intensifying Discrimination

Nicholas I (1825–55), certainly one of the most anti-Semitic Russian tsars, zealously changed the military draft laws. His confidential purpose was that "it will move them [the Jews] most effectively to change their religion." During his reign, Jews were prohibited from buying freedom from military service by paying a special tax, as had been a common practice, and a period of military service of twenty-five years became mandatory for Jewish men and boys. Boys from the ages of about eight or nine to eighteen years were sent to special preparatory "schools," after which they were transferred to regular units of the military. Alexander Herzen in 1835 recorded the process:

> The officer who escorted them said, "They have collected a crowd of cursed little Jewish boys of eight or nine years old." . . . The officer who handed them over said, "It's dreadful, and that's all about it; a third were left on the way" (and the officer pointed to the earth). "Not half will reach their destination," he said. "Have there been epidemics, or what?" I asked, deeply moved. "No, not epidemics, but they just die off like flies. A Jew boy, you know, is such a frail, weakly creature, like a skinned cat; he is not used to trampling in mud for ten hours a day and eating biscuit—then again, being among strangers, no father nor mother nor petting; well, they cough and cough until they cough themselves into their graves. And I ask you, what use is it to them? What can they do with little boys?"

Additional discriminatory actions of Nicholas I included barring Jews from settling within thirty miles of the western frontier (lest they engage in smuggling), prohibiting their employment of Christian domestic servants, prohibiting the building of synagogues near churches, censoring Jewish publications, and establishing schools in the Pale for the purpose of inculcating Christian teaching. Even Alexander II, whose reign Jews remember as a "golden age," commented in 1856 that his own policy was "to revise all existing legislation regarding the Jews so as to bring it into harmony with the general policy of merging this people with the native population, so far as the moral status of the Jews will allow it."

The 1888 Report

In 1888, a tsarist commission published the results of an investigation of the policy of the government toward the Jewish community since the time of Catherine the Great. After five years of lengthy interviews and in-depth study, the commission praised "the purity of . . . [Jewish] morals, their high respect for learning, their absolute sobriety, their thrift and constant activity." Yet the members of the commission—largely moderates—concluded that Jews had the following characteristics:

> (a) . . . isolation and exclusiveness; (b) a tendency to get control of the economic strength of the population; (c) a tendency to shirk state obligations; and (d) avoidance of physical, muscular labor.

The report continued:

> The passion for acquisition and money-grubbing is inherent in the Jew from the day of his birth; it is a characteristic of the Semitic race, manifest from almost the first pages of the Bible.

Such views provided fertile soil for persecution. Under Nicholas II (1894–1917), quotas on Jewish admission to higher education were stiffened, and Zionism was outlawed. Jews were imprisoned without charge and harassed with a host of limitations on their social and physical mobility. Anti-Semitic pogroms were now being prepared and carried out with the cooperation of local and national authorities, not merely their passive compliance, as in years past. The League of the Russian People, founded in 1904, counted among its members chief organizers of pogroms and, later, even the tsar and tsarevitch (the crown prince).

Perhaps most infamous among tsarist anti-Semitic activity was the notorious *The Protocols of the Elders of Zion*, a fabrication first published in 1903 by the reactionary publicist Pavel Krushevan. Based upon tales of German and French origin, the *Protocols* purported to outline a Jewish conspiracy for world domination. Its impact was felt during the Civil War in 1918–20 in the Ukraine, when 30,000 Jews were massacred and more than a quarter of Jewish homes were destroyed. Later, the *Protocols* would become the basis for Adolf Hitler's "Final Solution."

THE REVOLUTION TO KHRUSHCHEV'S FALL (1917–64)

After the fall of the monarchy in March 1917, Jews greeted enthusiastically the provisional government headed by Kerensky. The discriminatory policy under which they had lived for so long was replaced with the right of equality under law.

When the Bolsheviks came to power in October of the same year, many Jews were in leadership positions within the Party. This offered grounds for optimism, even though the great majority of these Jewish party leaders—such as Trotsky—did not identify with the Jewish community in any way. In addition, the new government immediately pledged

> the removal of every and any national and national religious privilege and restriction . . . the free development of the national minorities and ethnographic groups living within the confines of Russia.

The Bolshevik authorities initially did not interfere at all with the extraordinary growth of Hebrew culture in Russia that followed the March 1917 revolution. The Hebrew Tarbut movement at that time was a network of 200 educational institutions. By April 1918, the Tarbut in the Ukraine alone had 119 kindergartens, 118 elementary schools, and seven universities, colleges, and institutes.

Jewish Communists

During the 1880s and 1890s, which saw the beginnings of Russian Jewish involvement with the socialist movement, a wedge had been driven between the Jewish religious establishment and the Jewish working class. The establishment feared persecution by the tsarist government if Jews showed socialist leanings. In addition, from the mid-nineteenth century the Jewish *haskalah* (enlightenment) movement had generated an intellectual orientation that was avowedly secular and anti-religious.

These two traditions came together at the time of the Revolution to provide a foundation for the involvement of Jews in the Bolshevik regime and for the formation of Jewish Sections of the Communist Party, which would employ many of the methods popular with anti-religious propagandists of the time in the campaign against Jewish religion and culture. By 1919–20, Jewish Communists had encouraged the outlawing of Zionist parties as a threat to national unity and defense; earlier they had adopted as their specific domain anti-Judaic agitation and propaganda.

The campaigns of the Jewish Sections seemed to have little influence on the personal convictions of believers; but the effort did prove effective against institutional Jewish life, driving religious education underground, isolating Jewish community leaders from Western contact and even from much internal discussion, and sealing Russian Judaism into an increasingly obsolete 1917 form. As a result,

> Judaism could be convincingly portrayed as time and culture-bound, truly a "survival of capitalism" and *shtetl* culture, irrelevant to the brave new world of Soviet socialism. The impossibility of adaptation has meant that Judaism in the USSR today is much as it was in 1917—except shorn of its institutions, functionaries, and capacity for theological and social self-renewal. No reformist-adaptative movement of any kind has developed, in contrast to the West, and adaptation has come only in the form of necessary tactical compromises with the pressures exerted by the regime [Zvi Gitelman, "Judaism and Modernization," in Dennis Dunn, ed., *Religion and Modernization in the Soviet Union* (Westview Press, 1971), p. 294].

During this early period the Hebrew language came to be linked with Zionism, seen then as a bourgeois-nationalist ideology that must be destroyed. Yiddish, in contrast, was seen as a language of the masses and was therefore approved. At first, Hebrew was restricted to secondary schools. Then in 1919 the Commissariat of Education issued decrees that by the following year put an end to all Hebrew schools. Most other Jewish institutions were soon abolished, along with a majority of synagogues, and religious activity was severely curtailed. Although every religious body in the USSR suffered similarly under the extreme pressures of this period, Judaism had some particular disadvantages—its lack of a centralized, hierarchical body such as the Orthodox Church had, and the vehement anti-Semitism evident in the population.

Resumption of Persecution

The anti-Semitic prejudice of the masses expressed itself all too clearly in a revival of pogroms, for the most part in the Ukraine, exacerbated by the Civil War. In 1919, some 685 pogroms were carried out against Jews, plus numerous incidents of minor violence. Between 1918 and 1921, perhaps as many as 150,000 Jews died as a result of anti-Semitic violence, leaving tens of thousands of orphans and homeless people.

In November 1926, the chairman of the Central Executive Committee of the Soviet regime acknowledged that Soviet white-collar workers were "more anti-Semitic today than . . . under tsarism." An official "survey of anti-Semitism among trade union members," conducted in February 1929 in Moscow, found that "anti-Semitic feeling among workers is spreading, chiefly in the backward sections of the working class that have close ties with the peasantry." At the heart of the prejudice, as in the 1880s and afterwards, was "talk of Jewish domination."

A crippling blow to the Jewish community was the removal of any semblance of an organizational or coordinating structure. The Law on Religious Associations of April 1929 permits

> religious communities of the same denomination . . . [to] form religious associations which may or may not coincide geographically with the administrative subdivisions of the Union of Soviet Socialist Republics . . . and may set up *religious centers*. . . . These religious centers, which are governed by their own rules and regulations, may hold republic or All-Union congresses, church councils, and all other conferences on matters related to the administration of church affairs [italics added].

The order further noted that "religious centers" may publish "periodicals and the necessary devotional literature." In August 1919, however, the Soviet government banned the existing central Jewish body, the Central Board of Jewish Communities, and no coordinating body has been permitted since, in contrast with other recognized religious groups. A Conference of Rabbis of the Soviet Union met for the last time in 1926 at Korosten, with twenty-five rabbis as delegates and ninety other rabbis as guest.

The "Jewish Autonomous Region"

In 1927, a desolate area near the Chinese border was set aside for Jewish resettlement as a method of responding to perceived threats, both internal and external. This region, known as Biro-Bidzhan, was to be an alternative to a Zionist homeland, providing for the economic development and normalization of the Jewish community within a territory that would preserve their national/cultural identity. In addition, the state had specific economic and foreign-policy objectives: the natural resources of the region would be developed, the border would be secured from an increasing Chinese and Korean emigration, and the area, with an expected population of a million or more, could help to resist Japanese expansion. Previously the area had been inhabited only by some 1,200 Koreans, Kazakhs, and primitive tribesmen, because of the difficult environmental conditions.

A severe climate, lack of roads, and inadequate housing stifled any serious development. Nonetheless, Biro-Bidzhan was proclaimed a Jewish autonomous region in 1934 without a Jewish majority. The undertaking proved to be a failure, as expressed by an anonymous former settler and Communist Party member:

> If this is supposed to represent a Jewish Autonomous Region, then to hell with it. I am no longer buying this travesty. We are ready to accept a non-Jewish existence in a non-Jewish milieu: that is a clear-cut situation. But Biro-Bidzhan is a fake.

Far removed from the major Jewish population centers in the western part of the country, with only minimal Jewish cultural influence, Biro-Bidzhan some fifty years after its establishment would have a population only 5 per cent Jewish, making up only 0.7 per cent of the total Russian Jewish population.

Judeophobia had already become part of official USSR policy by the end of the 1930s; it did not, as is often assumed, develop in May 1948 when the State of Israel was established. According to Hitler, Stalin told Nazi foreign minister Joachim von Ribbentrop in the fall of 1939 that he would oust Soviet Jews from leading positions the moment he had enough qualified non-Jews to replace them. Stalin's promise was more than a mere diplomatic gesture to placate his racist ally. In 1942, one year after the Nazi invasion of Russia, Soviet authorities handed down a secret order establishing quotas for Jews in particularly prominent posts. Still, as machinery for the Second World War moved desperately into place, Judaism along with other religious traditions enjoyed for the most part a respite from the persecution.

The Post-War Years

In the immediate post-war period, however, when the state gave "favorable treatment" to Russian Orthodoxy, Islam, and other religious groups, Judaism was held in "disfavor." Walter Kolarz concludes: "Stalin anticipated that religious Judaism would disappear much more quickly than other religions . . . and he was determined to hasten this natural process as effectively as possible."

In 1945, according to Igor Gouzenko, a former Soviet diplomatic official in Canada who later defected, the Central Committee sent "confidential" instructions to directors of all factories to remove Jews from responsible positions. According to Milovan Djilas, Stalin boasted to him that "in our Central Committee there are no Jews!" Stalin's daughter revealed that after the war, "in the enrollment at the university and in all types of employment, preference was given to Russians. For the Jews, a percentage quota was, in essence, reinstated."

The Jewish Anti-Fascist Committee, established in 1941 to win Jewish sympathy in the Western world for the Soviet cause, was liquidated in November 1948. Composed of leading Yiddish artistic and literary figures, the committee constituted the Jewish "address" in the USSR for as long as it existed. Soon, nearly all Yiddish writers were imprisoned, and by 1952 they had either been tried and executed or sent to labor camp, where they perished from the severe conditions. This meant the extinction of a once-thriving Yiddish culture.

Prejudice reached especially intense levels during the "anti-cosmopolitan" campaign of 1949–53, climaxed by the notorious "Doctors' Plot." The fabricated charge accused nine of the most prominent physicians in Moscow—six of whom were Jewish—of murdering two Soviet officials and planning the deaths of Stalin and other state leaders. *Pravda* reported:

> Their foremost intention was to undermine the health of Soviet leading military cadres in order to weaken the defense of the Soviet Union. . . . The wrecker doctors were closely connected with the international Jewish bourgeois nationalist organization which bears the name "Joint," which was set up by American intelligence agencies [to conduct] . . . extensive espionage, terrorist, and subversive activity in a number of countries, including the Soviet Union.

In the dramatic secret report of Nikita Khrushchev to the Twentieth Congress of the Communist Party in February 1956, Stalin's sinister activity was exposed:

> Present at this Congress as a delegate is the former minister of state security, Comrade Ignatiev. Stalin told him curtly, "If you do not obtain confessions from the doctors we will shorten you by a head."
>
> Stalin personally called the investigative judge, gave him instructions, advised him on which investigative methods should be used; these methods were simple—beat, beat, and once again, beat.
>
> Shortly after the doctors were arrested, we members of the Political Bureau received protocols containing the doctors' confessions of guilt.

Fortunately for the accused, on March 5, 1953, the day hearings were set to begin, Stalin suffered a stroke and died. Within two months, the defendants were acquitted and released. Had Stalin not died when he did, there would certainly have been, according to his distinguished British biographer Isaac Deutscher, "only one sequel: a nationwide pogrom."

The Khrushchev Years

While Khrushchev did not adopt such an extreme action, his treatment of religious bodies was very harsh, in sharp contrast to the relative progessiveness expressed in his political and economic reforms. Synagogues, virtually the only remaining Jewish institutions in the USSR, were the target of particularly severe administrative measures during the 1959–62 drive against houses of worship. The pattern was this: First, letters and articles would appear in the press citing alleged illegal activities or pro-Israel propaganda in the synagogue; then letters from readers, including "religious believers," would ask for the liquidation of the "nest of corruption"; then information regarding the "nest of anti-Soviet propaganda" would be published; finally, local authorities would "bow to the ardent wishes of the community" and padlock the synagogue doors.

By the time the campaign ended, the number of synagogues in the USSR was drastically reduced. An official report to the United Nations in 1956 referred to 450 synagogues; by 1961, the total was down to 100. Nine years later, only 62 synagogues remained, a number that has remained relatively constant. Today, almost half of the synagogues in the USSR are in Georgia, the northern Caucasus, and the Central Asian republics, where only about 5 per cent of the Soviet Jewish community—some 100,000 Oriental (Sephardic) Jews—resides. The rest of the synagogues are expected to serve those who are religiously observant among the 1.7 million European (Ashkenazic) Jews, in widely scattered areas.

The extent and character of the propaganda attack upon Judaism was striking. A bibliographical study reveals that between 1958 and 1967, books and pamphlets attacking Judaism constituted 9 per cent of all anti-religious literature at a time when religious Jews amounted to only 2 per cent of the total religious population. Seven times as many copies of books attacking Judaism as books attacking Islam were published, and twice as many as the number of copies attacking Christianity.

Poet Yevgeny Yevtushenko penetrated to the Russian soul with his "Babi Yar" in 1961. The Russian people are "blemished" by anti-Semitism, says the poem; the Communist song, "The Internationale," can "thunder forth" only when Jew-hatred is "buried for good." When Khrushchev objected to Yevtushenko's raising the shameful issue, the poet would not be silenced. The popular hate must be faced, he said, for "we cannot go forward to Communism with such a heavy load as Judeophobia."

Many of the broadsides directed at Judaism suggest that it is regarded as more harmful and reactionary than the other recognized religions in the USSR. A Soviet "authority" writing in the leading newspaper of Byelorussia declared that "there is no crime that has not been justified by the Holy Book of the Israelites." The introduction to a book published by the Ukrainian Academy of Sciences states: "Judaism has incorporated and condensed everything that is most reactionary and most antihumane in the writings of contemporary religions." Lev Korneyev's book *The Class Essence of Zionism*, published in 1982, says:

> The Talmud idolizes private property, proclaims the cult of the division of people into the rich and the poor. According to the Talmud, money is the criterion not only for material values but also for spiritual ones, and the basis of all human worth, morality, and history.

Anti-Semitism as State Policy

The emergence of discrimination against Jews as state policy in the late 1930s and early 40s certainly cannot be considered a function of the foreign policy of the USSR. That policy had swung from a pro-West position ("collective security") to a pro-Nazi position (the Nazi-Soviet Non-Aggression Pact) and then back to a pro-West position (the Grand Alliance). During these fluctuations, official anti-Semitism, which denied the civil rights of Jews as individuals, developed along a single line. Only in the realm of collective ethnic and cultural rights were the Jews accorded some equality.

The government's policy of discrimination against Jews as individuals was largely a function of two internal developments in the Soviet Union at the time: (1) deepening Russian nationalism (bordering on xenophobia, as often in the Russian past) and (2) the formation of a totalitarian structure.

The new *Russian nationalism* was a dominant characteristic of the struggle against the Old Guard's "internationalism." Suspicion fell equally upon those suspected of harboring sympathies with various non-Russian nationalities of the USSR and those linked, in one way or another, with the West. Anti-

Semitism went hand in hand with this official Russian chauvinism, as it had during the tsarist era. Certainly it was not accidental that in 1926, when Stalinist forces were attempting to inculcate a national pride in the doctrine of "socialism in one country," official anti-Semitism made its first, if then only momentary, appearance.

Chauvinism catered to and fed upon popular prejudices. The war years were replete with examples of bigotry linked to nationalistic fervor. Many of the partisan units, for example, were riddled with anti-Semitism. Khrushchev in 1956 acknowledged to a visiting French socialist delegation that popular prejudice against Jews did play a role in the state's discriminatory policy:

> If the Jews now want to occupy the highest positions in our republics, they will naturally be looked upon with disfavor by the indigenous peoples. These pretensions will be coolly received especially since these people do not consider themselves any less intelligent or less capable than the Jews. Or, for example, in the Ukraine, if a Jew is named to an important post and he surrounds himself with Jewish collaborators, it is quite understandable that there will be jealousy and hostility toward the Jews. But we are not anti-Semites.

The other internal development contributing to official anti-Semitism was the erection of a *totalitarian structure* aiming to mobilize mass energies for party-determined purposes. Totalitarianism, of course, can tolerate no social units independent of the central manipulators of power. With ethnic groups centered in one geographical area, dismantling their autonomous communal structures was a long-term process, difficult to complete. But with the dispersed Jewish community the task was simplified. Their communal establishment could simply be pulverized.

That the Jews were particularly suspect in a totalitarian structure impregnated with a distinct chauvinistic character is not surprising, for they were indeed a minority with an international tradition and world-wide religion. Jews everywhere had cultural, emotional, and even family ties that transcended national boundaries.

Furthermore, Hannah Arendt has noted that totalitarianism requires an "objective enemy who, like the 'carrier of a disease,' is the 'carrier' of subversive 'tendencies.' " This aspect of totalitarianism had a distinctive impact on the state's relationship to the Jews. The very nature of a system that claims both a monopoly on truth and the control of the "commanding heights" by which the preordained may be reached precludes human error or inadequacy. Only plots and conspiracies by hidden forces could hinder or defeat "scientifically" planned programs. Stalin even considered his daughter's marriage to a Jew a "Zionist plot." Other Soviet leaders may not necessarily have perceived Jews as "plotters" but may have cynically accepted the functional usefulness of such a perception. Jews were cast in the role of scapegoats, to be blamed for failures or difficulties in the regime's internal and foreign policies.

Provincialism of Party Leaders

The background of the party leadership that came to power after the late 1930s might help to explain the persistence of folk imagery about the Jew. With the influx of this group, the wide cultural and intellectual horizons that had characterized the pre-Purge party leaders gave way to views that were provincial and cramped. On both national and regional levels, almost half of the top party executives in the early sixties had peasant backgrounds. Only 6 per cent had white-collar origins, while a little more than a quarter came from the proletariat. Most likely, many of them learned their negative Jewish stereotypes in their own homes, their own neighborhoods, their own towns.

Moreover, almost 40 per cent of party leaders either had no education beyond secondary school or had attended only a party school. Of those who completed college, 40 per cent studied engineering and 30 per cent agronomy—narrowly specialized and highly applied skills. Training in the broad humanistic disciplines was negligible. About a third of the leaders studied specialized skills in farming, a third in industry, and a third in ideology. Most conjoined their specialized experience with work in the organizational apparatus before reaching their top posts. Clearly, this pattern of training and experience did little to broaden their scope.

In the narrow range of outlook, the traditional conception of

Jews, imbibed as it were from the environment, emerges as an accepted and acceptable model. That over 90 per cent of all top party posts on the national level are held by ethnic Russians helps to reinforce these attitudes. If this figure clearly bares the post-war trend toward Great Russian chauvinism, it just as clearly reflects one of the principal tendencies inherent in such chauvinism—anti-Semitism.

A future party leader is subjected to totalitarian indoctrination from the day he first embarks upon the course that will enable him to perform the function of a high party *apparatchik*, whether in the central secretariat or in the provinces. This creates the classic authoritarian personality—rigid, disciplined, obedient, adoring of the symbol of his own nationality, suspicious of the alien and the outsider. The Jew, especially the "cosmopolitan" and "international Zionist" Jew, becomes the embodiment of all the evil fantasies conjured up as threats to the socialist "motherland." Government policy reflects this deeply entrenched view.

The Modern Period (Since 1964)

Why has Judaism, at least until the late 1980s, been the target of an especially vicious anti-religious campaign? An "old Bolshevik," speaking to an American visitor in the offices of *Pravda*, summed up the answer neatly:

> Synagogues are in themselves of no consequence. But they serve as the last assembly for our Jews, often for those who are no longer religious. They help maintain cohesion, to nurture the feeling of belonging to a distinctive Jewish entity. And this is exactly what we are trying to prevent.

Judaism is sharply attacked "not so much because it is a religion as because of its effect in unifying Jews." Clearly, the primary enemy is not the Russian Judaic establishment *per se*, which has been based on the synagogue or, more likely, on institutions tolerated by the state over the last four decades, such as the Yiddish monthly *Sovietishe Heimland*. This was a force that the Soviets correctly assess has all but disappeared through the state's campaign of extermination and assimilation. Rather, the target is the Jewish population as a distinctive ethnic group within which an active interest in Judaism has been revived outside the normative synagogue establishment. Indeed, the force of Judaism is now really independent of the traditional Russian Jewish/Yiddish community, which has virtually disappeared. More than the synagogue, the unifying factor is now the tripartite theme *Israel-emigration-Hebrew*, especially the study of Hebrew.

Between Khrushchev's removal from power in 1964 and the Gorbachev era, anti-Semitism varied little in form from that experienced by previous generations, though there were fluctuations in intensity. The absence since 1919 of a central or federative structure for Judaism remains fundamental to the fragmentation of religious life and limits effective resistance to the Party's anti-religious campaign.

Lack of Literature and Religious Articles

The lack of a central structure also makes the enjoyment of specified as well as unspecified rights difficult if not impossible. For instance, while the "religious centers" of other faiths are able to publish periodicals and devotional literature, Judaism finds this virtually impossible. It publishes no periodical. It has not published a Hebrew Bible since the late 1920s. By contrast, the Russian Orthodox Church in 1957 printed 50,000 copies of a 1926 edition of the Bible, and in 1958 the Baptists printed 10,000 copies of the Bible. The Muslims in 1958 printed 9,000 copies of the Koran in 1958 and another edition in 1962.

Despite progress in the Gorbachev era, Jewish prayer books are still scarce. Many brought into the country by visitors have been confiscated; numerous prayer books remain locked in storage in Moscow and Leningrad. Although the state has assured those faiths having no "religious centers" a supply of the "necessary paper and the use of printing plants," this privilege has been extended to Judaism in a most restrained manner. In 1957, for the first time since the 1920s, an edition of the *siddur* (prayer book) was permitted, but of only 3,000 copies. Another edition of 5,000 appeared in 1968. Since there are an estimated

200,000 religiously observant Jews, the number published is distinctly inadequate. In partial response to the need, and to intervention by other countries, the authorities permitted 5,000 prayer books and Old Testament Bibles to be shipped in from the United States and elsewhere.

Without a "religious center," Judaism has also been deprived of the opportunity to produce such essential devotional articles as the *talith* (prayer shawl) and the *tfilin* (phylacteries). The Soviet government says it extends to "religious organizations" the right "to set up undertakings, such as candle factories and icon painting studios, for the manufacture of the requisite articles for religious worship." The right becomes meaningless, however, without a "religious center."

Lack of Outside Contact

The existence of "religious centers" enables the religions of the USSR to have formal contacts with their co-religionists abroad. A lengthy report on this subject by the Soviet government to the United Nations in 1963 says in part:

> Religious centers in the USSR maintain extensive communications with kindred international ecclesiastical organizations and take part in international ecclesiastical congresses, councils and conferences. . . . The Russian and Georgian Orthodox churches, the Lutheran Church of Estonia and Latvia, the Armenian Church, and the Church of Evangelical Christians–Baptists are members of the World Council of Churches. The Christian Churches of the USSR—Orthodox, Armenian, Lutheran, Old Believer, Reformed, and Evangelical Christians–Baptists—are members of the International Association of Christian Churches called the "Prague Christian Movement for Peace." . . . The All-Union Council of Evangelical Christians–Baptists are members of the World Union of Baptists and the European Baptist Federation. The Buddhist Central Religious Authority in the USSR is part of the World Brotherhood of Buddhists. The Mohammadan ecclesiastical authorities in the USSR take an active part in the Islamic Congress. The Catholic Church in the USSR participated in the first session of the Second Vatican Council.

There is no mention of Jews, because this religious community has not been permitted to have formal affiliations with any external body of its co-religionists. At a U.N. seminar in Yugoslavia in 1965, the Soviet representative insisted that individual persons have no status in international law and that, consequently, members of an ethnic or religious group cannot be accorded the right of association with international bodies of the same ethnic or religious affiliation. Only organizations have such status, he argued. Without a "religious center" in the USSR, no members of the Jewish community have the right to have an "association" with co-religionists abroad. The inclusion of a rabbi in a religious delegation from the USSR to the United States in 1984 was the first time in twenty years that any cleric of the Jewish community made an official visit abroad. In the following years, the rabbis of Moscow went to the United States on several occasions. They also met with Jewish communal leaders from other countries who were visiting the Soviet capital.

Besides permitting formal contacts with external co-religionists, the Soviet government also allows theological students of many faiths to journey abroad to study at religious institutions. Again, Judaism is notably absent from the 1963 report from the Soviet government to the United Nations:

> The Soviet Government does not impede the training of ministers at theological institutions abroad. In the last five years students from religious groups in the USSR have studied at the following educational establishments abroad: the Muslim Theological Seminary in Cairo, Baptist colleges in the United Kingdom, the Theological Faculty of Oxford University, the Lateran University of the Vatican, Göttingen University (Federal Republic of Germany), Bethel Theological Seminary, McMaster University (Canada), and the Muslim University of Syria.

In 1971, American rabbi Arthur Schneier initiated discussions with Soviet authorities to permit Jews seeking rabbinical training to go to Hungary, where training facilities are available. Since then, several Soviet Jewish students have been admitted to the Hungarian rabbinical seminary, the only one in Eastern Europe, and four now function as rabbis.

Lack of Theological Training

In the training of theological students, Judaism operates under a heavy burden. Only one *yeshiva* has been allowed to operate, and permission for that was not granted until 1957, while the Orthodox Church, for example, was allowed to establish a number of seminaries immediately after the war. In over thirty years, this *yeshiva* has ordained only two students. Of the thirteen students who were enrolled in April 1962—eleven of them over forty—nine students from communities in Georgia and Dagestan were prevented by Soviet authorities from coming to Moscow on grounds of a housing shortage. Between 1965 and 1972, no students were reported to be attending the *yeshiva*. In 1972 its doors were opened to permit six students—none rabbinical students—to study. Today the *yeshiva* is virtually defunct.

However, in February 1989 Rabbi Adin Steinsaltz opened a Judaic Studies Center in Moscow whose mission is to train orthodox rabbis and teachers. The center, the equivalent of a *yeshiva*, is attached to the Academy of World Civilization, a part of the Academy of Sciences.

As the Soviet authorities fully realize, the lack of theological training seriously affects the future course of organized religious practice, and Judaism faces the possibility of being without meaningful spiritual leadership. There are only four known ordained rabbis serving in pulpits in the Soviet Union. They are all recent graduates of the seminary in Budapest. Two officiate in Moscow, one in Leningrad, and one in Riga. In areas of Central Asia, an unknown number of *hahamim* (literally, "wise ones"), though not ordained, attempt to meet the religious needs of congregants.

All religions are affected by a state law that forbids "any teaching of a religious belief to children or persons under age, done in governmental or private teaching establishments or schools." Only in a family setting is such teaching allowed. The chairman of the USSR Supreme Court's Collegium for Criminal Cases has emphasized that only "the raising of children in a religious spirit when carried out by parents and other relatives does not constitute a crime."

Pressure Against Religious Rites

Significantly, the two Jewish religious rites that have been subjected to the strongest administrative pressures and propaganda have a distinctive national character: the Passover service and circumcision. Passover is in many ways a national holiday, recalling the historical experience of the liberation of the Jewish people from Egyptian bondage. It is at least minimally commemorated, if not religiously observed, even by secular and atheistic Jews wherever they may be.

Central to the Passover observance is *matzoth*, unleavened bread. The state's treatment of this article is a measure of its extraordinary concern about the holiday. In a report to the United Nations in 1956, the Soviet government said that on days preceding Passover, the stores of "the State trading organizations sell . . . *matzoth* . . . to enable worshipers to perform the appropriate ritual."

But in 1957, restrictions on the public baking and sale of *matzoth* began to appear, first in Kharkov and then in other cities. By 1962 the ban virtually blanketed the country. In March 1963, Rabbi Yehuda Levin, then the chief rabbi of Moscow's central synagogue, formally announced that the authorities had banned entirely the public baking and sale of *matzoth* and that congregants should bake the unleavened bread at home. Three months later, four elderly Jews were convicted of "illegal profiteering" in the sale of *matzoth*. The trial was the first of its kind in forty-five years, according to the chief rabbi. The defense attorney pointed out that the accused sold *matzoth* "not for profit but for their religious beliefs; they used no hired labor, they distributed the production which they didn't use themselves."

In 1964, the Moscow Jewish community was suddenly permitted, prior to the Passover, to rent a small bakery to produce *matzoth*. Since only a limited amount could be made, the chief rabbi granted special dispensation to religious Jews to eat beans and peas instead. After an outcry from abroad, in 1965 synagogues in a few major communities were given the right to bake *matzoth* for the Passover. At that time the chief rabbi told an American delegation that the authorities had assured him of adequate supplies of flour to bake *matzoth* in the future (an assurance that did not, however, extend to the rest of the country).

These few concessions concerning *matzoth* did not affect the propaganda campaign. Agitation in the press directed against Passover continued to be vindictive. The traditional phrase "Next year in Jerusalem" was singled out for the sharpest condemnation, less for its seemingly Zionist flavor than for its implication that Jews everywhere are loyal to a symbol that memorializes the ancient struggle for freedom and group integrity.

The rite of circumcision is even more characteristic of Jews, whether religious or not. Soviet authorities have described ritual circumcision as a "barbaric practice" that is injurious to health. They even frown on medical circumcision, and the Soviet medical encyclopedia has no entry on the subject. Yet in many parts of the world today non-Jewish as well as Jewish male infants are circumcised, for health reasons.

Soviet law does not specifically prohibit circumcision, probably because the regime is reluctant to antagonize its 47 million Muslim citizens. The vast majority of Muslims, even those who are party members, practice the rite freely. Although Oriental Jews living in areas with large Muslim populations benefit from the leniency shown the Muslim population, European Jews in the USSR face the harshest social consequences should they have their newborn sons circumcised. Party members are expelled; non-party members may be demoted in their jobs, lose opportunities for advancement, or be kept from acquiring a new apartment, and they face social ostracism for themselves and their families. The *mohel*, the person who performs circumcisions, is subject to strong pressure unless he is among the fortunate few in large towns who are granted official permits. He may be punished for performing surgery without a license or for functioning as a clergyman without registering.

The Assault on Hebrew

Central to the human rights of a cultural minority, as specifically defined in international law, is the assurance that its language or languages will not be subject to discrimination. Officially, the USSR recognizes Hebrew as a living language, intimately linked to the culture of the Jewish people. But that recognition is accompanied by systematic and gross discrimination against the use and teaching of the language by Soviet Jews. To the extent that Hebrew is subject to discrimination, the very culture of the Jews as an ethnic and religious minority is endangered.

The religious dimension is clearly crucial. Hebrew is not only the language of ancient and modern Jewish culture, an important unifying factor for Jews throughout the world, whatever their national languages; it is also the sacred language of Judaism, the language of prayer and of the *Torah*.

Legal Guarantees

Under international law, therefore, religious rights must include, for any Jewish community, the right to use and teach Hebrew. Although not binding, the Helsinki Final Act does obligate participating states to respect the freedom of the individual to *profess* and *practice* a religion of choice. Such activity for Jews requires the use and teaching of the sacred language.

This obligation is consistent with domestic legal provisions in the USSR. Article 36 of the 1977 Soviet Constitution guarantees Soviet citizens of different nationalities "the possibility to use their native language and the languages of other peoples of the USSR." This right is reiterated in Article 34 of the constitution of the Russian SFSR and no doubt appears in similar articles in the constitutions of the other republics.

Article 45 of the Soviet Constitution focuses upon education. It assures students "the opportunity to attend a school where teaching is in the native language." Statutes stipulate that where there are at least twenty-five pupils of the same nationality (and age group), the Soviet state is required to establish a separate school in which the language of instruction is the language of the nationality involved.

Communist ideology also publicly endorses the principle of the use and teaching of all minority languages. The official Program of the Communist Party of the Soviet Union vigorously affirms the right of every citizen "to speak and write in any language." Even more significant is an authoritative article that appeared in the government organ *Izvestia* on December 24,

1976. This lengthy article, "The Indestructible Power of Soviet Culture," declared that "no one in the Soviet Union is forbidden to study any language, including Hebrew or Yiddish." The statement served the additional purpose of indicating official awareness that the Hebrew language is closely tied to Jewish culture. The assertion was made in the context of an elaborate discussion of the cultural development and expression of the Jewish people in the USSR.

Evolution of the Policy

The Soviet regime's attitude toward Hebrew is marked by radically changing perceptions. In the early days after the March 1917 revolution, Hebrew culture in Russia experienced a remarkable growth. Then, owing in part to the increase of cultural and national tensions during the Civil War, Hebrew schools were abolished in 1919. Yet Hebrew did not disappear from the curriculum of higher education; it was dealt with as a foreign language linked, at least to some degree, with the Jewish people. A high official of the Communist Party's Jewish Section in 1926 stated that "Hebrew is still tied to our Yiddish language and cultural creation." He noted that Hebrew was recognized in the state's department of education, taught in the teachers' colleges and in the Odessa and Kiev institutes of social sciences, and available elsewhere as an elective.

Soviet sources also reveal that Hebrew was included in the curriculum of Moscow State University well into the 1920s and Odessa University until 1941. As part of research programs in linguistics and archeology, Hebrew as a language is currently taught in several institutions, among them Leningrad State University and Tbilisi State University, as well as at Moscow State University's Institute of Asian and African Countries and the Moscow Institute of International Relations. Significantly, neither of the two Moscow institutes has any known Jewish students. Key religious institutions authorized by the Kremlin also include Hebrew in their curricula: the Russian Orthodox theological academies in Leningrad and at Zagorsk (outside Moscow), and, of course, the nearly defunct *yeshiva* established in 1957 in Moscow. The most notable illustration of the acceptability of Hebrew as a living language is the authorized publication in 1963 of a Hebrew-Russian dictionary. Accurate and thorough, the acclaimed dictionary, prepared by the Russian-Jewish scholar F. Shapiro, constituted a testimonial to the vitality of the language. In addition, Moscow Radio broadcasts Hebrew-language programs to Israel, and the journal of the Soviet-dominated international Communist movement, *Problems of Peace and Socialism* (printed in Prague), is published in Hebrew, among other languages. By no means, then, can it be said that Hebrew as a distinctive foreign language has been eliminated by Soviet authorities. The *Izvestia* article of December 1976 linked the language to the Jewish people and acknowledged that there are Jews who want to study Hebrew.

The Disabilities

But Hebrew has also been subjected to an extraordinary set of discriminatory disabilities, designed to undermine its role as a conduit for Jewish heritage and communication. The same 1976 *Izvestia* article observed that "the Soviet public cannot tolerate" the alleged plan of "Jewish nationalists" to use "Hebrew study groups for propagandizing the Zionist ideology and for cultivating a spirit of national exclusiveness and open racism." Apparently Jews were to be allowed to study Hebrew in private but not in groups, and without teachers. Formal, organized classes for study of the language have been disallowed, and no Hebrew textbook or literature is officially available even for private study.

In 1985, thirty-three Jewish activists from Moscow and Leningrad wrote to the government department responsible for the distribution of reading material requesting a list of publications in the Hebrew language that had been officially approved, and information on where they could be obtained. A response to the inquiry was sent by the director of *Glavizdatexport* (State Publications Export):

> Jewish citizens, like citizens of other nationalities in our country, are able to study and read literature and newspapers in their national language. The national language of the Jews living in the USSR is Yiddish. Our Central Publishing House publishes books in Yiddish,

> and in the Jewish Autonomous Region Yiddish newspapers appear and programs in Yiddish are broadcast. The Central Publishing House has prepared a Russian-Yiddish dictionary to be issued in 40,000 copies, and by 1988 will publish a self-study book of the Yiddish language.
>
> As to Hebrew, which you are asking about, that language was never spoken by the Jews in Russia. That language is being used here, and in other countries, for religious rituals. In 1963 a Russian-Hebrew dictionary by Shapiro was published in 25,000 copies for experts. This dictionary can be found in many libraries and in second-hand shops. We do not plan to issue a further edition, nor do we intend to import books in the Hebrew language [Keston News Service, no. 245].

Some years earlier, in February 1972, forty-nine Moscow Jews asked the Municipal Department for People's Education to establish a course in Hebrew, asserting that interest in the language "has steeply risen among a part of the Jewish population in Moscow." A month later, forty-seven Minsk Jews wrote to the Byelorussian Party Central Committee and the Byelorussian ministries of education and culture requesting "evening courses for the Hebrew language." They complained bitterly about the closing of two private and presumably modest-sized Hebrew study groups that had been created in January 1972.

Official reaction was typical. A reply to the Moscow Jews stated that the teaching of foreign languages is regulated by the program of study of Soviet ministries of education; therefore the private teaching of Hebrew is unlawful. The contents of this letter were disclosed in a 1974 report prepared by the distinguished Swedish parliamentarian Per Ahlmark for the Consultative Assembly of the Council of Europe. In his view, the teaching of Hebrew in the USSR was forbidden.

But clearly the ban was not total. Individuals do study, and tiny groups studying Hebrew have not been driven out of existence; their tenacity has so far been greater than the authorities' persistence in trying to discourage them. In 1980, in Moscow alone, some 1,000 persons were reportedly studying Hebrew under the direction of an estimated eighty teachers. Until the late 1980s, however, most were severely harassed and their teachers judicially punished. Ahlmark's 1974 report noted:

> The police break into homes where Hebrew classes are held, conduct a house search, and arrest the occupant. In the proceedings, he is then accused of possession of anti-Soviet publications although they are merely simple Russian-Hebrew dictionaries or language textbooks.

Prosecution takes place under Article 70 of the Russian SFSR criminal code, which bans anti-Soviet agitation and propaganda, or Article 190, which forbids the circulation of information known to be falsely defaming the Soviet system. Also used are allegedly fabricated charges of possession of narcotics or firearms, as in the 1984 sentencing of three young Hebrew teachers.

Arbitrariness of Application

What narrows even further the rigidly restricted right to learn Hebrew is the reportedly capricious manner in which the teaching of Hebrew is handled by state authorities. Private tutors of Hebrew may sometimes discreetly "advertise" their services, but in other instances teachers have been intimidated and harassed. In the cases of Josyf Begun and Pavel Abramovich, the authorities at first threatened to apply Article 209 of the Russian Republic's penal code, the "anti-parasite law." According to the Presidium of the Supreme Soviet of the RSFSR, a "parasitic way of life as envisaged in Article 209" is

> living by an adult person capable of working for a protracted period (more than four months in succession or adding up to a year's duration) on unearned income with avoidance of socially useful work, persisted in after an official warning on the inadmissability of this style of life.

A person found to have violated Article 209 is given one month to find employment. If at the end of the month he is found still to be unemployed, the authorities issue a warning that he will be liable for criminal prosecution should he not be gainfully employed by the end of a second month. Persons convicted under Article 209 have been sentenced to two years' exile in Siberia.

Soviet authorities sometimes refuse to accept the private teaching of Hebrew as a socially useful form of employment. Arbitrariness prevails in the responses of local government agencies. For example, appropriate agencies approved the private teaching of Hebrew by Vladimir Prestin (Moscow, 1971) and by Lev Furman and Mark Nosovskii (Leningrad, 1977). But the experiences of Josyf Begun and Pavel Abramovich, two scientists who also had applied for permits to leave for Israel, illustrate a harsher approach.

The Begun and Abramovich Cases

Josyf Begun applied for an emigration permit in 1971. His request was denied, and subsequently he was fired from his job as a senior scientific worker in mathematics with the Central Science Research Institute of Economics. The same year, Pavel Abramovich was fired from his job as an electronics engineer after his request for emigration was denied on grounds of "access to state secrets." Both men then took up the private teaching of Hebrew as a means of livelihood. They were arrested in 1977 for "systematically engaging in vagrancy."

Begun was informed by a local party official that he had no right to teach Hebrew as he did not have a degree in the subject he was teaching. Abramovich was told by the finance department of the local Moscow district that the government could not register him as a Hebrew teacher or accept payment of taxes from him on income earned from teaching because he did not "have the specialty of the pedagogue." Abramovich rejected the charge on the grounds that it was not within the competence of the finance ministry to determine his qualifications to teach Hebrew.

If unpublished Soviet statutes stipulate that a prerequisite for permitting the teaching of a subject on a private basis is that it is already being offered in an institution of higher learning, the teaching of Hebrew meets this requirement. To refuse to recognize the private teaching of Hebrew as "socially useful work" appears to be both arbitrary and discriminatory.

Even more serious, rejection of the private teaching of Hebrew violates established international law regarding the free choice of employment. The right of the individual freely to choose his or her own employment was first recognized in 1948 under Article 23 of the Universal Declaration of Human Rights.

The right became binding for contracting parties of the International Covenant on Economic, Social, and Cultural Rights. The language is clear and precise. Its Part III, Article 6, reads:

> 1. The states parties to the present covenant recognize the right to work, which includes the right of everyone to the opportunity to gain his living by work which he freely chooses or accepts, and will take appropriate steps to safeguard this right.

The Soviet Union ratified this covenant in October 1973. Furthermore, a 1964 International Labor Organization convention, the Convention Concerning Employment Policy, requires member states, of which the USSR is one, to pursue "as a major goal an active policy designed to promote . . . freely chosen employment."

On June 1, 1977, Begun was found guilty of pursuing a "parasitic form of life" and sentenced to two years' exile in Siberia. He addressed the issue of private Hebrew instruction in his final statement to the court:

> I began teaching in private. I insist that it be admitted that the teaching of Hebrew is socially useful work. It was precisely because they refuse to register Hebrew that this trial was rigged up. There is no public way of studying the language of the Jews. There are no courses, and Hebrew is not taught in the schools. For the overwhelming majority of the people, there is no possibility to study the language. The fact that the financial offices refuse to register incomes from teaching Hebrew has completely deprived people of the possibility of studying their own language.

After completing his sentence, Begun returned to teaching Hebrew. He was again arrested in 1982 and was charged with "anti-Soviet agitation and propaganda," which subjected him to a long sentence of detention. In the changed atmosphere of *glasnost*, he was released and early in 1988 was allowed to leave for Israel.

The anti-Hebrew campaign of the early 1980s became more concerted and severe when it appeared that the harsh sentence imposed on Begun in 1982 was not deterring the younger generation of Hebrew students and teachers. Of the eight Hebrew teachers arrested between 1982 and 1985, one was charged with resisting the militia, another with possession of drugs, and four with anti-Soviet slander. The anti-parasite law ceased to be used.

In a shift of policy, since 1986 all the Hebrew teachers have been released, and no others have been arrested. The Hebrew study groups have once again been allowed to function, though without official approval.

Suppressing Yiddish

Not only has Hebrew been subject to discrimination. Yiddish, too, the officially recognized Jewish language in the USSR, and all aspects of Jewish institutional life, were victimized by a powerful state-administered assault. Today there is not a single formal Yiddish language class in European Russia for the world's third-largest Jewish community and for the Soviet Union's sixteenth-largest nationality. All Jewish communal and institutional structures except the Yiddish literary journal *Sovietishe Heimland* and the Yiddish newspaper *Biro-Bidzhaner Shtern* have been liquidated. Near the end of 1988, there was discussion of proposals to reconstruct some of the facilities and to create a Jewish Center in Moscow. There is still no Jewish publication in the Russian language, which 97 per cent of all Soviet Jews speak. None of the other more than one hundred nationalities in the USSR has been stranded in such a cultural desert.

In an official Soviet statement that appeared in a booklet published by the party-sponsored *Znanie* society in 1967, M. N. Andryukhin characterizes "the destruction of a people's language" as a national cultural genocide. This, he says, is a "crime of the same order" as "physical genocide."

Emigration: A Privilege, Not a Right

In chapter five, Philip Walters outlined five responses of Soviet religious bodies to the anti-religious posture of the state: undiluted loyalty, discretionary accommodation, constrained accommodation, dissent, and emigration. Since there are only four ordained and active rabbis in the entire European portion of the USSR, to apply such a division to the Jewish situation is rather artificial. Still, the first position, "undiluted loyalty," would probably best describe the only viable option for ordained Jewish leaders; the community is presumably too small and isolated to support a much more courageous stand. Leaders within this category understand not only the letter but also the spirit of Soviet legislation on religion and generally abide by both.

Little is known, however, about Jewish life in Central Asia, which is distant from Moscow's oversight, and where local tradition allows the leadership of rabbis not formally ordained; perhaps some among these, though they cooperate with authorities, nevertheless take some initiative in their religious responsibilities. Indeed, Georgian and Bukharan Jews have managed to preserve their identities to a greater extent than other Jewish communities in the USSR, and certainly not without some creative and probably courageous leadership.

Unlike the Christian community, Soviet Jewry has few members who choose the fourth option, dissent, except as expressed in behavior unacceptable to the authorities. There are some who lead an underground religious existence, observing the traditions and rites and instructing children in the faith. Others are teaching or learning Hebrew or Jewish history. But as Soviet Jews have found an identity in the tripartite theme *emigration-Israel-Hebrew*, few feel compelled to attempt to change the political system.

Many Jews—and certainly the vast majority of religious ones—desire only to leave the country. The main motive for many is to reunite with relatives, many of whom left during the peak emigration years of 1978 and 1979. By 1980, when Soviet toleration of some emigration virtually ended, more than 350,000 persons were known to have requested affidavits from Israel in the first step of an arduous journey—and one that most did not expect to complete. In 1988, as some restrictions were eased, there was an upsurge in new and resubmitted requests for affidavits, estimated at 100,000.

The right to emigrate from the Soviet Union is not guaranteed to all citizens but is permitted only for the purpose of "reunification of families" or "repatriation to one's homeland." The peak year for Jewish emigration was 1979, when 51,320 Jews left. In 1984, however, fewer than 1,000 were permitted to leave, and in 1985 only some 1,100. But in 1987, there was an easing of barriers, and the figure rose to 8,000. By the last quarter of 1988 the monthly rate had reached more than 2,000.

The reasons given for the denial of emigration requests vary. Caprice and arbitrariness prevail. In many cases the applicant is told he had "access to state secrets." During the months and probably years of waiting for an exit visa, most refuseniks have found it difficult to continue working at meaningful occupations, and some have had trouble finding even the most menial employment. In the past, some professionals and academics had their credentials revoked; others faced discrimination in educational opportunities. Many refuseniks have faced a routine of repeated questionings. In the 1970s and early 1980s, some who campaigned for the right of Jewish emigration faced charges of "parasitism," "hooliganism," and even treason.

The Outlook

During the late 1980s, a sense of ethnic and cultural identification has been awakened among some Jews, notably young ones, and they have attempted to regularize and improve Jewish life in the USSR. Activity has centered on the creation of Jewish cultural associations in several cities. Some of these have been officially accepted by local authorities. These associations are part of a network of Jewish groups acceptable both to the authorities and to Jews, without the taint of those institutions, both religious and non-religious, that continued to function in the post-Stalin decades.

Other forms of Jewish expression have come into existence outside this newly developing establishment network. Most of them have not received official approval but are tolerated. A Soviet-Israel Friendship Society was formed early in 1988, with several hundred members in more than twenty cities. This was followed several months later by a Union of Hebrew Teachers. While the bulk of the union's members are in Moscow and Leningrad, 40 of its approximately 100 member teachers are from a dozen other cities. Some 600–800 students are involved. The aim is to spread the Hebrew language among the Soviet Jews as well as to foster the teaching of Jewish history and traditions.

While hinting at the possibility that Hebrew could be taught at proposed Jewish cultural centers in Moscow, officials have refused to recognize Hebrew as a national language (perhaps alongside Yiddish, which is known only to Jews in the western republics) of Soviet Jews. Indeed, Hebrew teachers, although increasingly tolerated, are still not given official recognition.

Other small, independent groups are operating also, in cities far from the main population centers, where the official and semi-official groups have not penetrated. With loose ties to the larger groups, they function mostly as seminars in Hebrew and forums for the discussion and teaching of Judaism and matters relating to Israel.

In 1988, officials in Moscow, in talks with Western officials and Jewish leaders from other countries, expressed a willingness to allow development of a Jewish religious establishment and a framework for Jewish cultural life. The authorities seemed to accept the notion that Jews could once again conduct an autonomous communal life in the USSR, but within the framework of a solution to the much broader problem of demands by other national minorities that lack their own territory within Soviet borders. The opening in February 1989 of a Judaic Studies Center to train rabbis (see page 235) was an encouraging development.

As we have seen, the especially disadvantaged position of Soviet Jews as compared to other ethnic and recognized religious groups is due in part to a long-standing anti-Semitism that goes back to the introduction of Byzantine Orthodoxy into the region a thousand years ago. This anti-Semitism has been preserved through centuries of tsarist and Soviet regimes. Another strike against Judaism is that it is tied inextricably to Israel; Judaism is "international" and "cosmopolitan," in contrast to such indigenous traditions as Russian Orthodoxy and, in Central Asia, Islam.

To the extent that Jewry has maintained any life-breath at all in the Soviet Union, Zvi Gitelman argues that this is a function largely of its renouncing its claim to "proclaim a truth basis for general social relation," and limiting its domain in such a way that conflicts with the state are minimized. Gitelman continues:

> The problem in the Soviet Union is not the confrontation between modern relativism and traditional religious dogmatism. It is, in fact, the problem of conflicting dogmas in a system which has little tolerance for relativism. When religion confronts the Soviet state there is a conflict not quite between the secular and the religious, but between a secular ideology which has the *behavioral characteristics* (and even some of its structural ones) of a religion, and a "traditional" religion [Zvi Gitelman, "Judaism and Modernization," in Dennis Dunn, ed., *Religion and Modernization in the Soviet Union* (Westview Press, 1971), p. 284].

At least as significant as the anti-religious discrimination and persecution to Judaism in the USSR, however, has been the toll exacted by modernization. The anti-Semitism of the tsarist period did at least have the positive effect of preserving the *shtetl* (the rural Jewish towns and villages), along with its myths, rituals, and world view. With the coming of the Soviet period, however, a massive movement of Jews took place; they left the villages of the Pale of Settlement and entered areas formerly forbidden them. This process probably did more to break up the traditions and community than any other factor. Jews intermarried, spoke Russian in everyday conversation, became urbanized, and more than ever before entered the economic and social mainstream, leaving behind both their religion and a closely knit community founded upon a history of diaspora.

The inability of Marxism-Leninism to fill "three-dimensional space" previously occupied by powerful religious symbols is widely perceived. The Soviet experiment has underscored the inadequacy of an economic and political ideology for addressing questions of meaning, purpose, and value, and there is evidence of significant discontent on this level. While consumerism and materialism are widespread responses in the USSR—as in the West—to the need to find meaning, intellectuals and others also attempt to fill the "soul-space" with traditional symbols, as expressed in Judaism and other religions.

In the end, as religion has been relegated to the periphery of social concern, there may be less societal pressure—as opposed to "official" state pressure—to conform to an atheistic ideology than in the past. Many Soviet citizens simply do not care about such matters. Concern over belief, of whatever nature, has been replaced in part by a concern for a better life. This situation may indeed allow more opportunity for the development and exercise of a religious world view.

10

The Religious Renaissance: Myth or Reality?

Jane Ellis

THE SUBJECT of a religious renaissance, or religious revival, in the Soviet Union has attracted increasing attention from Western commentators in recent years. While much that has been written is inspiring, much is superficial, and some is misleading. At the same time, some commentators both in the USSR and in the West deny that such a phenomenon exists. The earliest evidence for a religious reawakening came years ago from lone voices that for a long time were largely ignored in the West. Preaching in his Moscow church in 1969, Father Vsevolod Shpiller said this:

> I believe that a new chapter is beginning in the history of our church. . . . More and more frequently and unexpectedly you meet people of the most varied ages and situations who have gone through deep inner spiritual, mental, and emotional crises, sometimes through tragic conflicts which they have found insoluble in a non-religious framework. Not infrequently now, here and there, maybe in a muted and novel way, sometimes questioningly, the poet's words can be heard: "Not long ago I was secretly told, Christ is soon returning." The religious thought of great minds, faithful to Christ, is becoming a vital subject for those who are asking the Church about different things, more and more frequently, more and more deeply, more and more earnestly.[1]

Jane Ellis is a senior researcher at Keston College. She is the author of *The Russian Orthodox Church: A Contemporary History*. Previously the editor of Keston's journal *Religion in Communist Lands,* she now edits *Frontier*.

Several years later, in 1977, a Christian layperson wrote in a similar vein. At the time Igor Shafarevich was a renowned mathematician, a lecturer of many years' standing at Moscow University, and a member of the Academy of Sciences. In an interview published in *samizdat*, he stated:

> Religion now plays an entirely different role from the one it used to play in Russia before the Revolution and probably from the one it plays at present in many Western countries. Religion in our country has to satisfy much higher spiritual demands. Many are drawn to religion through a search for spiritual values, after having been disillusioned by the materialist way of life. Many are drawn to the Orthodox Church by a wish to get into touch with the history of their native land, with the national traditions of Russia. And of course the church fulfills many other functions besides the basic task, that of creating a link between man and God.
>
> It is this which turns the church into such an enormous force, and this force finds its outward expression in the great numbers of children and adults baptized, in the way young people are attracted to the church, in the crowded churches and the huge masses of people who gather around the churches on feast-days.[2]

These views of Orthodox Christians were supported by a non-believer who played a leading role in the dissent movement, Lyudmilla Alexeyeva. When she emigrated from the Soviet Union in 1977, Alexeyeva confirmed that there was a general religious rebirth in the USSR, especially among the intelligentsia. It was now taken for granted that such a person could be baptized and go to church, she said.[3]

Dissenting Voices

Many more people have testified that a substantial movement toward religion is taking place in the Soviet Union. Yet there are also dissenting voices. Valeri Chalidze, a leading figure in the human-rights movement until he left the USSR in 1972, wrote after arriving in the United States that there was no such thing as a "Russian Orthodox revival":

> The émigré press is full of reports on the great number of Russian Orthodox believers, and the influx of youth into the church, although there are no statistics to confirm this. But this merely parallels their interest in all "unofficial" spiritual phenomena: non-Marxist philos-

ophy, Buddhism, Yoga, spiritualism, and the like. We know of unofficial groups and seminars devoted to the study of Orthodoxy as well as to other religions, instances of the baptism of young intellectuals, and an interest in religious subjects on the part of non-conformist artists. But there has been nothing like a large-scale return to the Orthodox religion. No more grounds exist for calling the current heightened religious interest an Orthodox revival, than for calling the human-rights movement a political revival.

The philosopher Aleksandr Zinoviev, a 1978 émigré whose *samizdat* satirical novels have been translated into English, shares Chalidze's skepticism:

> As far as the phenomenon of "religious renaissance" in Russia is concerned, it is basically an inadequate form of expression for social dissatisfaction and a tribute to fashion (especially where intellectual circles are concerned). Only in part is this an expression of a psychological need for something resembling religion.[4]

Another writer who has denied that there are grounds for speaking of a religious revival, though for quite different reasons, is the human-rights activist and Orthodox Christian Adel Naidenovich. In a *samizdat* article dated September 1978 she wrote:

> Is the vitality of the church felt among the many millions of people in the cities? Seek for it on a building site, in any office, on a collective farm, in any interweaving of masses of humanity. . . . All around is religious paralysis. . . . We have been reduced to a situation of great sorrow and the total victory of godlessness.[5]

Unlike Chalidze or Zinoviev, she would clearly like a religious revival to take place but sees no evidence of it at present.

Can these three latter statements be reconciled with the three preceding ones? Some allowance must be made for the writers' different standpoints. Anyone whose life has been greatly affected by a religious reawakening will not fail to put an extremely high value upon that experience and upon its potential for transforming the lives of others. On the other hand, anyone not involved in this process can point to the multitudes of people as yet unaffected. While significant numbers of people are undoubtedly experiencing some kind of religious revitalization, then, it would be misleading to suggest that it is a mass movement.

Seeking a Name

What should this revitalization be called? The Orthodox Christian and writer Andrei Sinyavsky speaks to this point:

> In contemporary Russia there is neither a renaissance (even a religious one) nor a revolution (even a moral one). . . . There really is, however, . . . an enlivening of religious feeling and consciousness in Russia today (and this is good!). This is expressed by a turning among a part of the intelligentsia—above all the young and most intellectual ones—to forgotten values, to the church, to religious philosophy.
>
> Children educated in atheism have somehow comprehended something in the darkness and aspired to read the Bible, which they had never read before, to go to church, to cross themselves, to pray, to think things over.[6]

In Russian, the word writers usually use to describe the phenomenon is *vozrozhdeniye,* customarily translated either "revival" or "renaissance"; others simply use the Russian transliteration of "renaissance"—*renessans*. "Renaissance" is probably the more satisfactory translation. "Revival," in customary English usage, suggests something more sudden and dramatic. But "renaissance," while it applies to some religious groups, may be inappropriate for others. "Reawakening," "revitalization," and "rebirth," with their more tentative, less dogmatic overtones, probably come closer to the mark and will be used in this chapter. Yet the term "renaissance" has now been so widely used, by both Soviet and Western writers, that we cannot reject it—as the chapter title shows.

Background of the Reawakening

Whatever name is given to the phenomenon we are considering, the fact of its existence is remarkable. In the Soviet Union since 1917 there has been a determined, brutal attempt to eradicate religion. Atheistic propaganda, often virulently antireligious, has been the norm. The massive attempts to eradicate institutional religious life in the 1920s and 30s, to the point of causing the violent deaths of millions of believers, have now ceased, but believers continue to suffer persecution and even death for their faith. Against such a background, the survival of a few small, scattered groups of religious believers would be remarkable enough. The fact that nearly all religious groups have survived, and that many, probably most, of them are growing, is one of the most remarkable developments in the religious world today. The refusal of vast numbers of ordinary, humble believers to abandon their faith during decades of mass persecution meant that there would be a church still in existence to which newer generations would be able to turn. The *samizdat* author Gennadi Shimanov has attempted to put this into perspective:

> The most sensitive people, those who yearn most for sense in this general senselessness and are incapable of living for the sake of base profit, have begun gradually, one by one, to return from the "far country" to the Orthodox Church. . . . We can note here only a few of . . . the most common "channels" through which the truth about God has streamed out. First of all, there are the old women *[babushki]*. Their role, until now valued by only a few, is indeed a great one. In the intolerable years the *babushki* have borne and still bear on their frail shoulders, crushed by life, the edifice of the Church. . . . What kind of enemy of godlessness can they be? The wind could blow them down, they are powerless. . . . Any of them would die of a flick of the fingers, turning up their toes on the spot. . . . But no. One just can't do that to them. And so they live. . . .
>
> Yes, the *babushki* have done great harm to godlessness. But what can be done; after all, they can't all be shot on reaching pensionable age. . . . And so like it or not one has to be patient, resign oneself, and wait until they all become atheists. Only one will have to wait a long time.[7]

Yevgeny Vagin, who before emigrating served a labor-camp sentence for his oppositionist activity, based on his Christian beliefs, agreed that it is the millions of ordinary believers who have kept the church alive. He writes:

> If all this time there had not been the *faithful*—piously preserving the Orthodox faith, never retreating, following it to fatal torments, establishing it by the sacrifice of their blood—would it have been possible to say that Russia is alive, and believes, and has a great future?. . . These unseen millions form a kind of natural foundation,

a spiritual basis for the religious quest of the "solitary" intellectuals.[8]

Beginning of the Reawakening

After years of persecution so severe that institutional religious life had been almost eliminated, the practice of religion was allowed to resume during and after the Second World War. This took place within the narrow limits decreed by the state. The church had been so devastated before the war, however, that there was considerable room for expanding its activities before it began to come up against the limits. The masses of the faithful, having never abandoned their beliefs, were once more able to practice them fairly openly.

And there were new members as well. At about the end of the 1950s small numbers of young inquirers or converts began to meet together to discuss the faith. Sometimes a circle would form around a priest, if one could be found willing to take the risks involved in active work among young people. As these groups multiplied during the 1960s, some of the intelligentsia, both young and old, began to take religion seriously. This coincided to some extent with the severe anti-religious campaign of 1959–64, inaugurated by Khrushchev. Instead of deterring new seekers after faith, this campaign may have spurred them on. The quality of the anti-religious propaganda was so low that no thinking person could take it seriously, and people may well have been inspired to look more closely at something that their government was so determined to destroy.

After the end of the anti-religious campaign, and especially during the 1970s, the number of converts began to grow more noticeably, and, as far as one can tell in the absence of statistics, the number of Christian discussion groups increased significantly. This coincided with the rise and expansion of the human-rights movement. Mikhail Meerson-Aksyonov, who emigrated in 1974, described the early years as follows:

> [In the mid-sixties] it was more or less impossible to meet any young people in the churches except for the same few who came just out of curiosity. But in the following years the situation changed, so that it became commonplace to see young men and women in many

> Moscow churches each Sunday, taking part in the services and receiving Holy Communion. Around certain priests groups of a hundred or more young people have gathered. Father Dmitri Dudko, who is known in the West, has drawn around himself in the past several years a group of young intelligentsia of several hundreds; and he is far from the exception. On such great feasts as Easter the churches are packed with young people, so much so, that the elderly are lost among them. . . .
>
> This frequenting of the churches by the youth is not confined to the capital. At one time I worked in a small village church outside Moscow where every Sunday a good number of young people confessed and communicated. This impressed me the more in that they had little chance of understanding the meaning of their faith, for the clergy of that parish were frequently changed and were not at all concerned about the religious instruction of their flock, not to mention not being inspired by a missionary spirit.
>
> In the course of these years, groups of Orthodox youth were formed in other cities. I will speak only of those known personally to me, whose leaders visited me in Moscow for religious literature. They came from Leningrad, Grodno, Tomsk, Gorky, Odessa, Yaroslavl, Vologda, and more.[9]

In the much more repressive atmosphere of the early 1980s, the public activity of religious activists, as of human-rights activists, diminished considerably; but while the Christian discussion groups adopted a much lower profile than formerly, their activities continued.

Causes of the Reawakening

The religious reawakening can be attributed to several factors. For many people, the initial impulse was a very simple one: *disillusionment with Marxism-Leninism*. Having lost whatever faith they may once have had in the only state-approved system of beliefs, such people were obliged to seek, alone and often painfully, for something to make life meaningful. For very many, though not all, the search has ended in the embrace of some form of religious belief. This point was made by General Pyotr Grigorenko, who was cashiered from the Red Army when he became openly involved in the defense of human rights. During an interview in 1978, after his emigration, Grigorenko said:

> I am no longer a Communist, although I professed this teaching almost my entire conscious life. . . . I see no Communist state system which has not stifled its people, deprived them of their human rights, liquidated freedom and democracy, established the complete supremacy of a party-state bureaucracy. . . . If I must call myself anything, I would agree simply to take the name "Christian."[10]

Another cause of a turn toward religion has been *atheism's lack of appeal.* Atheism, an essentially negative philosophy, failed to provide an adequate view of life. In particular, many have found its answer to the problem of death quite unsatisfactory. A resilient religious element in Russian literature and art, and the fact that Russians are supposed, by themselves as well as others, to be naturally religious, also work against the acceptance of atheism. Added to this is the singularly arid, repetitive, and uninspiring character of atheistic propaganda—a fact borne out by frequent criticisms in the Soviet press as well as by the comments of disenchanted readers. The negative response to atheism was summed up by Vladimir Osipov, the Orthodox and Russian nationalist writer who served eight years in a labor camp for editing the *samizdat* journal *Veche*:

> On no battlefield has anyone yet cried "For atheism!" And the Russian air has not been sanctified with this cry. Atheism is something alien, imported, not part of us. I think that atheism was imposed on the Russian land and did not take root in it.[11]

Regarding the aridity of materialism, Yuri Mamleyev, a *samizdat* author who emigrated from the USSR in 1975, writes of two realities that "shatter the position of materialism and atheism in the USSR":

> On the one hand, there is the aspiration towards knowledge and towards truth: already there has been accumulated a sufficient quantity of experiments in parapsychology and of theoretical conclusions on matter in science itself (in physics, for example) to be able to see . . . how naïve and primitive are the dogma sent down from the heights of Marxism, how they fetter people's creative energy.
>
> The second reason, leading right to the sources of the present renaissance, is in spiritual and moral thirst and the absolute impossibility of slaking it with the help of materialism. . . .

> This is why, for example, the more and more frequent articles in the Soviet press, where attempts are made to reconcile with death the soul of a person brought up on atheism, are meaningless. Usually these attempts go no further than empty assertions that we will "continue" to live in our actions, in our descendants, and so on. It is clear that this is not an answer to the question but an evasion of it.[12]

The *strong religious element in Russian culture* is another cause of interest in religion. Among those who choose to reject Marxism-Leninism, many feel a need to look into their past to discover a sense of their own identity. They cannot believe that history began in 1917, and they eagerly seek their historical, cultural, and spiritual roots in earlier times. In doing so, they come across Christianity at every turn. Many begin their religious quest, and others are converted to Christianity, through reading Russian nineteenth-century authors, above all Dostoevsky. Some people, though seized by the religious values of Russian culture, remain on the fringes of the church—indeed, culture itself in a way becomes their religion. Others, however, embrace a deep Christian commitment.

Another reason for interest in religion has been the *growth of nationalism* in many areas of the USSR. Nationalism and religion are often closely intertwined, sometimes inextricably so. The assertion of nationalistic values—language, culture, religion—is one of the ways in which Soviet citizens express their dissatisfaction with Soviet ideology and "sovietized" culture. Additionally, in many areas of the USSR, nationalism is an expression of dissatisfaction with rule by Moscow and the overt russification that accompanies it. In Ukraine, Estonia, Latvia, Lithuania, Georgia, and Central Asia there are people who strongly resent having to conduct much of their daily business in the Russian language, with the concomitant debasement and impoverishment of their own language and, consequently, their own culture. They also resent the political control exerted by Moscow, the capital of a foreign country. Some of the strongest nationalists even advocate secession from the USSR.

It is not surprising that, as they have sought to rediscover and preserve their national traditions, the nationalists have come upon the religious beliefs and practices of their forebears. For example, Roman Catholicism remains as strong among the highly patriotic Lithuanians as it does in Poland. The population of the four Central Asian republics, and to a lesser extent of Kazakhstan, remains strongly wedded to the Muslim way of life and resistant to atheistic propaganda. Russian nationalism is also growing, at least partly in reaction to the nationalistic trends.

The Question of Timing

The question remains, however, why these impulses toward religion began to make themselves felt at a particular time, namely, the late 1950s and early 1960s. There are two principal reasons. First, young people of that period belonged to the first generation under Soviet power that had the leisure time required to *think*. Since 1917 the population of the USSR had endured war, revolution, civil war, large-scale famine, political terror, war again, and then the final years of Stalinism. No doubt these experiences strengthened many religious believers in their faith, and inspired some non-believers to adopt some form of faith. But they did not permit significant groups within society to rethink the basis of their lives in a way that has subsequently become possible.

Even people who did embrace religious faith during the years of hardship would have had little or no opportunity to communicate it to others. People learned to guard their thoughts and beliefs jealously for fear of denunciation, and there was thus no basis for any kind of religious movement or even exchange of views about religion. Only after the defeat of Hitler and the demise of Stalinism was anything remotely resembling normal intellectual and spiritual life able to reemerge.

Another factor that contributed to a reawakening of interest in religion at this particular time was destalinization, commencing with Nikita Khrushchev's famous "secret speech" at the Congress of the Communist Party of the Soviet Union (CPSU) in 1956. It was an unprecedented happening. For the first time a Soviet leader, one who had previously been exalted to almost godlike proportions, was revealed to have been fallible, even mistaken. For the entire generation that had grown up under Stalin's leadership and also for older people, the shock was immense. Something that had been pressed upon them all their lives was revealed overnight to be false. Realizing that they had been systematically lied to for almost three decades, these people would be unlikely ever again to take any official statement on trust. If they had been lied to once, they could be lied to again. Thinking people now wanted to reason for themselves and work out their own values on which to base their lives.

This opened up an attitude of inquiry that would lead in many different directions. Religion was only one of these directions. Nonetheless, the crisis of confidence had been so great that a very considerable number of people were newly interested in religion. They blazed a trail for others to follow, and so the move back to religion gained momentum with the passing years.

Perhaps the most significant fact about the religious reawakening is that, according to Marxist-Leninist dogma, it should not, indeed could not, have happened. The view of the CPSU was that, under conditions of socialism and with atheistic propaganda, the ground for nurturing any kind of religious belief would disappear and religion would wither away. The first date set for this to happen was 1937, by which time an entire generation would have grown up under socialism and would feel no need of religion. When the census of 1937 showed that a large proportion of the population remained believers, however, this goal was hastily revised (and the census unpublished), while systematic atheistic propaganda continued. Khrushchev's antireligious campaign of 1959 to 1964 was certainly intended as a final—albeit quixotic—campaign to eradicate religion. But the growth of interest in and commitment to religion over the last twenty-five to thirty years has been a most decisive rejection of Communist theories about religious belief.

Scope of the Reawakening

The Russian Orthodox Church is the largest religious group in the USSR, and it is in this community that the evidence of spiritual reawakening has been most obvious. Most of what we have said so far, and all of the quoted comments, have been about the Orthodox Church. But there are also signs of renewal in other religious bodies.

The largest religious faith in the Soviet Union is, of course, the Christian. The Russian Orthodox Church probably has at least 50 million adherents. There are about 5.5 million Roman (Latin-rite) Catholics and possibly 1.5 million or more Eastern-rite Catholics (Uniates), who are outlawed. There are probably about 5 million Protestants—more than 3 million Baptists, half a million Pentecostals, and smaller numbers of Seventh-Day Adventists, Lutherans, Mennonites, Methodists, and Jehovah's Witnesses. The Old Believer Churches (formed by a schism within the Russian Orthodox Church in the seventeenth century) are of unknown size but could have as many as a million adherents. There are also unknown numbers of True Orthodox (who left the Russian Orthodox Church in the 1920s to go underground) and other sects of earlier Orthodox origin. There are strong national Orthodox churches in both Georgia (population 5 million) and Armenia (population 3 million); church attendance in both these nations is reportedly high, but some allowance must be made for nominalism. People of Muslim background form the second-largest religious group in the USSR, numbering between 45 and 50 million, with a high birthrate. They are not all practicing believers, but the Islamic tradition and way of life remain strong. There are at least 1.8 million Jews (other estimates are higher, from 2.25 to 3 million), not all of whom are religious. There are about half a million Buddhists in the Soviet Far East, but no Hindus. The last few years, however, have witnessed the rapid growth, without previous roots, of the Hare Krishnas, a Hindu sect.

The above estimates, imprecise though they are, add up to between 110 and 120 million religious believers. This rough estimate derives some support from another estimate, equally tentative, of 115 million believers, made by a Western scholar on the basis of Soviet sociological data.[13] This is a significant proportion—41 per cent—of the current Soviet population of 280 million. Soviet sociologists who have surveyed religiosity have in recent years estimated that between one in five and one in three of the population are believers.

Does this large number of believers reflect significant growth through religious reawakening, or have the religious communities maintained or increased their numbers mainly through family tradition? A rough categorization of four types of growth or non-growth suggests itself.

1. Membership Decline

Some groups appear to be declining in membership. The Buddhists and the Lutherans are included here. Although Buddhist decline has been offset somewhat by an intellectual interest in Buddhism among the urban intelligentsia in some Russian cities, this has not swelled the Buddhist communities of the Soviet Far East. Membership of Lutheran churches in their heartlands of Estonia and Latvia is decreasing. Although new Lutheran churches have been registered in Central Asia, these are communities that have been there, unregistered, since they were deported by Stalin, not new churches. We assume that Old Believers, True Orthodox, and other sects of Orthodox origin are declining, or certainly not growing. The tiny group of Methodists, numbering just over 2,000, may have increased its numbers slightly over the last few years, but even if its handful of congregations continues to grow, it is unlikely to make much impact beyond its present locations in Estonia and Transcarpathia (though the Methodist church in Tallinn, Estonia, has one of the liveliest congregations anywhere in the Soviet Union). We will therefore place the Methodists in this first category.

Religious groups in the second and third categories appear to be maintaining their numbers or growing. In the second category, this is due primarily to ethnic or national allegiance, while in the third it is the result of evangelism.

2. Growth Through Ethnic or National Allegiance

Pre-eminent in the second category are the Muslims. While there may be no doubt of their implacable resistance to both russification and Soviet atheistic propaganda—and also of the influence upon them of the Islamic revival, particularly in Iran—

it is difficult if not impossible to disentangle nationalism (or sometimes tribalism) from religion in seeking to know what motivates them (see chapter eight). Religious fervor is certainly present, as evidenced by the widespread Sufi brotherhoods; but a high birthrate without doubt plays an important role in the growth of Soviet Islam.

It is difficult to know whether the Georgian and Armenian Orthodox churches, as well as the Catholic churches in Lithuania, western Ukraine, and elsewhere, are increasing their numbers or not, but they clearly are maintaining their memberships and continuing to exhibit a spiritual strength and vitality that has ancient and vigorous roots. As we have seen, there are close ties between religious and nationalistic sentiments in these areas. The same is true of the Russian Orthodox Church, and it may be that the members who were raised in the church, as distinguished from the converts, should be included in this category. Finally, the Mennonites probably belong in this second category as well. Though numbering not more than 50–60,000, they are maintaining their numbers in the ethnic and German communities where they have traditionally been based. With the introduction of Russian-language services in some congregations, they may have some potential for adding Russians as well as Germans to their ranks.

3. Growth Through Evangelism

In the third category are the groups whose numbers appear to be increasing as a result of evangelism: Baptists, Pentecostals, and, probably, Seventh-Day Adventists and Jehovah's Witnesses. Since evangelism is illegal in the USSR, these groups render themselves liable to severe penalties, which they suffer in substantial numbers and with great fortitude. It is impossible to estimate how great the growth has been within these communities. In the case of the Baptists and Pentecostals (both registered and unregistered) there have over the years been so many reports of new converts, expanding congregations, and the opening of new churches that it seems safe to say there has been significant growth. The much smaller Adventist group is probably growing also; the greatest growth is likely to be among the unregistered congregations, known as the True and Free Seventh-Day Adventists, who are noted for their zeal in producing *samizdat* Christian literature. The Jehovah's Witnesses are outlawed, and growth is therefore difficult to verify; but reports in the Soviet press over the years suggest that their efforts to increase their numbers—a practice in which they are as zealous as their fellow Witnesses elsewhere in the world—are arousing some degree of alarm among the authorities and are therefore almost certainly meeting with some success.

Perhaps we should tentatively add the Hare Krishnas to this third category. Their existence within the Soviet Union appears to date back no more than ten years, but during that short time they appear to have won a not insignificant number of converts.

What is seen in the second and third categories may perhaps be not the revival of faith but "only" growth. This is not to underestimate the significance of the large numbers of persons who are seeking and finding religious faith; it is simply an attempt to describe the phenomenon as precisely as possible. The process of growth means that there are many moving and inspiring stories of individual conversions.[14] To take just one example from many: in 1980 it was reported that 600 people were converted in two weeks as a result of Baptist outreach in Alma-Ata, Frunze, and other Central Asian cities. Tents erected for evangelistic meetings were reportedly full to overflowing.[15] Such reports continue to arrive from all over the Soviet Union. Clearly, growth, particularly among the Baptists and Pentecostals (and, latterly, the Hare Krishnas), is significant, and a cause for great joy among members of the communities. This growth is remarkable given the persistent atheistic propaganda and the severe penalties against active proselytism. The fact that many people are ignoring or rejecting a Marxist-Leninist world view in favor of a religious one is important for understanding the factors that will shape Soviet society in the future. And it clearly worries Soviet officialdom.

The reason for not calling this a "revival" or "renaissance" is that essentially nothing new is happening in these groups. They have always used the opportunities for outreach available to them, and added to their numbers. They have never had any nationalist affiliations (even though all the evangelical groups are strongest in Ukraine, they are basically a-nationalist in outlook), and have reached out to surrounding unbelievers regardless of their locale. This process did not cease even during the harshest years of persecution—the 1920s and '30s—as accounts by recent émigrés make clear.[16] What has happened in the last two decades or so is that the scale has been increasing: proselytizing has attracted more converts than formerly. But there has been no *qualitative change* in either the methods of outreach of these groups, their membership, or the converts they attract.

4. Growth Through Renewal

Precisely this fact of qualitative change distinguishes the members of the fourth category. With both the Russian Orthodox Church and religious Jews there is a firm basis for speaking of spiritual renaissance. Here something new and unexpected has happened: there has been a reversal of established trends. Not long ago, in both groups, religious fervor appeared to be on the wane and the capacity for spiritual renewal seemed virtually non-existent. These expectations have been confounded in a surprising way.

A. Judaism

Religious Judaism has persisted throughout the Soviet period, but its strength has gradually been dissipated. It has suffered both from the secularization to be found in Jewish communities in the West and from the anti-religious persecution common to all believers in the Soviet Union. The Christian denominations, at the end of the Second World War, were strengthened by the existence of flourishing Christian communities in the territories acquired by the Soviet Union on its western borders, but the situation was very different for the Jews, for several reasons. First, the Jewish communities in some of these areas had suffered from Soviet depredations during the period of annexation by the USSR (1939–41) as a result of the Nazi-Soviet Non-Aggression Pact. Second, in the territory that came under Nazi occupation—and this included large areas of the western part of the Soviet Union within its pre-1939 borders—Jewish communities were almost exterminated. In the post-war decades, the anti-Jewish sentiment fostered during Stalin's last years was followed by greater or lesser manifestations of the anti-Semitism that has long been present among many members of the Slavic peoples among whom most Soviet Jews live. This has been a deterrent to any revival of religious Judaism. A further deterrent has been the deliberate Soviet policy of keeping the numbers of rabbis and synagogues to a bare minimum, and restricting the production of Jewish religious literature and of objects and foods required for worship and a kosher diet.

Despite this unpromising background, there has been a resurgence of Jewish religious life over the past two decades. The prime catalyst has undoubtedly been the growth of the State of Israel, with the single most important stimulus being Israel's stunning victory in the Six Day War of 1967. This gave Soviet Jews reason to be proud of their identity, to explore their Jewish roots and their religious as well as national heritage—if the two can be distinguished. A British visitor to Moscow described the change in attitude:

> In Moscow during the 1960s there were only a handful of religious Jews and some other Jews who were interested in Judaism only as a philosophy. Hebrew studies, mostly self-taught, began in 1968, with the practical purpose of using the language in Israel, where Jews wanted to go. . . . Between 1971 and 1976 several young Jews began to study Judaism and to observe Jewish religious law on their own. By 1977 religious seminars and lessons were taking place on a regular basis. The group was composed of about fifteen men. . . . By 1981 the number had increased to a hundred, all of whom were observant Jews. . . . A religious Jew in Moscow nowadays is thought of as an intellectual, deep-thinking, and cultured person.[17]

Although the Hebrew classes and religious seminars were the target of KGB reprisals, and several of the leading Hebrew teachers were imprisoned in labor camps, the newly awakened religious zeal seems unlikely to abate. This is, however, an unofficial movement: though its members may attend synagogues, their religious life centers around meetings in private homes. There does not appear to have been any spiritual rejuvenation within the registered synagogues.

Most if not all of those involved in the unofficial religious movement are primarily motivated by the desire to emigrate to Israel, and so the future of religious Judaism in the USSR remains open to question. While Jews who have become religious undoubtedly have been influenced by the factors, mentioned above, that have influenced other Soviet citizens to turn to religion, clearly the current political circumstances have been the strongest influence upon them. If all the Jews who wish to emigrate to Israel were allowed to do so, undoubtedly the most religiously zealous Jews would be among them. The basis for the continuation of Jewish religious life in the Soviet Union would then be very weak.

B. Russian Orthodoxy

The increasing number of converts to Russian Orthodoxy is due in part to a rejection of Marxism-Leninism, but it is more than that. It is also a rejection of the course upon which the majority of the Russian intelligentsia had been set since about the middle of the nineteenth century.

By and large, the intelligentsia rejected the church, which they saw as backward, intellectually inadequate, and subservient to tsardom, with wholly inadequate answers to the questions they were asking about the future of their society. For those answers they looked to the West and embraced the rationalist ideas of the Enlightenment. Such great thinkers as Khomyakov, Solovyov, and Dostoevsky spoke out against this attitude, propounding the virtues of the church, but their words fell upon stony ground. There seemed to be no reason why the Russian intelligentsia—in common with secularized intelligentsia in any other country—should ever return to the church.

An unexpected development, however, occurred at the turn of the century: several leading Marxist thinkers—Struve, Bulgakov, Berdyaev, Frank, Lossky—entered the Orthodox Church. This served to show that the Christian community was not simply the tradition-ridden, moribund body that many had taken it to be.[18] Indeed, these thinkers' embrace of the church marked the start of a creative process that could well have led to widespread renewal within[19] had the process not been truncated by the revolution.

Intellectuals who convert to Orthodoxy today regard these thinkers as their natural antecedents.[20] The religious renaissance of today, however, may well represent more than the continuation of the earlier, truncated movement: it may include representatives of the intelligentsia akin to those who chose *not* to follow Struve and his fellow thinkers into the church. In other words, with illusions about Communism shattered, the Orthodox Church may hold more attraction for intellectuals than it did early in the century.[21]

The move back toward the Orthodox Church is most noticeable among the urban intelligentsia, particularly among young people. Information on what happens outside the larger cities is very difficult to obtain. Urban believers seem to have no clear idea of what is happening in the churches *v glushi* (in the backwoods). But without doubt the vast bulk of the church's membership continues to come from the peasant and worker classes; the religious tradition is passed on from generation to generation, as it has been for centuries.

Role of the Administrative Church

The Moscow patriarchate is the church's administrative and spiritual center. In recent years, some foreign observers have assumed that the spiritual reawakening within the church has led to an increase in the patriarchate's "influence" or even "power" in relation to the state. Almost the opposite seems true. Concessions won by the church in recent years—more space for its central administration, more students training for the priesthood, opportunities to publish more Bibles and liturgical books (though still a grossly inadequate number)—have been at the price of even greater subservience to the state and even more vocal support for Soviet foreign policies. The church leadership remains as captive as ever: the state's firm control of the hierarchy enables it to limit church life effectively in many different ways.

The events of 1988, the Millennium year, have altered this picture somewhat without changing it substantially. Considerable publicity was given to the Orthodox Church before and during the main Millennium celebrations in June and July. Gorbachev met church leaders—the first such meeting since Stalin summoned the three senior bishops in 1943—and publicly stated that believers had a right to their views.[22] Konstantin Kharchev, chairman of the Council for Religious Affairs, made it clear that the government was looking for the support of the country's 70 million believers for *perestroika*.[23] Also, the church was able to hold a *sobor* (national council) in June, the first since 1971 and only the fourth during the Soviet period. The atmosphere was relaxed and open, and senior hierarchs made frank speeches about the need to improve theological education for future priests, to open more seminaries, to improve the low quality of church restoration work, and to expand the church's publication program, which was strongly criticized.[24] The *sobor* adopted a new Orthodox Church Statute that was much more comprehensive and precise than its previous instrument of government, adopted in 1945. The new statute actually contained some provisions that contradict the Law on Religious Associations—the possibility of church involvement in charitable activity, of the church's right to own property, and of the church's having juridical personality. This created expectations that these rights will be granted when the revised law is finally published.

These developments signify a more relaxed attitude toward the church on the part of the authorities, but within the existing framework. As of fall 1988, the basic ground rules, including strict state supervision of the hierarchy, do not appear to have changed. Independent thinkers within the church continue to criticize hierarchs for subservience to the authorities and for failing to seize initiatives presented by the new climate. Moreover, it is not yet clear whether the greater degree of tolerance shown by the state was for the period of the Millennium celebrations only, or is intended to inaugurate a new phase in church-state relations. Favorable press coverage has not been in evidence since the end of the celebrations, and the much discussed new law has still not been published.

Thus, much of the revitalization of spiritual life continues, as before, to occur independently of the hierarchy. In fact, the noted church dissident Father Gleb Yakunin, in a detailed *samizdat* report analyzing church life, concluded that the Moscow patriarchate was so weakened that it was incapable of responding to, much less leading, the renaissance that was bringing new converts into the church.[25]

In many cases the reawakening begins outside the organized church. People searching for a meaning to life have found it in the church, joined the church, and swelled its ranks. The church's role has been the essentially passive—though vitally important—one of receiving the seekers and then teaching and nurturing them. This role reflects not only the fact that evangelization is illegal in the Soviet Union but also some characteristics of Orthodoxy. Though by no means inward-looking, Orthodox congregations have traditionally not proselytized in the way that evangelical denominations, such as Baptists, have. The congregation's role has been to create a center of spirituality that draws in the needy, the troubled, the seekers after truth. The church is the salt of the earth, the leaven in the bread, ready to be found by those who sense impoverishment in their lives.

Yet the missionary impulse that took Orthodoxy across the Ural Mountains to spread through Siberia to the shores of the Pacific, and on into Japan, Alaska, and California, is not dead. Although many clergy are too cowed by state pressure to do more than officiate at services, a number of leading spirits do reach out to unbelievers, especially young people, and draw them into their churches. Father Dmitri Dudko has become by far the best known of such priests, but there are others.[26] Such active clergy, however, are constantly under the eye of the Council for Religious Affairs (CRA), which takes measures to limit their impact—by moving them to another parish, for example, or threatening them with reprisals. Like Father Dmitri, such priests may even have to pay the price of imprisonment. Evidence for the close supervision of the clergy is provided in a secret report prepared by the CRA itself, the so-called Furov Report, described in chapter three.[27]

The missionary impulse is also present among many of the church's new converts. Having found great satisfaction in their changed lives, they want to share this experience with others and encourage them to join the church too. In time, this may come to be seen as a second phase in the revitalization of the Orthodox faith.

Bishops and the Renewal

Some bishops, including several who travel abroad frequently, have spoken in a positive way about spiritual revitalization in the church, while remaining cautious about its extent. Archbishop Pitirim of Volokolamsk, chairman of the church's publishing department, said in an interview with a Soviet English-language periodical:

> The church has always been replenished with young people, but my generation and my elders were mostly successive church members following family traditions. While the people of my generation had parents or grandparents who were believers, nowadays the grandchildren of unbelieving grandparents sometimes come to the faith. . . . We should not speak of a quantitative "boom," but we should speak and think of a qualitative addition to the church.[28]

Archbishop Kirill, when he was rector of the Leningrad Theological Academy, made a similar comment in an interview with Westerners. Asked if it were true that, as sometimes reported in the Western press, there was a "religious boom" among Soviet young people, Archbishop Kirill replied:

> It is obvious that now in our church there is a renewal [in this] generation. . . . I don't think we have characterized this phenomenon, the interest of young people in church, as a special religious "boom." That might be wrong and too victorious. I would prefer a more modest estimation of reality.[29]

There is no reason to doubt the sincerity of these comments; certainly church leaders are glad to see their church grow. One must question, however, why they are willing to make such positive statements in public to foreigners. Foreign travel for church leaders (as for other Soviet citizens) is conditional upon "proper" behavior while abroad, and therefore one may assume that Soviet authorities have given traveling church leaders permission to make such statements. The authorities no doubt reason that if bishops talk about the growing numbers of young people entering their churches, Westerners will conclude that the church's lot cannot be such a bad one after all—and, sadly, all too many Western believers oblige them.

The bishops vary in their capacity and willingness to assist the movement of educated young people into the church. Some do more in quiet ways, behind the scenes, than others do. Still, the bishops are under even closer observation by the CRA than the clergy, and sooner or later their activities will be the subject of a report to Moscow. The Furov Report's division of the bishops into three categories according to their degree of compliance with state regulations limiting church life makes this explicit (see chapter three).[30] Under these circumstances, Father Gleb Yakunin's conclusion that the Moscow patriarchate can respond only in a limited way to the influx of new converts is correct. The bishops know this, too. This necessary corollary to the fact of church growth, however, is naturally omitted from their public statements.

The Role of Study Groups

The church's limited capacity to respond to the needs of new converts underlies the considerable growth of informal discussion groups. Starting on a small scale at the beginning of the 1960s, these have grown steadily, meeting needs that the registered churches cannot meet: the need to borrow, read, and discuss Christian books, to ask questions with a hope of getting honest answers, to receive guidance from older believers, to spend time in a relaxed atmosphere with others who share one's beliefs. These study groups and seminars help with what is probably the main difficulty in the revitalization of spiritual life in the church: a deficit of teaching. A person with an atheistic upbringing may be ignorant of the most elementary teachings of Christianity, may perhaps never have seen a Bible. The church labors under a great disadvantage in attempting to meet this deficiency. The severe shortage of Bibles is only one part of the problem.

The following extracts are from letters sent to a Christian activist in the Soviet Union after an open letter he had written was broadcast by Western radio stations beaming Russian-language programs to the USSR.[31] The first is from a twenty-two-year-old university graduate in the Leningrad region:

> Although I could not say that I am a believer, even less am I an atheist. Potentially I am a believer, but I'm hampered by gaps in my knowledge and ignorance of traditions. Therefore I do not think I have the right to call myself a believer. Nevertheless, what you are doing is of great interest to me. . . . I am in total support for your aims . . . and am ready to give you any assistance in my power, small as that may be.

The second writer is a polytechnic student from Kirov:

> I would put myself in the "wavering believers" category. In other words, those who believe in God, and yet don't. . . . I think these doubts flourish because people lack information, are ignorant about religion. . . . Many have never so much as seen a Bible—including myself—yet isn't the Bible the main source of all religious information? . . . But although I am far from God, I am quite certain that religion brings only good to people. It brings out the best in them, it raises them, encourages them to forsake bad ways, makes the good even better.

There is not space here to examine the problem of teaching and other problems that have come about as the result of the spiritual reawakening, but their existence should be noted. It is certainly not true that once a person has entered the church, his or her religious problems are over. State pressure upon the churches is far too great for that to be possible. Moreover, the influx of a number of people with widely differing opinions and life experiences into a church that has only recently emerged from a prolonged trauma when its very existence was imperiled can hardly be expected to proceed without conflict. It is perhaps significant that the best known of the discussion groups adopted the title "Christian Seminar on the *Problems* of the Religious Renaissance" (italics added).[32]

Reaction of the Authorities

Recent changes in the Soviet Union have brought about a more positive, though still uncertain, attitude toward religion. Before that, however, the Soviet authorities reacted somewhat ambiguously to the growth of interest in religion. They were, and still are, eager to promote the impression that there is freedom of religion in the Soviet Union and that religious life proceeds normally. Yet the Communist Party of the Soviet Union has remained firmly wedded to the belief that religion is obsolete and is doomed to die out—though no dates have been set for its demise.

Furthermore, in contradiction to its propaganda about freedom of religion, the Soviet press for many years frequently ran reports complaining about the growth of religion and urging more vigorous measures to combat it. These reports made it clear that the authorities continued to fear the influence of religion and were determined to take strong measures to counteract it—though the fact that the same complaints appeared for years and years strongly suggests that the measures taken have proved largely ineffective. It was clearly embarrassing for Soviet authorities to have to admit in print that religion is proving so resilient. The customary way out of the dilemma has been to blame Western propaganda for the continuing vitality of religion. Because it is ideologically impossible to admit that there could be any ground on which religion could flourish under the conditions of victorious socialism, the blame had to be transferred to some outside force. Therefore, there have been many impassioned but repetitive displays of invective against "bourgeois clericalism," "imperialistic reaction," "bourgeois propaganda," "ideologues of anti-Communism," and "clerical anti-Communism." The whole phenomenon of the religious renaissance is said to be nothing but a "myth" created by "bourgeois clerical myth-makers."[33] Although it is true that more sophisticated analyses of the reasons for religious belief have been published periodically over the last two decades, they have not been influential enough to prevent the continued publication of the much cruder propaganda.

It is now generally admitted that the 1929 Law on Religious Associations is out of date and does not correspond to current needs. For the majority of believers, however, the admission is long overdue. Igor Shafarevich pointed this out as long ago as 1977. In an interview with Father Gleb Yakunin, he said:

> When one becomes acquainted with the legislation on religion and when one hears how this legislation is put into practice, one gets the feeling that we are not living now but in the 1920s or 1930s. . . . One would think that now, when religion is on the upsurge and can no longer be crushed by any force, it would be realistic to act on this basis instead of living under the illusion that religion will cease to exist in our country within a few years. And yet the laws on religion which exist at present can only be characterized as being based on this illusion.[34]

In action, as opposed to words, however, the Soviet authorities' behavior has been anything but ambiguous. The practice of imprisoning leading religious activists intensified markedly in the 1980s. Activists could expect to be arrested more quickly after they began to engage in public activity, to be sentenced to a longer term, and perhaps to be resentenced within the labor camp before they finished the first sentence. Not until nearly two years after Gorbachev came to power did this practice begin to change. A number of political and religious prisoners were released early. However, in September 1988 there were still 175 known religious prisoners, though new arrests had virtually ceased. Overt repression of religion was no longer deemed appropriate, but the will to eradicate the residual consequences of past repression was lacking.

The marked public changes during 1988 in the attitude toward religion have not yet established themselves as the norm for the future. It is clear that Gorbachev's conciliatory attitude has come about for entirely pragmatic reasons—he needs all the support he can get, including that of believers, to push through his reform program. Kharchev has now admitted that a quarter of the Soviet population, 70 million people, are believers, whereas the previous practice was to play down their numbers as much as possible. But this does not mean that opponents of religion have changed their views. Articles critical of religion continue to be published alongside favorable ones. There has certainly not been a total change of attitude or policy; the change is that there is now debate on the subject. Official recognition of the role played by religion has been confined so far to an acknowledgment that it is persisting. So far there has been no admission that it may be growing, nor any reference to a renaissance or reawakening of faith.

Nonetheless, the growth of interest in religion in the Soviet Union is almost certain to continue. This spiritual revitalization after the decades of persecution and enforced atheism undoubtedly has great significance for the future of both Communism and religion. As for the Russian Orthodox Church specifically, let us give the final word to one of its priests:

> This generation gained its conversion to Christ on its own, by way of the most profound reflections and inner trials. . . . This is what is new in our church; it can be slowed down, of course, . . . but no one in this world has the power totally to stop it. This movement has begun and it will be accelerating, for behind it is the charisma and power of Our Lord Jesus Christ, who has seen the confession of faith by his people; who has put his people to the test in humiliation, difficulties, in such conditions that for a while it appeared that just a little more and the end would come. . . .
>
> Yes, historically the Russian church has sinned a lot. But the Lord sees how she has been passing through the crucible. . . . Thus the Lord has seen the faith of his people and now tells it: "Your sins are forgiven—get up and walk!"[35]

11

Gorbachev's Reforms and Religion

Pedro Ramet

MIKHAIL GORBACHEV'S program of *perestroika* (restructuring) affects all spheres of Soviet reality, from economic management to foreign policy to the media to nationalities policy to religion. *Perestroika* is necessarily all-inclusive because the crisis of the Soviet system is all-inclusive, and because policy spheres cannot be isolated from one another. However, it is not applied in the same way in all spheres. Nor, in the religious sphere, is it applied in the same way toward all groups. The Russian Orthodox Church has been the chief beneficiary of *perestroika* in the religious sphere, and unregistered (hence illegal) religious groups have not benefited at all.

Perestroika has created intense controversy between advocates of liberalization and hard-liners. *Moscow News*, *Ogonyok*, and *Literaturnaya gazeta* have been the leading platforms for pro-*perestroika* "liberals," while *Komsomolskaya pravda* and *Molodaya gvardia*, among others, have represented more conservative views. *Perestroika* has been subjected to diverse interpretations, clarifications, and applications that are at times in discord. However, there is one point upon which everyone can

---

Pedro Ramet is an assistant professor in the Jackson School of International Studies, University of Washington. He is the author of *Cross and Commissar: The Politics of Religion in Eastern Europe and the USSR* (1987) and *Nationalism and Federalism in Yugoslavia 1963–1983* (1984).

agree: in no sphere is *perestroika* intended to dismantle the Communist power monopoly or to create conditions in which genuine pluralism might take root. Atheism can be expected to remain the *de facto* ideology of the state and the *de jure* ideology of the Party, and *perestroika* enthusiasts will talk not of scuttling atheistic education but of making it more effective.

The first year and a half after Gorbachev's accession to power in March 1985 brought few signs of improvement in religious life. On the contrary, fresh reports of arrests and harassment of believers invited skepticism as to whether religion was to be included in the reform. On September 28, 1986, for example, a front-page *Pravda* article criticized the church's claim to be "the sole custodian of cultural values" and stressed that party, trade union, and Komsomol organizations "must not farm out problems of ethics and morality to religion."

The Public Debate Begins

The opening up of debate about the status of religion in Soviet society can perhaps be dated to the publication of a long article by poet Yevgeny Yevtushenko in *Komsomolskaya pravda*, December 1986. Yevtushenko suggested that if church and state are separate, atheism too should be separable from the state. He noted that the source of morality is culture, which in turn has its source in religion. Yevtushenko also called for publication of the Bible by state publishing houses. His article was coupled with a sophisticated rebuttal by Suren Kaltakhchyan, which pointed out that any culture has both positive and negative elements and that, to progress, one should try to discriminate between those elements. By extension, any religion includes both positive and negative elements; according to Kaltakhchyan, only a detached secularism can view religion objectively, discarding the negative while preserving the positive.

The publication of this debate was quite remarkable. Not only was a major and largely hard-line newspaper publishing a spirited defense of religion by a major cultural figure, but the article was given the courtesy of a dignified reply.

The exchange was important in at least two respects. First, it opened up discussion of the role of religion in Soviet society and thus signaled a possible liberalization of the state's religious policy. Second, it gave vent to views in intellectual circles and elsewhere that there is a moral and spiritual crisis in the Soviet Union—a crisis not infrequently blamed on Communist ideology.

A few months later, *Komsomolskaya pravda* refuted the notion that atheism has created a "moral vacuum" and that morality derives from religion. Then in September 1987 academician Dmitri Likhachev entered the fray. In an interview with *Literaturnaya gazeta* he criticized Soviet atheistic propaganda as "ignorant . . . not only of church history but of history as a whole, . . . ignorant of culture, of the culture of democracy."[1] Likhachev recalled the role of the monasteries in fostering investigations in genetics, horticulture, and agriculture, and drew a pointed contrast with the Lysenko affair (in which the state adopted as Marxist orthodoxy the scientifically deviant view of agronomist Trofim Lysenko that acquired characteristics are inherited) and with the destructive role played by Soviet pseudoscience under some of Gorbachev's predecessors. Likhachev called on the state to stop interfering in church affairs, and said there should be a *real* separation of church and state.

That same month, *Moscow News* carried an interview in which Russian Orthodox Metropolitan Aleksii of Leningrad-Novgorod noted that "sometimes on the spot, in obvious contradiction with the fundamentals of the socialist state of all the people, believers are treated as 'second class' citizens and are regarded with some suspicion and caution."[2] That this admission, even in its qualified form, could be printed in a Soviet newspaper, and later carried by the Tass international news service, was dramatic enough. Then a few months later, the head of the government's Council for Religious Affairs, Konstantin Kharchev, publicly conceded that the description was fair. In Kharchev's view, *perestroika* promises to remedy this situation and, in his words, "remove [believers'] present status as second-class citizens."[3]

Early in 1988 Volodymyr Tancher, head of the atheism department at Kiev State University, put forth a series of concrete proposals. If adopted by the regime, the proposals could significantly improve the situation of the registered religious organizations. Writing in the Ukrainian atheistic monthly *Lyudyna i svit* (Man and the world), Tancher proposed that the state: (1) enact a new, comprehensive law on religion, spelling out the rights of believers; (2) grant juridical status to the churches, defining more clearly their right to own property; (3) let believers be represented on local Councils for Overseeing Adherence to Soviet Legislation on Religious Cults, and on the Councils for Religious Affairs; and (4) allow the churches to engage in charitable work.[4]

Changes Already in the Air

There had already been signs of change in at least three of these four areas, so that Tancher's article is interesting not so much for being novel as for weaving together several strands into a unified policy package.

First, as early as January 1986, the *Journal of the Moscow Patriarchate* published an article entitled "The Rights and Duties of a Religious Community" that said in part:

> A religious society enjoys the rights of juridical persons and as such may, if need arises, build or purchase, with its own money and according with the law, necessary premises; acquire means of transport, church requisites, and objects of religious cult with the right of ownership. The purchase by a religious society of a building for its needs is legalized by a notarized deal. The building thus acquired becomes the property of the religious society.

The January 1918 decree on the Separation of Church From State and School From Church expressly denied that churches enjoy the rights of juridical persons, and the 1929 Law on Religious Associations, even as revised in 1975, did not establish any such rights. The journal's reference to these rights was therefore new. Also new was the suggestion that churches enjoyed the right to acquire property; up to now they have had to lease buildings from the state or use them rent-free.

Second, several officials, including Kharchev and Gorbachev,[5] have confirmed that new legislation on religion is being drafted. Although discussion started in 1986, work on a draft bill was held up, according to Kharchev, by the broader political struggle over *perestroika*. By May 1988, work on the draft legislation had begun, and Fedor Burlatsky, chairman of the official Soviet Human Rights Commission, suggested that it could be ready for ratification in 1989, if not by the end of 1988.[6] Various drafts of this legislation are discussed in chapter three and in the appendix. According to Kharchev, the legislation will ease some of the restrictions under which the churches have operated. Its primary aim, however, as he told students of the CPSU's Higher Party School in spring 1988, is to make the state's regulation and containment of religion more effective.[7]

Third, there has also been movement toward permitting churches to carry on charitable activities. In March 1988, *Meditsinskaya gazeta* published an interview in which Vladimir Sorokin, rector of the Leningrad Theological Academy, urged that the churches could make themselves useful to Soviet society by engaging in charitable work and providing community services—which the legislation of 1929/75 expressly forbade. In June, a special Russian Orthodox ecclesiastical council adopted a new Orthodox Church Statute affirming the church's *duty* to perform charitable works and also its priests' right to administer their churches (a prerogative entrusted, up to now, to a committee approved by the authorities). In 1988, Moscow churches were able, for the first time in Soviet history, to send volunteers to help in local hospitals; the government encouraged it. An Italian newspaper reported that Moscow had given permission for Mother Theresa, the world-renowned Catholic nun from Yugoslavia, to open a charity mission in Moscow at some unannounced date.[8]

Other Concessions

Other concessions by the regime have contributed to a more relaxed atmosphere. Various religious dissidents—such as Ukrainian Uniate Josyf Terelya, Russian Orthodox Fr. Gleb Yakunin, Lithuanian Catholic Fr. Alfonsas Svarinskas, and, in summer 1988, a number of Baptists—were released from prison. In summer 1987 the state decided to move a military firing range away from the sixth-century monastery complex Davit Garedzha in southern Georgia. Permission was given to reopen some long-closed churches in Ukraine and elsewhere. The Council for

Religious Affairs registered some 104 new parishes in 1987 and another 160 (90 of them Russian Orthodox) in the first six months of 1988. Public religious processions, long barred, have taken place with the acquiescence of the authorities. In May 1988, Kharchev told an American diplomat that the authorities were considering a proposal to allow religious instruction outside the home, and to permit Bible-study groups.[9]

On December 25, 1987, Tass for the first time reported on the Protestant and Catholic observance of Christmas, and in April 1988 parts of a Russian Orthodox Easter service were broadcast on Soviet television. Previously, the official media had reported what churchmen had to say only when it concerned the abolition of nuclear weapons or Soviet peace proposals, but in December 1987 *Pravda* published an article by Archbishop Mikhail Mudyugin of Vologda and Velikii Ustyug on the problems of Soviet youth.

Also, in November 1987 the atheistic monthly *Nauka i religiya* published some statistics for religious organizations covering 1961–86; many of these statistics had not been published previously in the USSR. Of more general importance is the fact that under Gorbachev, Soviet atheistic writing has become more scholarly and less agitational. The government authorized the launching of two new publications: the *Moscow Church Herald*, published by the Moscow patriarchate in five languages, and *Religion in the USSR*, published by Novosti publishing house in six languages.

The Soviet academic journal *Sotsiologicheskie issledovaniya* set an important precedent in summer 1987 with three articles about religion, one contributed by an American academic.[10] In a further twist, the author of one of the other articles criticized the American for his allegedly uncritical use of official Soviet sources that underestimate the number of believers in the Soviet Union and their educational level.[11]

With the general tendency under Gorbachev to criticize Stalin and Brezhnev has come a need to deal with the history of religious repression in the USSR. The process got under way with a lengthy article in the CPSU Central Committee organ *Kommunist* in March 1988. The unsigned article described Stalinist excesses against religion as a "distortion of the party line" that contradicted party decrees, often the fault of local party workers. The article also claimed that some party members tried, at times, to prevent certain oppressive policies from being carried out.

Not all party members have wanted to admit past excesses or to distance themselves from them. These more conservative circles were responsible for the reissue, in 1987, of Roman Plaksin's 1968 diatribe against the Russian Orthodox Church, which among other things denied there was any persecution of the church and said charges to that effect were "filthy fabrications" spread by "priests and other White Guard scribblers."[12]

Stricter Adherence to Law

Under Gorbachev there has been a new emphasis on strict observance of legal codes. This has allowed *Moscow News* and *Literaturnaya gazeta* to publish articles defending the rights of religious communities against "dirty tricks" campaigns and illegal obstructionism by local authorities. An article in the January 1987 *Moscow News* told about Orthodox Christians in the town of Oktyabr'sky who had met all the legal requirements to register a new parish but had been intimidated and blocked by local authorities for four years. In July, *Literaturnaya gazeta* published a letter from Orthodox Christians who described how, even after their congregation had obtained official permission to make major repairs on their church, the district committee tried to prevent the builders from completing the work. And in October 1987, *Literaturnaya gazeta* charged local party barons overseeing the Ukrainian village of Barvenkovo with setting up illegal roadblocks to prevent worshipers from attending Sunday services, and with slandering the local parish priest, whom *Literaturnaya gazeta*, by contrast, praised. These examples—and others could be cited—constitute clear signals from the Gorbachev regime that local authorities cannot ignore the law and that guarantees to believers must be honored.

This has encouraged believers, of course, and one result has been a series of petitions addressed to Gorbachev or to then president Andrei Gromyko. Early in 1987, Father Gleb Yakunin, newly released from confinement in Siberia, wrote to Gorbachev asking for the extension of *perestroika* to religious policy. A few months later, some thirty-eight Orthodox, Catholic, and Protestant theologians and believers addressed a more formal appeal to both Gorbachev and Gromyko. Among the eleven things they asked the state to do were: grant the church the rights of a juridical person; rescind the nationalization decree of 1922 and return confiscated properties to the church; give religious propaganda the same tolerance as anti-religious propaganda; allow the church freedom to develop contacts with individual believers and church bodies in other countries; and stop interfering in the internal affairs of the church.

Later, toward the end of 1987, Archbishop Feodosi of Astrakhan and Yenotayenka appealed to Gorbachev for the return of the Kiev Monastery of the Caves—a request that was subsequently granted.

Encouraged by *glasnost*, in July 1987 Orthodox dissident Aleksandr Ogorodnikov and a small group of other religious activists launched an unofficial magazine called *Bulletin of the Christian Community*. In its first issue, of which twenty copies were produced, the 200-page *Bulletin* included accounts of religious activists still in prison and a discussion of the Millennium of the Christianization of Kievan Rus'. But in an open letter dated January 12, 1988, Ogorodnikov lamented that "democratization" in the religious sphere was "an exercise . . . meant to give a cosmetic touch-up to the facade of the ideology, without actually changing its substance."[13] He concluded that fundamental change in religious life cannot come from above; it must come from the grass roots.

Russian Orthodoxy and Perestroika

On April 29, 1988, General Secretary Gorbachev held a formal meeting with Patriarch Pimen and other members of the Synod of the Russian Orthodox Church. It was the first such encounter since September 1943, when Stalin received three senior prelates of the church and encouraged their support for the war effort. To many, the meeting—televised on the evening news—seemed to confirm a new status for the church in Gorbachev's USSR.

With the return of several monasteries to the church (including Optina Pustyn in Kaluga region, the Tolgsky convent in Yaroslavl region, part of the Monastery of Kiev-Pechersky, and one of the monasteries on the Solovetsky islands in the White Sea near Arkhangelsk), monastic life may be able to revive. More important may be the fact that authorities have allowed "significant" increases in enrollments at the Moscow, Leningrad, and Odessa seminaries.[14] Church leaders anticipate being able to open church hospitals and perhaps to undertake joint research with the USSR Academy of Sciences on Russian historical themes.

The 1988 celebration of the Millennium of the Christianization of Kievan Rus' provided an occasion for the regime to showcase the Russian Orthodox Church and to influence both domestic and foreign opinion, and for the church to recall its central role in developing Russian culture. The official festivities took place June 5–16 in Moscow and Kiev, with additional celebrations in Leningrad and Riga. They were attended by representatives of all the Orthodox churches and major Christian communities, and by ecclesiastical and other public figures from many countries. There were speeches, liturgical services, concerts, and the laying of wreaths. The Central Documentary Film Studios announced it was making several full-length films on the Christianization of Rus'. Suffragan Bishop Palladi of Kiev revealed that "75,000 prayerbooks are being prepared for publication; the New Testament in Ukrainian is coming out in Kiev, [and] other publications are planned, including a catechism."[15]

The millennial celebrations were profusely reported by *Pravda, Izvestia, Moscow News,* and *Golos rodiny*, and full-page articles about the church were published in a number of newspapers. The celebrations were also televised. All this contributed to the prestige of the Russian Orthodox Church, which encourages optimism for its future.

A few words of caution should be registered, however. First, the Russian Orthodox Church has shown no sign of interest in improving the lot of other religious bodies. Some of the new Russian Orthodox parishes that have opened in the Ukraine (specifically in the villages of Nahachiv, Ustia, Starychi, and

Kalinovka) are using reopened church buildings that while padlocked had been used clandestinely by Ukrainian Greek Catholic priests and believers. (The Ukrainian Greek Catholic Church was dissolved by the government in 1946 and has operated only underground since then.)

Second, despite some concessions to the church and some promises of change in legislation, believers are still subject to prejudicial treatment in education and careers. This necessarily sets limits on any church revival.

And third, the Orthodox hierarchy, while daring to suggest the return of certain facilities and prerogatives, remains aware of its dependence on the state. Hence, while many churches in the West reacted to the Chernobyl nuclear disaster of April 1986 with frank discussions and probing questions, the Russian Orthodox Church maintained a circumspect silence. And yet, when Patriarch Pimen was interviewed by *Izvestia* in April 1988, after making the customary endorsement of *perestroika* and *glasnost*, he spoke of numerous "unsolved problems" in church-state relations. "It is especially difficult," he said, "to obtain permission to open new parishes where there have not been any parishes before."[16]

Some Russian Orthodox priests and laypersons would like their leaders to be much more outspoken. In June 1988, seven suspended priests met with laypersons in a Moscow apartment to celebrate illegally a counter-"Jubilee Mass" in protest of the official millennial celebrations. At the same time, dissident Aleksandr Ogorodnikov and the editors of the *samizdat* Orthodox magazine *Vybor* organized an unofficial conference on the Millennium. Participants criticized the church leadership for not taking proper advantage of the Millennium and for failing to protest the continued imprisonment of about 200 persons for religious reasons. There was also criticism of the June 1988 special Orthodox council for failing to debate the most salient questions confronting the church, for taking no steps to dissociate the church from its 1949 "canonization" of Stalin, and for its general reserve on the matter of religious freedom.

Islam and Parallel Islam

As noted earlier, *perestroika* is by no means a homogeneous policy to be applied in the same way toward all religious groups.

Nor will liberalization and concessions for one group necessarily produce liberalization and concessions for others. For Islam, *perestroika* has brought little change.

Gorbachev's first public statement on Islam came in November 1986, when he told a gathering of party officials in Tashkent that local conditions in Muslim-populated Uzbekistan demanded "a determined and pitiless combat against religious manifestations" and an improvement in atheistic activity.[17] Many local party committees in Central Asia have been inclined to turn a blind eye toward unregistered religious associations, the participation of party members in religious rites, and even the use of state enterprises for the production of religious artifacts and souvenirs. A plenum of the Uzbek Central Committee in January 1988 addressed this problem directly. According to republic First Secretary Rafik Nishanov, "many Communists" have

> withdrawn from the struggle with Islam and other religions, with attempts to pass off religious patriarchal customs as national traditions. . . . Even for many Communists, the Muslim "science of life" is more authoritative than the party rules and the norms of socialist morality. . . . The former first secretary of the Samarkand district party, M. Sherkulov, personally took part in the construction and organization of the so-called holy place, while the former deputy chairman of the Samarkand regional *soviet,* I. Kurandykov, illegally redirected considerable material resources to the construction of a mosque.[18]

The CPSU has sought to discipline these wayward members. In a six-month period in 1987, fifty-three Uzbek party members lost their party cards for having taken part in religious rituals. In a related move, K. Nurulhakov, a senior member of the philosophy department of the Tadzhik Academy of Sciences, instructed party activists in Tadzhikistan to take specific measures to counter the strong religiosity of Central Asian women. In particular, he suggested reviving the "tens" system, first introduced in 1981, under which every district of the republic is divided into groups of ten households, with a permanent corps of anti-Islamic agitators and informers appointed to monitor religious life in the groups.[19]

At least two factors prejudice the authorities against Islam.

The first is that Muslim religious identity and Muslim ethnic identity are inseparable. Islam is therefore a part of the state's nationalities problem. It is both ironic and indicative that Soviet authorities have been attacking Islam as a "destroyer of national culture." In February 1986, for example, the Georgian-language party daily in Tbilisi wrote that "Islam has been and remains one of our spiritual and physical subjugators, the destroyer of our purest national faith and the untiring enemy of our mother tongue."[20]

Second, the authorities have tended to see Islam as a "brake" on social and economic development and the source of backward practices (such as the series of immolations of Central Asian women reported during 1987). *Pravda* in January 1987 refuted the notion that Islam could be credited with any "civilizing" effects and attributed to Islam the economic lag in Central Asia, Afghanistan, and Iran. The Muslim Religious Board for Central Asia and Kazakhstan even came under fire for trying to "modernize" official Islam in its publication *Muslims of the Soviet East*.

Yet despite the regime's continued hostility toward Islam, certain Soviet writers have introduced new elements into the discourse. In May 1987, Igor Belyaev, the head of *Literaturnaya gazeta*'s foreign department, gave generous credit to several Western specialists on Islam in the USSR, describing French scholar Alexandre Bennigsen in particular as "an authoritative expert on Islam."[21] A month later Belyaev noted that the closing of officially registered mosques, a feature of the late Khrushchev years, merely resulted in a growth in the number of unregistered "parallel" mosques. Belyaev suggested that these "parallel" mosques be legalized and that the administrative harassment of Muslim believers stop—a suggestion later seconded by Talib Saidbaev, director of the Institute of Philosophy and Law of the Uzbek Academy of Sciences.[22]

The Catholic Church

Throughout 1985 and 1986, there was little sign that the Catholic Church was to benefit from *perestroika*. On the contrary, those years saw the death of Father Juozas Zdebskis, one of the most active members of the Lithuanian Catholic dissident movement, in a suspicious automobile accident, and the arrest and the trial of five Lithuanians for illegally printing prayer books and other religious materials. The *samizdat Chronicle of the Lithuanian Catholic Church* dated April 23, 1986, reported that the KGB was waging a "revenge campaign" against Father Jonas Kauneckas, an active member of the Catholic Committee for the Defense of Believers' Rights. As late as May 1987, a Western observer could claim that the Catholic Church had not benefited at all from *perestroika*.[23]

But in mid-1987, civil authorities announced that they would return to church authorities the Queen of Peace Church in Klaipeda, which the state had confiscated for use as a concert hall immediately after its duly authorized construction in 1960. Secular organizations cooperated with the church in celebrating the 600th anniversary of the Christianization of Lithuania, and the state publishing house issued a high-quality book with color photos of some 150 Lithuanian churches. (The involvement of the secular organizations may have been a mixed blessing, since they were evidently instructed to play up the non-Christian elements of Lithuania's cultural heritage.) In September 1987, the Presidium of the Lithuanian Supreme Soviet held an unprecedented two-hour meeting with Archbishop Liudvikas Povilonis, Bishop Antanas Vaicius, and other representatives of the church. Not only did the authorities not lecture the clergy; they actually admitted mistakes. The clergy raised serious issues, including slanderous attacks on priests made in the party press.

On October 22, 1988, Soviet authorities returned Vilnius Cathedral to the Catholic Church. The cathedral had been closed since 1950. Some new Catholic parishes are said to have been granted registration.

For the Greek Catholic (Uniate) Church in Ukraine, the situation remains far more complex. The church, which numbers three to five million adherents, has been illegal since 1946. Soviet authorities received Ukrainian Catholic leaders in a secret meeting in August 1987 but rejected their appeal for re-legalization. Four months later, Ivan Hel, chairman of the Committee for the Defense of the Rights of Believers and Church in Ukraine, delivered another appeal for re-legalization to the USSR Supreme Soviet. More significantly, Russian Orthodox leaders, no doubt under pressure from the authorities, agreed in June 1988 to meet with Vatican representatives to discuss the status of Ukrainian Catholicism.

Since the confiscated Uniate parishes of the western Ukraine have given the Russian Orthodox Church its strongest base, Orthodox leaders are unlikely to be very receptive to compromise. In July 1988, Kharchev (head of the state's Council for Religious Affairs) told a journalist from *Le Monde* that the government had no objection to re-legalization of the Greek Catholic Church but that the Moscow patriarchate was strongly opposed. Kharchev suggested that the conflict might be resolved in time. In the meantime, he indicated that the authorities proposed to turn a blind eye toward Ukrainian Catholics and that the believers therefore "run no risk of persecution by the authorities."[24]

The Jewish Community

Much of the life of the Jewish community centers around applications for emigration to Israel, and here significant gains have been made. In August 1988, Jewish emigration, after eight successive monthly increases, reached an eight-year high of 1,864. In February 1989 a Judaic Studies Center was opened in Moscow. It will train rabbis and teachers.

At the same time, however, the new openness in Soviet society seems to have stirred up anti-Semitism, especially among Russians. Pamyat (Memory), a conservative unofficial organization concerned about preserving the environment, the church, and the Russian cultural heritage, is overtly anti-Semitic. As Dimitry Pospielovsky notes,

> The movement proclaims Masonic-Zionist internationalist forces as Russia's enemy number one, allegedly aiming at the destruction of Russia, Russian culture, and Russian spirituality, including the Orthodox Christian Church. . . . According to some unofficial reports, at their meetings speakers have on occasion condemned Christianity as a Jewish legacy and as too internationalist to serve Russian national interests, preferring a revival of old paganism.[25]

In spring 1988, leaflets distributed around Moscow called for "death to Jews" and promised to mark the Millennium with anti-Jewish pogroms, but the Millennium passed without incident. Subsequently, Pamyat held a noisily anti-Semitic meeting in a Leningrad park. In this atmosphere, Moscow Jews have started to express concern and to admit to feelings of disquiet. Several government newspapers, including *Izvestia*, have reprimanded Pamyat for its anti-Semitism. In August 1988, *Moscow News* published letters from Soviet citizens that condemned Pamyat as racist and fascist. One letter claimed that a speaker at a Pamyat rally on July 7 had demanded the deportation of Jews and other "alien races." On August 13 *Izvestia* accused Pamyat of stirring up ethnic hatred and demanded that it be disciplined.

Other Groups

The effects of *perestroika* on other religious groups will depend on whether they are registered (legal) or unregistered (illegal). Registered groups automatically benefit from changes in the general political climate and will benefit from any legislative changes. The Baptists, for instance, have already begun sending volunteers to assist in state hospitals. And in early 1987 it was announced that the Seventh-Day Adventists had received permission to open a theological training institute—for the first time in fifty-seven years.

With unregistered religious groups, an important distinction must be made between groups that want to register legally and to observe the legal codes but for various reasons have been refused registration, and groups that simply do not want to register. The leading example of the latter is the unregistered Baptist community, which continues to experience difficulties. For example, in April 1986, an illegal prayer house in Odessa was bulldozed and a number of Baptists were arrested. The Odessa community was repeatedly harassed during 1987 and 1988, and some of its prayer meetings, held illegally in the home of V. D. Konomenko, were interrupted by police. The community was fined a total of 350 rubles in the first four months of 1988. And yet, authorities seem to be offering a carrot along with the stick: during 1987 and 1988 it has steadily released unregistered Baptist pastors and laypersons from prison.

The Hare Krishnas have repeatedly applied for registration and been turned down. Finally, in May 1988, in a surprise development, the Council for Religious Affairs told members of the Moscow community of Hare Krishnas they would be allowed to register, to build a temple, and to import religious literature.[26] Authorities have been said to be considering the legalization of the Jehovah's Witnesses as well.

The Outlook

In February 1986, the CPSU convened its Twenty-seventh Party Congress and adopted an amended party program. In the section on atheistic upbringing, party officials had added an additional sentence to the original draft:

> The party will use all forms of ideological influence for the wider propagation of a scientific understanding of the world, [and] for the overcoming of religious prejudices, without permitting any violation of believers' feelings.[27]

This sentence captures the core of Gorbachev's vision for religion: continued atheization, but within the context of stricter adherence to Soviet law.

The main beneficiary of *perestroika* is the Russian Orthodox Church. Other groups, such as Catholics and Baptists, have experienced only slight improvement. For Muslims, there has been little change. Some Jews fear that their lot may actually be worsening. And the situation of unregistered religious communities remains fraught with risk.

In October 1988, Gorbachev retired five members from the Politburo (Gromyko, Dobrynin, Solomentsev, Dolgikh, and Demichev) and reassigned his rival, Yegor Ligachev. Previously responsible for ideology and supervision of the party machinery, Ligachev was put in charge of agriculture. This, together with the promotion of reliable Gorbachev allies, amounted to a political coup. It seemed to throw open the doors to potentially far-reaching change and to an acceleration of *perestroika*.

A Soviet joke that was popular in the 1970s held that under

Communism, the past was always changing but the future remained unchanged. Now, under Gorbachev, the future, too, may be changing. In his speech to the United Nations in December 1988, Gorbachev said that his country was "deeply involved in building a socialist state based on the rule of law":

> Work on a series of new laws has been completed or is nearing completion. Many of them will enter into force as early as 1989, and we expect them to meet the highest standards from the standpoint of ensuring the rights of the individual.
>
> Soviet democracy will be placed on a solid normative base. I am referring, in particular, to laws on the freedom of conscience, *glasnost,* public associations and organizations, and many others. In places of confinement there are no persons convicted for their political or religious beliefs. Additional guarantees are to be included in the new draft laws that rule out any form of persecution on those grounds.
>
> Naturally this does not apply to those who committed actual criminal offenses or state crimes. . . .

The seventy-one-year Soviet record on the treatment of religious organizations is one of hatred, lying, judicial murder, mass discrimination, and de facto relegation of believers to second-class status. It is also a record of policy inefficiency and miscalculation. Soviet constrictions have deepened the faith of many in the churches, driven others into the much less controllable underground, and left at least some of the atheized citizens spiritually rootless and drifting.

Under Gorbachev, much is changing. Three and a half years into his rule, the direction of change is clear enough, but its extent and ultimate consequences cannot yet be predicted.

APPENDIX

Further Drafts of New Law on Freedom of Conscience

John Anderson

This commentary by a Soviet researcher at Keston College is from the March 2, 1989, edition of Keston News Service.

Within the last week Keston College has seen two versions of a draft USSR Law on Freedom of Conscience. The first, published in the February issue of the journal *Sovetskoe gosudarstvo i pravo* (Soviet state and law), was written by jurist Yuri Rozenbaum, someone who has been involved in the field of religious legislation since Khrushchev's time and is believed to be a member of the commission drafting the new law. The second draft remains unpublished but is apparently the text given to church leaders by Konstantin Kharchev, chairman of the Council for Religious Affairs, at a meeting held during the second week of February. Those present at the meeting were told to make comments and suggestions within a week. What is less clear is whether this latter version is *the* proposed draft or simply the version favored by the CRA. (The rest of this commentary will refer to it as the CRA version.)

In both style and content there are differences between the two. The CRA version speaks of the need to bring the continuing application of Leninist principles into line with "the contemporary stage of development of Soviet society" but is often rather vague and ambiguous. Rozenbaum's version, as might be expected from someone with a legal training, reveals a greater precision in its wording and is accompanied by a commentary. In a number of their provisions, both versions go some way toward meeting the criticisms of existing legislation made by believers, although some clauses are open to differing interpretations. On occasion the two drafts are in direct disagreement with each other, as well as with existing legislation on religion.

1. Freedom of conscience appears to have a broader interpretation, entailing the right not only to profess any or no religion but also "to propagate religious or atheist views" (CRA) or "to carry out religious or atheist education" (Rozenbaum). The CRA version claims that this right is exercised "in accordance with the Constitution," though Article 52 of the 1977 constitution defines freedom of conscience in terms of "performing religious worship or carrying out atheist propaganda." Rozenbaum points out that this constitutional formulation has been criticized on the grounds that it puts believers and atheists in an unequal position, and notes that the 1918 and 1925 constitutions permitted "freedom of religious and anti-religious propaganda."

2. Both versions include strongly worded guarantees against discrimination on religious grounds and prohibit the bringing of any civil or criminal cases against citizens simply on the grounds of their religious faith.

3. Both versions restore to religious organizations the right of "juridical personality," taken from them in the 1918 Decree on the Separation of Church From State, and only partially restored in later unpublished decrees.

4. The position of religious education is less clear. Article 3 of the CRA version speaks of parents or people substituting for them having the right "to ensure the religious and moral education, and the teaching of their children in accordance with their own convictions." The same version states that "citizens may teach or study religion privately as individuals or with others, at home or at the religious society" (Art. 7). Rozenbaum's draft takes a similar line while stressing that this excludes the creation of special institutions where more general educational subjects are taught (Art. 7). Article 17 of the 1929 (revised in 1975) Law on Religious Associations allows religious education of children only in the home and only by parents, and prohibits any form of group study of religion among adults. Now it should be possible to set up any number of adult study groups, and to organize catechism classes or Sunday schools in private flats or attached to places of worship. What will not be possible is the establishment of church schools.

5. A number of articles in both versions appear to give greater scope to charitable activities and literature production, though neither makes this greater latitude very explicit. Both omit the existing ban on religious organizations' carrying out charitable activities, and the CRA version speaks of church monies being used for "charitable aims" as exempt from taxation (Art. 24). Provision is also made for religious groups to participate in public life and social organizations.

With regard to literature, the CRA draft speaks of the right of all citizens to "freely acquire and use" religious literature in the language of their choice (Art. 3), though at the time of writing those wishing to set up religious publishing cooperatives have met with little success. Article 12 of the CRA version speaks of the possibility of using income from publishing activities for the upkeep of religious centers and administrations, which presupposes a wider field of publishing activity than is at present undertaken by religious groups.

6. A more significant change comes in Article 5 of the CRA version, which states that while religious convictions cannot be used as a means of avoiding one's civil obligations, "exceptions to this can be made in terms of exchanging one civic responsibility for another, with each case to be decided in court"; i.e., it may be possible for conscientious objection to be recognized.

7. While the above points relate to general principles of freedom of conscience, the bulk of both versions deals in some detail with the way in which religious organizations come into being and operate. The first change is basically semantic. The old law spoke of two types of "religious associations": "religious societies" and "religious groups." The CRA draft describes all religious institutions from parish to patriarchate as "religious organizations," while reserving the name "religious society" for the local unit—as opposed to Rozenbaum, who retains "association" for the latter. Article 8 of the CRA version, which defines religious organizations, gives explicit legal recognition to monasteries and theological institutes. At the local level religious societies are set up by a group of ten adult citizens who apply for registration with the local *soviet,* who must reply within a month. If they refuse, the believers can appeal to the "state organs of the USSR for religious affairs" (CRA, Arts. 10–11). In Rozenbaum's version it is not the "association" that is registered but the statute *(ustav)* of the body, and he suggests that a typical *ustav* should be attached to the Law on Freedom of Conscience.

What many believers will be unhappy with is that the continuing requirement for religious societies to register still appears to take the form of a sanctioning act rather than a simple recognition of an existing community, and that the final court of appeal in cases where registration is refused will be the state organs dealing with religious affairs. While in the present political climate the central authorities are likely to take a sympathetic view of such appeals, many believers would probably prefer Rozenbaum's proposal that in the last resort they can take their cases to the courts (Art. 18).

8. The CRA draft permits rites and ceremonies to be performed in private homes, which was explicitly denied by the old law, and suggests that they can also be performed in hospitals, old people's homes, and prisons if the relevant administration admits it. This marks little change from the old system, leaving permission for such rites up to the discretion of the appropriate authorities. Interestingly, neither draft makes it clear whether such rites have to be performed by clerics belonging to registered congregations or whether, for example, Ukrainian Catholics or unregistered Baptists would find themselves liable to prosecution for conducting services in private apartments. Rozenbaum makes additional suggestions with regard to the participation of children in religious rites, suggesting that from the age of ten upwards they themselves must agree to any participation in such activities (Art. 19).

9. Both drafts comment on the need to make changes in the way legislation on freedom of conscience is monitored. Rozenbaum suggests that it should be left to the local *soviets* and the legal organs away from the center, but that a new State Committee for Religious Affairs should be set up attached to the Presidium of the Supreme Soviet. The CRA version, perhaps not surprisingly, is less explicit as to what form its successor should take, referring simply to the "state organ for religious affairs."

10. Rozenbaum's draft includes three articles on the right to atheist convictions and education that spell out, in far more detail than is the case for believers, the rights to which atheists are entitled (Arts. 20–22).

Though neither draft explicitly permits many of the activities believers would like to involve themselves in, many of the 1929 bans on their activities are absent. And, in a climate where it is said that in Soviet society everything that is not expressly forbidden is permitted, the new law seems likely to be a significant improvement on its predecessor, especially as the last article of the CRA draft states that should the USSR accede to an international treaty whose provisions differ from the Law on Freedom of Conscience, then the former shall be applied.

Yet one must express certain reservations about the ambiguous phrasing of some of the CRA draft and note that while Gorbachev has expressed the desire to create a "law-governed state," many officials remain reluctant or psychologically unable to commit themselves to such a formula. For this reason, party policy seems likely to remain more important than law for the immediate future.

Notes

Chapter 2:
Sorokowski, "Church and State 1917–64"

1. Dimitry Pospielovsky, *The Russian Church Under the Soviet Regime, 1917–1982* (Crestwood, N.Y.: St. Vladimir's Seminary Press, 1984), p. 37.

2. Bohdan R. Bociurkiw, "The Ukrainian Autocephalous Orthodox Church, 1920–1930: A Study in Religious Modernization," in Dennis Dunn, ed., *Religion and Modernization in the Soviet Union* (Boulder, Colo.: Westview, 1977), pp. 317–18, 323–24; reprinted in Bohdan R. Bociurkiw, *Ukrainian Churches Under Soviet Rule: Two Case Studies* (Cambridge, Mass.: Harvard University Ukrainian Studies Fund, 1984).

3. Robert Conquest, ed., *Religion in the U.S.S.R.* (New York: Praeger, 1968), p. 14; Pospielovsky, *The Russian Church*, p. 38.

4. Pospielovsky, *The Russian Church*, p. 99.

5. Ibid., p. 100, citing Soviet sources.

6. Ibid., pp. 103–4.

7. William C. Fletcher, *A Study in Survival: The Russian Orthodox Church, 1927–1943* (New York: Macmillan, 1965), pp. 28–32.

8. Pospielovsky, *The Russian Church*, pp. 108–10.

9. Bociurkiw, "The Ukrainian Autocephalous Orthodox Church," p. 315.

10. Nadezhda Teodorovich, "The Byelorussian Autocephalous Orthodox Church," in *Religion in the U.S.S.R.* (Munich: Institute for the Study of the U.S.S.R., 1960, p. 72—hereafter *Religion in the U.S.S.R.* (Munich); Harvey Fireside, *Icon and Swastika: The Russian Orthodox Church Under Nazi and Soviet Control* (Cambridge, Mass.: Harvard University Press, 1971), p. 140. For the history of this church under Soviet rule, see also Walter Kolarz, *Religion in the Soviet Union* (New York: St. Martin's Press, 1962), pp. 124–27.

11. Rafael Ivanitsky-Inguuilo, "The Georgian Autocephalous Orthodox Church," in *Religion in the U.S.S.R.* (Munich), pp. 72–78. For a brief history of this church, see also Kolarz, *Religion in the Soviet Union*.

12. Conquest, *Religion in the U.S.S.R.*, pp. 100–101; J. A. Hebly, *Protestants in Russia* (Belfast: Christian Journals, 1976), p. 105.

13. Kolarz, *Religion in the Soviet Union*, pp. 218–26. Among the other

Eastern Catholic activists of the time was Mother Catherine Abrikosov, who founded the first and only Russian Eastern-rite Catholic women's order.

14. Pospielovsky, *The Russian Church*, pp. 164–65 and Appendix 6.

15. Ibid., p. 175.

16. Titus Hewryk, *The Lost Architecture of Kiev* (New York: Ukrainian Museum, 1982), pp. 8–10.

17. Pospielovsky, *The Russian Church*, p. 230.

18. Teodorovich, "The Byelorussian Autocephalous Orthodox Church," p. 73; see Fireside, *Icon and Swastika*, pp. 139, 141–43.

19. Pospielovsky, *The Russian Church*, pp. 234, 236.

20. Fireside, *Icon and Swastika*, p. 140.

21. Conquest, *Religion in the U.S.S.R.*, p. 34.

22. Fletcher, *A Study in Survival*, p. 118.

23. Pospielovsky, *The Russian Church*, pp. 317, 324, 327.

24. Kolarz, *Religion in the Soviet Union*, pp. 162, 167; Sarkis Torossian, "The Apostolic Church of Armenia," in *Religion in the U.S.S.R.* (Munich), p. 129. On the Armenian Apostolic Church see Kolarz, pp. 150–75; Torossian, pp. 126–30.

25. Kolarz, *Religion in the Soviet Union*, pp. 316–18.

26. Casimir C. Gecys, "The Roman Catholic Church in the Lithuanian SSR," in *Religion in the U.S.S.R.* (Munich), pp. 111–12. See generally pp. 103–16.

27. Leu Haroska, "The Roman Catholic Church in the Byelorussian SSR," in *Religion in the U.S.S.R.* (Munich), p. 100. See generally pp. 93–102.

28. Bohdan Bociurkiw, "The Uniate Church in the Soviet Ukraine: A Case Study in Soviet Church Policy," in *Canadian Slavonic Papers* VII (1965), pp. 89–113; reprinted in Bociurkiw, *Ukrainian Churches Under Soviet Rule*.

29. Pospielovsky, *The Russian Church*, pp. 343, 349; Philip Walters, ed., *Religion in the Soviet Union and Eastern Europe* (Keston, England: Keston College, 1985), sec. 2.

30. Torossian, "Apostolic Church of Armenia," p. 128.

31. *Religion in Communist Dominated Areas*, vol. XIII, nos. 5–6 (May-June 1974), pp. 75–78 (text of letter). For a comparison of the 1960 statutes and the 1963 amended statutes, see Michael Bourdeaux, *Religious Ferment in Russia* (New York: St. Martin's Press, 1968), Appendix I, pp. 190–210.

32. Published in *Bratsky Listok*, nos. 2–3 (1965); quoted in Bourdeaux, *Religious Ferment in Russia*, p. 20.

33. Hebly, *Protestants in Russia*, p. 130.

Chapter 3:
Anderson, "Legislative and Administrative Control of Religious Bodies"

1. On Soviet treatment of dissent, see two articles by Peter Reddaway: "Policy Towards Dissent Since Khrushchev," in T. Rigby, A. Brown, and P. Reddaway, eds., *Authority, Power, and Policy in the USSR* (London: Macmillan, 1980), and "Dissent in the USSR," in *Problems of Communism*, vol. 32, no. 6 (November-December 1983), pp. 1–15.

2. V. I. Lenin, "Socialism and religion," in K. Marx, F. Engels, and V. I. Lenin, *O religii* (Moscow, 1983).

3. F. J. M. Feldbrugge, ed., *The Constitutions of the USSR and the Union Republics: Analyses, Texts, Reports* (Alphen aan den Rijn [Netherlands], 1979), pp. 73–75.

4. *Pravda*, June 29, 1988.

5. For a general discussion of the 1977 Constitution, see Feldbrugge, *The Constitutions of the USSR.*

6. A typical Soviet discussion of the issue is provided in A. Barmenkov, *Freedom of Conscience in the USSR* (Moscow, 1979).

7. English translation in *Religion in Communist Lands*, vol. 6, no. 1 (Spring 1978), pp. 34–40.

8. *O nauchnom ateizme i ateisticheskoye vospitanii* (Moscow, 1974), p. 29.

9. The separation decree of 1918 explicitly denied religious associations the right of juridical personality. In January 1986, however, the *Zhurnal Moskovskoi patriarchii* carried an article entitled "The Rights and Responsibilities of a Religious Society" that said they did in fact enjoy a legal status. Although the article gives no reference to any law, the implication is that at the very least existing legislation has been reinterpreted.

10. The role of the CRA is discussed in more depth in W. Sawatsky, "Religious Administration and Modernization," in D. Dunn, ed., *Religion and Modernization in the Soviet Union* (Boulder, Colo.: Westview Press, 1977).

11. The English text of the Law on Religious Associations can be found in R. Marshall, ed., *Aspects of Religion in the Soviet Union, 1917–67* (Chicago: University of Chicago, 1971); the 1975 amendments in *Vedomosti verkovnogo soveta, RSFSR*, July 3, 1975, pp. 487–91.

12. Cf. *Sovetskoye gosudarstvo i pravo*, 1965/1, pp. 39–45.

13. E.g., Barmenkov, *Freedom of Conscience*, p. 174.

14. *Chronicle of Current Events* 41 (London: Amnesty International, 1976), pp. 125–27.

15. V. A. Kuroyedov and A. Pankratov, eds., *Zakonodatel'stvo o religion zykh kultakh* (Moscow, 1971).

16. Extracts from the Furov Report can be found in *Religion in Communist Dominated Areas*, 1980/9–12, pp. 149–61; 1981/1–3, pp. 4–13; 1981/4–6, pp. 52–57. The full Russian text is in the Keston College archive.

17. See M. Rowe, "The 1979 Baptist Congress in Moscow: A Western Observer Reports," in *Religion in Communist Lands*, vol. 8, no. 3 (Autumn 1980), pp. 188–200.

18. On the Georgian church "scandal" see *Religion in Communist Lands*, vol. 3, nos. 4–5 (July-October 1975), pp. 14–23, and vol. 3, no. 6 (November-December 1975), pp. 45–54. On the conviction of Gaioz see *Zarya vostoka*, June 14, 1979.

CHAPTER 4:
Sapiets, "Anti-Religious Propaganda and Education"

1. Karl Marx, *Introduction to a Critique of Hegel's Philosophy of Law*.

2. N. Robkowicz, "Karl Marx's Attitude Towards Religion," in *Review of Politics*, no. 3 (1964), pp. 319–20.

3. H. Fireside, *Icon and Swastika: The Russian Orthodox Church Under Nazi and Soviet Control* (Cambridge, Mass.: Harvard University Press, 1971), p. 34.

4. The Soviet book in which this exhibit is described and other atheistic books and articles are quoted is in the Keston College library and archive.

5. M. Bourdeaux, *Religious Ferment in Russia* (London: Macmillan, and New York: St. Martin's Press, 1968), p. 16.

6. Quoted in W. B. Walsh, *Russia and the Soviet Union* (Ann Arbor, Mich.: University of Michigan Press, 1958), pp. 427–28.

7. E.g., *Chronicle of the Lithuanian Catholic Church*, no. 48 (June 29, 1981; translation published in New York, 1981), p. 32.

8. D. E. Powell, *Anti-Religious Propaganda in the Soviet Union* (Cambridge, Mass.: MIT Press, 1975), p. 52.

9. *Materials on the Facts of State Atheistic Violence and Arbitrary Force Against the All Union Church of True and Free Seventh Day Adventists in the USSR, to the Participants of the Madrid Conference, samizdat,* 1980/81, p. 429.

10. *Materials on the Facts*, p. 273.

11. Ibid., p. 488.

12. *Chronicle of the Lithuanian Catholic Church*, p. 56.

13. *Materials on the Facts*, p. 360.

14. D. E. Powell, *Anti-Religious Propaganda*, p. 69.

15. Soviet article quoted by M. Bourdeaux, *Patriarch and Prophets* (London: Macmillan, 1979, and New York: Praeger, 1970), p. 156.

16. D. E. Powell, *Anti-Religious Propaganda*, p. 81.

17. Ibid., p. 143.

18. See William C. Fletcher, *Soviet Believers* (Lawrence, Kans.: Regents Press, 1981), pp. 67–70, for a presentation of these figures.

19. D. E. Powell, *Anti-Religious Propaganda*, p. 117.

20. Ibid., pp. 152–53.

21. *Sovetskaya Moldavia*, November 20, 1987.

22. *Kommunist Tadzhikistana*, September 27, 1987.

23. Ibid., March 12, 1988.

24. Ibid., March 18, 1988.

25. *Sovetskaya Moldavia*, January 14, 1988.

26. *Keston News Service*, no. 287, November 5, 1987.

27. *Ogonyok*, no. 21, 1988, pp. 26–28.

28. *Russkaya mysl*, May 20, 1988, p. 4.

29. *Express khronika*, July 17, 1988.

CHAPTER 6:
Rowe, "Anti-Religious Persecution and Discrimination"

1. *Webster's New World Dictionary* (1974), s.v. "persecute."

2. Extracts from the articles of the criminal codes are published in *Religious Prisoners in the USSR* (Keston College and Greenfire Books, 1987) and in *May One Believe—in Russia?*, edited by Michael Bourdeaux and Michael Rowe (London: Darton, Longman and Todd, 1980). The full text of the RSFSR

criminal code in English is in *Soviet Criminal Law and Procedure*, translated by Harold Berman (Cambridge, Mass.: Harvard University Press, 1972).

3. Their story and the circumstances of their case have been extensively documented in Lorna Bourdeaux, *Valeri Barinov* (Basingstoke, England: Marshall, Morgan and Scott, 1985).

4. See, in particular, Sidney Bloch and Peter Reddaway, *Russia's Political Hospitals* (London: Gollancz, 1977). U.S. edition: *Psychiatric Terror* (New York: Basic Books, 1977).

5. *Religion in Communist Lands*, vol. 8, no. 2 (1980), pp. 103–6.

Chapter 7: Bräker, "Buddhism"

1. *Frankfurter Allgemeine Zeitung*, September 15, 1982.

2. This incident gave rise to the British invasion into Tibet. The British set a price of 20,000 rupees on Doržiev's head. For the British assessment of Doržiev see P. Landon, *The Opening of Tibet* (New York: Doubleday, Page, 1905), p. 21f.

3. These figures and the following ones are from Walter Kolarz, *Die Religionen in der Sowjetunion*, p. 447f; translated from *Religion in the Soviet Union* (New York: St. Martin's Press, 1962). Kolarz relies on relevant Soviet publications.

4. For more on this congress see ibid., p. 449f.

5. For the development and destruction of Buddhism in the Soviet Union see two articles by Nicholas N. Poppe, "The Buddhists in the USSR," in *Religion in the USSR*, B. Iwanov, ed. (Munich: Institute for the Study of the USSR, 1960), pp. 168–79, and "The Destruction of Buddhism in the USSR," in *Bulletin of the Institute for the Study of the USSR*, no. 7 (1956), pp. 14–20.

6. The accusation that the lamas "had actively helped the Japanese and Atman Semenov as well as his comrade-in-arms Baron Ungern" is found in the article on Lamaism in the first edition of the *Great Soviet Encyclopedia*.

7. U Chan Htoon, "Buddhist Mission From Burma," in *World Buddhism*, no. 2 (1961).

8. Ernst Benz, *Buddhas Wiederkehr und die Zukunft Asiens* (Munich: Nymphenburger Verlagshandlung, 1963), p. 198f.

9. See two articles by Holmes Welch in the *Far Eastern Economic Review*: "Buddhists in the Cold War" (March 8, 1962) and "Asian Buddhists and China" (April 4, 1963).

10. See three articles by Holmes Welch that rely on the analysis of available Chinese publications: "The Reinterpretation of Chinese Buddhism," in *China Quarterly*, no. 22 (1965), pp. 145–53; "Buddhism Under the Communists," in *Asian Survey*, no. 2 (1961), pp. 1–14; and "Façades of Religion in China," in *Asian Survey*, no. 7 (1970), pp. 614–26.

11. The trial was reported in detail in *Samisdat*, no. 10 (1973). See also "Buddhism in the USSR: Alexander Pyatigorsky Interviewed," in *Religion in Communist Lands*, vol. 6, no. 1 (1978), and Janis Sapiets, "Buddhists Struggle for Survival in the USSR," in *Religion in Communist Lands*, vol. 2, no. 6 (1974).

Chapter 10: Ellis, "The Religious Renaissance"

1. *Vestnik RKhD*, nos. 104–5 (1972), pp. 5–41; this translation from *Religion in Communist Lands*, vol. 1, no. 3 (1973), p. 23.

2. From an interview with Father Gleb Yakunin, *samizdat*, 1977; copy in Keston College archive.

3. *Ostkirchlice Information*, no. VI (1977), pp. 6–7.

4. Alexander Zinoviev, *Kommunizm kak realnost'* (Lausanne, Switzerland: Editions l'Age d'Homme, 1981).

5. A. Naidenovich, "Skorb, kotoroi ne bylo ot veka . . ." (A grief such as there has never been), *samizdat*, Moscow, September 1978.

6. Andrei Sinyavsky, "Sny na pravoslavnuyu Paskhu" (Dreams at Orthodox Easter), *Russkaya mysl,* December 4, 1980, p. 10.

7. Gennadi Shimanov, "Vera v chudo" (Faith in a miracle), from *Protiv techeniya* (Against the current), *samizdat*, Moscow, 1975.

8. Yevgeni Vagin, "O veruyushchikh millionakh" (On the believing millions), *Russkoye vozrozhdeniye*, nos. 7–8 (1979), pp. 141–43.

9. Mikhail Meerson-Aksenov, "Religious Renaissance in the USSR," *Diakonia*, vol. 11, no. 1 (1976), pp. 9–10.

10. "Interv'yu s Petrom Grigor'yevichem Grigorenko" (Interview with Pyotr Grigorievich Grigorenko), *Kontinent*, no. 17 (1978), pp. 408–11.

11. Vladimir Osipov, "Zapiski russkogo khristianina" (Notes by a Russian Christian), *Veche,* no. 1, *samizdat*, Moscow, 1971; this translation from *Religion in Communist Lands*, vol. 1, no. 1 (1973), p. 22.

12. Yuri Mamleyev, "Dukhovnoye vozrozhdeniye v Rossii i sovremennaya tsivilizatsiya" (The spiritual renaissance in Russia and contemporary civilization), *Kontinent*, no. 39 (1984), pp. 328–39.

13. William C. Fletcher, *Soviet Believers: The Religious Sector of the Population* (Lawrence, Kans.: Regents Press, 1981), pp. 208–9, 211.

14. Among such stories are those to be found in: Michael Bourdeaux and Xenia Howard-Johnston, *Aida of Leningrad* (Reading, England: Gateway Outreach, 1972); Michael Bourdeaux and Katharine Murray, *Young Christians in Russia* (London: Lakeland, 1976); Anita and Peter Deyneka, *A Song in Siberia* (London: Collins, 1978); Michael Bourdeaux, *Risen Indeed: Lessons in Faith from the USSR* (London: Darton, Longman, and Todd, and Crestwood, N.Y.: St. Vladimir's Seminary Press, 1983); Philip Walters and Jane Balengarth, *Light Through the Curtain* (Tring, England, and Belleville, Mich.: Lion Publishing, 1985); Lorna Bourdeaux, *Valeri Barinov: The Trumpet Call*, (Basingstoke, England: Marshalls, 1985).

15. "Movement Towards Revival in Central Asia," Information Service of the German Evangelical Alliance, no. 3, January 28, 1980.

16. Georgi Vins, *Testament From Prison*, trans. Jane Ellis (Elgin, Illinois: David C. Cook, 1975). Several other memoirs have been summarized in Lawrence Klippenstein, "An Unforgettable Past: Recent Writings by Soviet Emigré Baptists in West Germany," *Religion in Communist Lands*, vol. 14, no. 1 (1986), pp. 17–32.

17. Faith Sussmann, "Jewish Religious Revival in Moscow," *Religion in Communist Lands*, vol. 11, no. 1 (1983), p. 90.

18. Evidence of the movement toward church renewal, which was summarily crushed, is given in James W. Cunningham, *A Vanquished Hope: The Movement for Church Renewal in Russia, 1905–1906* (Crestwood, N.Y.: St. Vladimir's Seminary Press, 1981).

19. For an account of this, see Nicolas Zernov, *The Russian Religious Renaissance of the Twentieth Century* (London: Darton, Longman and Todd, 1963).

20. See for example Alexander Solzhenitsyn et al., *From Under the Rubble* (London: Collins and Harvill, 1975). In his introduction to this English translation, Max Hayward has pointed out that the book's seven authors were consciously associating themselves with two books whose authors included the previously mentioned thinkers (Struve, Bulgakov, Beryaev, Frank, Lassky): *Vekhi* (Landmarks), 1909, and *Iz glubiny* (*De profundis*), 1918.

21. An interesting essay on the return of the intelligentsia to the church is: Mikhail Meerson-Aksyonov, "Rozhdeniye novoi intelligentsii" (The birth of a new intelligentsia) in P. Litvinov, M. Meerson-Aksyonov, and B. Schragin, comps., *Samosoznaniye* (Insights) (New York: Khronika Press, 1976). Meerson-Aksyonov points out that if the present-day church is insufficiently outward-looking and creative to hold the allegiance of such people, they will find their niche elsewhere. He suggests that this may already be happening as intellectuals identify with the human-rights movement rather than with the Moscow Patriarchate.

22. *Izvestia*, April 30, 1988, p. 1

23. *Ogonyok*, no. 21 (1988), pp. 26–28.

24. See press releases issued by the Moscow Patriarchate during the *sobor;* also, Helen Bell and Jane Ellis, "The Millennium Celebrations of 1988 in the U.S.S.R.," *Religion in Communist Lands*, vol. 16, no. 4 (1988).

25. Father Gleb Yakunin, "Doklad svyashchennika Gleba Yakunina . . . o perspektivakh religioznogo vozrozhdeniya v Rossii" (Report of Father Gleb Yakunin [to the Christian Committee for the Defense of Believers' Rights in the USSR on the current situation of the Russian Orthodox Church and] on the prospects for a religious renaissance in Russia), *samizdat*, Moscow, August 15, 1979; published in Documents of the Christian Committee for the Defense of Believers' Rights in the USSR (San Francisco, Calif.: Washington Research Center), vol. 11, pp. 1128–68; a partial but extensive English translation is given in the same volume, pp. xvi-xxx.

26. For example, Fr. Alexander Pivovarov from Novosibirsk; see Michael Bourdeaux, *Ten Growing Churches* (Bromley, Kent, England: MARC Europe, forthcoming). See also Jane Ellis, *The Russian Orthodox Church: A Contemporary History*, (Beckenham, Kent, England: Croom Helm, 1986), pp. 97–99.

27. V. Furov, "Extracts from Informational Reports of the Council for Religious Affairs Under the Council of Ministers of the USSR to the Central Committee of the CPSU," *samizdat*, Moscow, 1974. Copy in Keston College archive. Published in *Vestnik RKhD*, Paris, no. 130 (1979), pp. 275–344. English translation in *Religion in Communist Dominated Areas*, New York, vol. XIX, nos. 9–11 (1980), and subsequent issues.

28. Interview in *Soviet Life* (periodical published by the Soviet Embassy in the United States), October 1981.

29. Typescript of interviews recorded for film *Candle in the Wind* in 1982, tape 2, p. 4; copy in Keston College archive.

30. *Vestnik RKhD*, no. 130 (1979), pp. 216–18.

31. An English translation of these and other letters is in the Keston College archive.

32. For further information on the Christian Seminar, see Jane Ellis, "USSR: The Christian Seminar," *Religion in Communist Lands*, vol. 9, nos. 3–4 (1981), pp. 111–25. For an account of another seminar, in Leningrad, the "37" group, see Jane Ellis, *The Russian Orthodox Church*, pp. 391–97.

33. A. V. Belov and S. I. Shilkin, *Mif o "religioznom vozrozhdenii" v SSSR* (The myth about the religious renaissance in the USSR), *Nauchny ateizm*, no. 3 (1983).

34. From an interview with Fr. Gleb Yakunin, *samizdat*, 1977; copy in Keston College archive.

35. Protopresbyter Vitali Borovoi, during a sermon preached in London in 1978; text in *Russkoye vozrozhdeniye*, no. 9 (1980), pp. 38–43. Cited in Dimitry Pospielovsky, *The Russian Church Under the Soviet Regime 1917–1982* (Crestwood, N.Y.: St. Vladimir's Seminary Press, 1984), pp. 458–59.

Chapter 11:
Ramet, "Gorbachev's Reforms and Religion"

1. *Literaturnaya gazeta*, September 9, 1987, p. 2, as quoted in Dimitry Pospielovsky, "Some Observations on the Dual Revival of the Russian Religious and National Consciousness and the Gorbachev Era," paper presented at a conference on "Christianity, the State, and Society in Contemporary Russia: Sources of Continuity and Change," Monterey, California, January 17–20, 1988.

2. As summarized in Tass, September 16, 1987; trans. in Foreign Broadcast Information Service (FBIS) *Daily Report* (Soviet Union), September 18, 1987, p. 38.

3. In an interview with *Ogonyok*, quoted in *Financial Times*, London, June 11, 1988, p. 2.

4. Roman Solchanyk, "Restructuring Church-State Relations," in *Soviet Analyst*, vol. 17, no. 8 (April 20, 1988), pp. 6–7.

5. Kharchev cited in *Le Monde*, Paris, July 3–4, 1988, p. 3; trans. in FBIS *Daily Report* (Soviet Union), July 12, 1988, p. 72. Gorbachev cited in *New York Times*, April 30, 1988, p. 4.

6. *Le Monde*, May 17, 1988, p. 6; trans. in FBIS *Daily Report* (Soviet Union), May 18, 1988, p. 61.

7. *Le Monde*, May 27, 1988, p. 4; trans. in FBIS *Daily Report* (Soviet Union), May 31, 1988, p. 50.

8. *New York Times*, April 12, 1988, pp. 1, 4; and *La Repubblica*, February 4, 1988, as cited in Oxana Antic, "A Monastic Order of Mother Theresa in the USSR?," *Radio Liberty Research*, February 16, 1988, p. 1.

9. Vera Tolz, "The USSR This Week," *Radio Liberty Research*, May 20, 1988, p. 13.

10. U. Fletcher [William C. Fletcher], "Sovetskie veruyushie," in *Sotsiologicheskie issledovaniya*, no. 4 (July-August 1987).

11. S. N. Pavlov, "O sovremennom sostoianii russkoi pravslavnoi tserkvi," ibid.

12. Roman Plaksin, *Tikhonovshchina i ee krakh* (Leningrad, 1987), as quoted in Oxana Antic, "Book Republished Denying Persecution of Russian Orthodox Church After Revolution," *Radio Liberty Research*, December 3, 1987, p. 2.

13. Open letter on "Religion and *Perestroika* in the Soviet Union," by Aleksandr Ogorodnikov (Moscow, January 12, 1988), distributed at the conference on "Christianity, the State, and Society" (see note 1). Compare Ogorodnikov's observation with *Komsomolskaya pravda*'s comment the preceding October: "It is not difficult to see that 'new thinking' does not mean abandoning materialism, that the restructuring of ideological work does not mean abandoning our ideology, and that our thinking must develop further but in the same direction, that is, on a Leninist basis."—*Komsomolskaya pravda*, October 21, 1987, p. 4; trans. in FBIS *Daily Report* (Soviet Union), October 29, 1987, p. 57.

14. Solchanyk, "Restructuring Church-State Relations," p. 6.

15. *Literaturnaya Ukraina*, May 5, 1988, p. 2, as quoted in Oxana Antic, "Celebration of Millennium of the Christianization of Rus' in Kiev," *Radio Liberty Research*, June 21, 1988, p. 3.

16. Quoted in *Glas koncila*, May 1, 1988, p. 4.

17. Agence France Presse, Paris, November 28, 1986; in FBIS *Daily Report* (Soviet Union), December 1, 1986, p. 6.

18. Quoted in *Keston News Service*, no. 294 (February 18, 1988), p. 3.

19. *Tajikistan Agitator*, October 1986, as summarized in *Arabia*, March 1987, p. 23.

20. *Kommunisti*, February 1, 1986, as quoted in *Arabia*, June 1986, p. 31.

21. *Literaturnaya gazeta*, May 20, 1987, p. 12.

22. Ibid., June 10, 1987, p. 14.

23. Fr. Kasimir Senkus, a Lithuanian pastor in Rottenburg-Stuttgart, as cited in *Frankfurter Allgemeine*, May 29, 1987, p. 4.

24. *Le Monde*, July 3–4, 1988, p. 3; trans. in FBIS *Daily Report* (Soviet Union), July 12, 1988, p. 73.

25. Dimitry Pospielovsky, "The 'Russian Orientation' and the Orthodox Church: From the Early Slavophiles to the 'Neo-Slavophiles' in the USSR," in Pedro Ramet, ed., *Religion and Nationalism in Soviet and East European Politics*, rev. and exp. ed. (Durham, N.C.: Duke University Press, 1988), p. 91.

26. *Keston News Service*, no. 302 (June 9, 1988), pp. 6–7.

27. Quoted in ibid., no. 246 (March 20, 1986), p. 7.

Bibliography

Akiner, Shirin. *Islamic Peoples of the Soviet Union*. London: Kegan Paul International, 1983.

Altshuler, Mordecai. *Soviet Jewry Since the Second World War: Population and Social Structure*. New York: Greenwood Press, 1987.

Anderson, Paul B. *People, Church, and State in Modern Russia*. Westport, Conn.: Hyperion Press, 1981.

———. *No East or West*. Paris: YMCA Press, 1985.

Bayes, Norman H., and H. St. L. B. Moss, eds. *Byzantium—An Introduction to East Roman Civilization*. Oxford: Clarendon Press, 1949.

Beeson, Trevor. *Discretion and Valor*. Rev. ed. Philadelphia: Fortress Press, 1982.

Bennigsen, Alexandre, and Marie Broxup. *The Islamic Threat to the Soviet State*. New York: St. Martin's Press, 1983.

Benz, Ernst. *The Eastern Orthodox Church*. Garden City, N.Y.: Doubleday, 1963.

Billington, James. *The Icon and the Axe: An Interpretive History of Russian Culture*. New York: Random House, 1970.

Bociurkiw, Bohdan R. *Ukrainian Churches Under Soviet Rule: Two Case Studies*. Cambridge, Mass.: Harvard University Ukrainian Studies Fund, 1984.

———, and Strong, John W. *Religion and Atheism in the U.S.S.R. and Eastern Europe*. Toronto: University of Toronto Press, 1975.

Bourdeaux, Michael. *Risen Indeed: Lessons in Faith From the U.S.S.R.* Crestwood, N.Y.: St. Vladimir's Seminary Press, 1983.

Buss, Gerald. *The Bear's Hug: Religious Belief and the Soviet State*. London: Hodder and Stoughton, 1987.

Ciszek, Walter, with Daniel Flaherty. *With God in Russia*. New York: Doubleday, 1973.

Conquest, Robert. *The Harvest of Sorrow: Soviet Collectivization and the Terror-Famine*. Oxford: Oxford University Press, 1986.

Dunn, Dennis J. *The Catholic Church and the Soviet Government, 1939–1949*. Boulder, Colo.: East European Quarterly, 1977.

———, ed. *Religion and Modernization in the Soviet Union*. Boulder, Colo.: Westview Press, 1977.

Ellis, Jane. *The Russian Orthodox Church: A Contemporary History*. Bloomington, Ind.: Indiana University Press, 1986.

Eppler, Elizabeth. *Soviet Jewry*. London: Institute of Jewish Affairs, 1971.

Fedotov, George P. *The Russian Religious Mind*. New York: Harper, 1960.

Fireside, Harvey. *Icon and Swastika: The Russian Orthodox Church Under Nazi and Soviet Control*. Cambridge, Mass.: Harvard University Press, 1971.

Fletcher, William C. *Religion and Soviet Foreign Policy*. London: Oxford University Press, 1973.

———. *The Russian Orthodox Church Underground, 1917–1970*. London: Oxford University Press, 1971.

———. *Soviet Believers: The Religious Sector of the Population*. Lawrence, Kans.: Regents Press, 1981.

———. *Soviet Charismatics*. New York: P. Lang, 1985.

———. *A Study in Survival: The Church in Russia, 1927–1943*. New York: Macmillan, 1965.

Florinsky, Michael T. *Russia—A History and Interpretation*. 2 vols. New York: Macmillan, 1953.

Freedman, Robert O., ed. *Soviet Jewry in the Decisive Decade, 1971–1980*. Durham, N.C.: Duke University Press, 1984.

Hebly, J. A. *Eastbound Ecumenism: A Collection of Essays on the World Council of Churches and Eastern Europe*. Lanham, Md.: University Press of America, 1986.

———. *Protestants in Russia*. Belfast: Christian Journals, 1976.

———. *The Russians and the World Council of Churches*. Belfast: Christian Journals, 1978.

Heller, Mikhail, and Alexsandr Nekrich. *Utopia in Power*. New York: Summit Books, 1985.

Kolarz, Walter. *Religion in the Soviet Union*. New York: St. Martin's Press, 1962.

Konstantinow, D. *Stations of the Cross: The Russian Orthodox Church 1970–1980*. London, Ont.: Zaria Publishing, 1985.

Moroziuk, Russel P. *Politicized Ecumenism: Rome, Moscow, and the Ukrainian Catholic Church*. Montreal: Concordia University Press, 1984.

Obolensky, Dimitri. *The Byzantine Commonwealth*. New York: Praeger, 1971.

Pipes, Richard. *The Formation of the Soviet Union: Communism and Nationalism, 1917–1923*. Cambridge, Mass.: Harvard University Press, 1964.

Pospielovsky, Dimitry. *The Russian Church Under the Soviet Regime, 1917–1982*. 2 vols. Crestwood, N.Y.: St. Vladimir's Seminary Press, 1984.

Powell, David E. *Antireligious Propaganda in the Soviet Union*. Cambridge, Mass.: MIT Press, 1975.

Ramet, Pedro, ed. *Religion and Nationalism in Soviet and East European Politics*. Durham, N.C.: Duke University Press Policy Studies, 1984.

Rywkin, M. *Moscow's Muslim Challenge*. London: M. E. Sharpe, 1982.

Sawatsky, Walter. *Soviet Evangelicals Since World War II*. Scottsdale, Pa.: Herald Press, 1981.

Schmemann, Alexander, ed. *Ultimate Questions—An Anthology of Modern Religious Thought*. New York: Holt, Rinehart and Winston, 1965.

Seton-Watson, Hugh. *The Decline of Imperial Russia*. New York: Praeger, 1952.

———. *The Russian Empire*. Oxford: Clarendon Press, 1967.

Simon, Gerhard. *Church, State, and Opposition in the U.S.S.R.* Berkeley: University of California Press, 1974.

Smith, Hedrick. *The Russians*. New York: Ballantine Books, 1976.

Smolar, Boris. *Soviet Jewry Today and Tomorrow*. New York: Macmillan, 1971.

Solzhenitsyn, Aleksandr. *A Lenten Letter to Pimen, Patriarch of All Russia*. Minneapolis, Minn.: Burgess, 1972.

Spinka, Matthew. *The Church in Soviet Russia*. Westport, Conn.: Greenwood Press, 1980.

Stroyen, William B. *Communist Russia and the Russian Orthodox Church, 1943–1962*. Washington: Catholic University Press, 1967.

Szczesniak, Boleslaw. *The Russian Revolution and Religion*. Notre Dame, Ind.: University of Notre Dame Press, 1959.

Timasheff, Nicholas. *Religion in Soviet Russia*. Westport, Conn.: Greenwood Press, 1979.

Treadgold, Donald W. *Twentieth Century Russia*. 5th ed. Boston: Houghton Mifflin, 1981.

Walters, Philip, ed. *Religion in the Soviet Union and Eastern Europe*. Keston, England: Keston College, 1985.

Ware, Timothy. *The Orthodox Church*. Crestwood, N.Y.: St. Vladimir's Seminary Press, 1986.

Yakunin, Gleb, and Lev Regelson. *Letters From Moscow*. Edited by Jane Ellis. San Francisco: H. S. Dakin, 1978.

Zaslavsky, Victor, and Robert Brym. *Soviet-Jewish Emigration and Soviet Nationality Policy*. New York: St. Martin's Press, 1983.

Zernov, N. *Eastern Christendom*. New York: Putnam, 1961.

Index of Names